ANOTHER WILDERNESS

NEW OUTDOOR WRITING BY WOMEN

edited by Susan Fox Rogers

SEAL PRESS

Cover art by Kris Wiltse
Text and cover design by Clare Conrad

Library of Congress Cataloging-in-Publication Data

Another Wilderness : New Outdoor Writing by Women / edited by Susan Fox Rogers.   1. Outdoor recreation for women—Literary collections. 2. Wilderness survival—Literary collections.   3. American prose literature—Women authors.   4. Short stories, American—Women authors.   5. Outdoor life—Literary collections.   I. Rogers, Susan Fox.
PS648.088A56   1994   796.5'082—dc20   94-15168
ISBN: 1-878067-54-0

First printing, October 1994
10 9 8 7 6 5 4 3 2 1
Distributed to the trade by Publishers Group West
Foreign Distribution:
In Canada: Publishers Group West Canada, Toronto, Ontario
In the U.K. and Europe: Airlift Book Company, London, England

For my parents, Jacqueline and Thomas Rogers,
who gave me freedom to play outdoors

Not all those who pass
In front of the Great mother's chair
Get passt with only a stare.
Some she looks at their hands
To see what sort of savages they were.
                    - Gary Snyder

                              -To sarah
                              from emily

ACKNOWLEDGMENTS

First, I would like to thank Faith Conlon of Seal Press who encouraged me on this venture, and then went off to have her own adventure of child rearing, and Holly Morris, who adopted me and made me feel completely at home with Seal. Holly is really the second editor on this book as she read and reread all of these pieces, helped make difficult decisions as to what to include and not, and, above all, remained cheerful through it all.

This anthology was years in the making and many people helped to give it form, but I would especially like to thank the following people: John Fout and Michèle Dominy at the journal at Bard College for time and space to work on this (and a Xerox machine); John Councill for his computer wizardry; Moose Cat and Honey Bear for their inimitable company; and Tamela Sloan for her work and love throughout the process.

This anthology could never have happened without all of the submissions from women who love the outdoors. Thanks to everyone who helped spread the word and who shared their work with me. And thank you especially to the women I have included in this collection for offering your words and vision, for your patience as this book came to completion, for your enthusiasm along this rugged path.

Contents

INTRODUCTION
ix

SOLO
Lucy Jane Bledsoe
1

WHERE BEARS WALK
Sherry Simpson
10

NIGHT SKATES
Susanna Levin
23

AAMAA DIDI
Jean Gould
36

WOLF
Gretchen Legler
52

STONES ALL AROUND, AN ABUNDANCE OF WATER,
OF BUSHES, OF BIRDS
Deborah Abbott
63

A CITY GIRL DISCOVERS THE FOREST
Gabrielle Daniels
68

PAJARITOS
Terri de la Peña
90

MOUNTAIN BIKING AND THE PLEASURES OF BALANCE
Marti Stephen
99

THE BEDOUINS OF NEVADA:
FIVE WOMEN SNOWBOARD THE FIRST DESCENT OF WHEELER PEAK
Kathleen Gasperini
105

ENDURANCE ON THE ICE:
THE AMERICAN WOMEN'S ANTARCTIC EXPEDITION
Anne Dal Vera
111

IN THE CANOE ENDLESSLY PADDLING
Alice Evans
124

THE JADED DIVER
Nancy Sefton
131

SPIRIT WALK
Karen A. Monk
144

A GLACIER SUMMER
Barbara Wilson
151

LOOKING FOR DANIEL
Elizabeth Folwell
161

HOMEWATERS OF THE MIND
Holly Morris
174

WILDERNESS WAY
Meryem Ersoz
179

ONE STEP AT A TIME
Lydia B. Goetze
187

EYE OF THE MEADOW
Carolyn Kremers
195

SUPERIOR SPIRIT
Ann Linnea
212

STORMS WORSE THAN MY OWN
Clarice Dickess
230

RIVER OF FEAR, RIVER OF GRACE
Geneen Marie Haugen
255

CONTRIBUTORS
267

INTRODUCTION

In the fall of 1993, I visited Gladys, an older friend who was in the hospital. I have known her since I was born (something she reminded me of too often), so it was painful to see her in such a situation. But I was pleased to find her up, out of bed, though hooked up to oxygen. I stooped to speak with her and—as we so often do with people who are ill—I spoke as if she might be half deaf or only able to half comprehend. I spoke slowly, in simple sentences, of simple things. I searched for subjects to talk about in place of obvious ones: the dreary white hospital room, operations, pain, and how much food has been eaten. So I told her I was finishing my anthology on women and outdoor sports.

"What was the name of the first woman adventurer?" she asked. My mind flipped through its file of names, women who might be considered "the first." As I searched, I found it was an odd idea, that we might have designated one woman our first and foremost adventurer. I also was a little upset that I couldn't figure out who this might be—I should know these things, I reasoned. I scanned the Alps, I looked down the Nile, I trekked across the Himalayas, the eighteenth, nineteenth, twentieth centuries floated by. Who could she be?

"I have no idea, Gladys," I admitted.

"What was her name," Gladys mumbled. "Eve." She nodded her head as if she had settled on the right name.

I continued to look at her blankly. Eve, who, I wondered.

"Eve," she repeated, and a slight smile touched the corner of her dry lips.

I began to laugh, delighted by her sense of humor, embarrassed by my own slowness, and amazed at how absolutely right she was: Eve was our first adventurer.

Outdoor sports may have become enormously popular during the 1980s but women have from the beginning dared to adventure: to eat an apple, to travel into the outdoors, to push ourselves physically and emotionally on to new terrains. Much of what women have done may not be classified as adventure in the traditional sense but I consider a walk down a broad smooth path on a sunny clear day an adventure if, while on that walk, I think of my sister and connect with her in a new meaningful way, or if I am visited by thoughts (or, if you allow, spirits) of a loved one. My definition of adventure is, I realize, broad, and this collection reflects that: my only requirement for these pieces was that they take place outdoors, that the writer explore what it means to be a woman moving, playing, being in the outdoors.

What is "new" about this collection is not necessarily the adventure itself, though some of the means to adventure—a mountain bike, a snowboard, or Rollerblades—may be modern. What is new is the writing. This collection includes several first-time authors, as well as women who have been writing for years but have never found a place to publish their multilayered tales of outdoor play. But there are other, important ways that this writing and this collection itself are original.

That we are writing about outdoor experiences is in itself a relatively new phenomenon within the history of women's writing. Stories and books about strong, physically independent women seeking adventure in the outdoors are still few and far between; women's sports and outdoor books are too rare. The stories these books tell are by nature feminist because the women depicted in them are, I believe, the physical articulation of feminist ideas.

Within the tradition of outdoor writing this collection breaks new territory as well. Outdoor writing is written and read for many different reasons: vicarious thrills, to dream about what we could have done and also to share information about an area, a descent or ascent. I remember trying to tackle Shakleton's stories of his expeditions to the North Pole—a subject my father was fascinated by. What I remember of those accounts is mostly being appalled that they would eat seals and penguins. And I also found those accounts tedious, as they did not match my own experience and sense of outdoor adventure as being wild and exciting. For years, nothing I read corresponded to what I felt outdoors, and the language—"conquering" a mountain or "mastering" a river—had nothing to do with what I did outdoors. That, no doubt, was because I was reading what was available: accounts written by men of their experiences. In those early days, I never saw my own life reflected in outdoor writing. *Another Wilderness* is a collection I have been wanting to read for many years.

The stories in this collection offer some of the traditional aspects of outdoor writing: vicarious thrills and the invitation to dream. But they also offer a view beyond the physical to an awareness of our emotional and spiritual selves. It is my belief that physical experiences are heightened and strengthened when moving outdoors. It is through these experiences that our lives are transformed. These transformations are at the heart of this collection.

The idea for an anthology that brought together many different outdoor sports was born in my own experience: I was thirteen when I began backpacking, rafting, caving and canoeing with a youth group whose goal was to keep kids off the street. Then I discovered rock and ice climbing and cross-country skiing with a High Adventure Explorer Post (Boy Scouts for girls and boys). For years, it didn't matter what I did outdoors, as long as I was outdoors.

The summer of my fourteenth year I remember going on trip after trip: canoeing on the Delaware for a week, caving in West Virginia, backpacking the Black Forest trail in Pennsylvania for ten days. I would come home from a trip, unpack, wash my clothes, and pack again. Finally my father said no. No more trips. It seemed to be the most illogical of interdictions. Why stop me from doing what I loved most? I cried and carried on and, if I remember correctly, got my way. I imagine now that perhaps my father was worried that my enthusiasm for sleeping in a tent had more to do with drugs or kegs of beer or, most likely in his fatherly concern, boys. And he was right: I had fallen in love. But I had fallen in love with rocks and trees, wind and sunshine. I adored my pack and my sleeping bag, my taped up water bottle and all of my carabiners.

My parents, academics both of them, could not understand

these passions. Yet they were the ones who initially led me to the outdoors: there were the long summers at the shores of the Indiana Dunes, where my father had grown up. He initiated his two young daughters into the ritual of camping out in the dunes. We had enough food—marshmallows, Cokes and graham crackers —to last for weeks and cotton sleeping bags that were drenched with morning dew. We would drag ourselves home for breakfast and spend the day recovering from a sleepless night spent telling stories, performing séances, playing flashlight tag and then worrying about being raided by the local tough kids. These early camping trips made me feel at home outdoors. My parents made the outdoors familiar, comfortable; they planted the seed and then stepped back, perhaps alarmed at what was growing, but willing to let it grow. I was lucky.

Out of all the outdoor sports I tried, it was rock climbing that I chose, or that chose me, and so it was to rock climbing that I gave my body and soul for the next eighteen years. I never stopped paddling, hiking and biking but I was, above all, a rock climber. It was for the rock that I lived in the parking lot of Eldorado Canyon, eating rice with soup mix for dinner (like many early love affairs, this one led to an acute case of mononucleosis), and climbing every day. I hitchhiked to Yosemite, bicycled to local cliffs in central Pennsylvania, begged and borrowed cars to get me to the Gunks for long weekends.

On many of my adventures I was traveling solo, but most of the time I was with a partner and that partner was usually male. Climbing and most outdoor sports are in the hands of men, and it is from them that so many of us learn. There are wonderful aspects to this—being pushed in ways that you might not have gone on your own or with other women. But there is also a downside, as men cannot know what our bodies are capable of, cannot imagine that the equipment doesn't fit or work for our bodies, cannot intuit our fears or always allow us to listen to them.

Author Marti Stephen learned to bicycle from men. She repeated the ritual of turning to men for knowledge several times before she came to "own her own balance" and learned that there really was no "proper" approach or attitude. It is only in mountain bike racing against and with other women that she comes across a new definition, a feminist definition, of competition. Kathleen Gasperini, in her piece, finds that doing the first snow-board descent of Wheeler Peak is not about the doing, but about the bond that grew, the "secret agenda" that developed among the five women.

It never occurred to me, until I started climbing with women, that there were aspects of climbing that I could not, maybe should not learn from my male partners. Women have a lot to share and learn from each other and that is one of the goals of this collection: to pass along our stories, to share all of our various experiences and knowledge about the outdoors.

Climbing has informed every aspect of my life: emotional, physical, social, spiritual. Climbing has taught me how to face fear, to trust myself, to commit body and soul to one thing, if only to the next hold. Climbing is my gauge and barometer; when I am centered in my life, I climb with balance and ease. If you, like the women in this collection, have fallen in love with the outdoors, or with an outdoor sport, you will understand and say *yes,* that is how it is. Though the sport may be different, the language we use to talk about our sports, our experiences in the outdoors are similar: we feel the same passion, we use the same metaphors. We all have been transformed by our experiences outdoors.

Each of these stories addresses many themes and ideas—from the danger of the outdoors to the friendliness of the outdoors, from the thrill to the fear of high-adventure sports. As you read, you will see that the ideas and themes of these stories overlap. I am calling these *stories,* because that is what we tell about our experiences, though except for one piece, these are not fiction and most would be more accurately called nonfiction narratives. In these pieces I see meditations, spiritual journeys, essays, confessions.

For many women, the outdoors is unfamiliar, foreign, a place of fear. Despite my early experiences and my sense of comfort in the outdoors, I have had my moments of fear outdoors. I have spent hours lying awake, listening for footsteps outside my tent, or days trying to rig a system to keep my food from bears. But I've always been a little embarrassed about my fears. So initially I envisioned a collection that portrayed strong fearless women, super role models for us all. But I came to realize I was imagining something rather unreal and dismissing what is very real—fear. Fear was the dominant emotion in many of the stories submitted to this anthology. In reading through hundreds of women's experiences I learned that there are fears that we share: a fear of men, of animals (often bears), and of the physical demands of the activity undertaken. Though many of these stories are also about facing and overcoming these fears, ending with a celebration of the outdoors, the fear itself is vibrant, the guiding force of the experience and of the story recounted.

Gabrielle Daniels has written a multi-layered meditation that witnesses the outdoors through an urban black woman's eyes— what she is looking for behind a tree or around a curve in the path is her attacker; Sherry Simpson confronts her extreme fear of bears by having direct contact with them. These two pieces reveal what many women experience—that entering the outdoors is entering a fearful and dark world and that nature is mysterious, other, forbidden.

On a poetic level, our fears probably come in part from our unconscious, from myths that lie within us, but it is also born of reality: going into the outdoors does involve dangers, among them animals, both human and not. This is a part of our lives as women in the world, as women who venture out, and we cannot ignore or deny it.

Of course, fear does not always rule our outdoor experiences, and the outdoors is not always the locus of our dark imaginings. A more gentle, welcoming side of the outdoors is presented by Terri de la Peña as she watches the birds along the California coast. In so doing, she connects with the land, to her past, and she also steps into a world that she feels is nonjudgmental, one that is safe and free of racism, sexism and homophobia.

Other writers express their feelings of being at home in the outdoors. While guiding a rafting trip for people with disabilities, Deborah Abbott, who lives between many worlds—that of the abled and the disabled, as well as between land and water— finds herself physically at home among the stones, water, bushes and birds. Authors Barbara Wilson and Jean Gould find their homes in the far reaches of the world: Wilson in Norway one summer and Gould in Nepal, while Karen Monk finds a spiritual home in her own backyard in the Catskill mountains.

Several of the pieces explore the urge that we have to head out, that drive that makes us want more. For Nancy Sefton, she wants to dive deeper, further into the water, to encounter more exotic, more dangerous underwater animals. Author Susanna Levin strains at her urban confinement and then finds the perfect solution: rollerblading—at night—which offers the thrills that she seeks in the outdoors.

Our unique perspectives as women adventurers and the responsibilities that we feel, for ourselves and for others, is woven through the fabric of many of these stories. Through an experience she had searching for a missing man, Elizabeth Folwell muses on whether women head out with different agendas than men. She wonders, Why don't we get lost? Why don't we disappear in the woods?

Impressive physical feats are chronicled by Alice Evans who describes her struggle to finish a paddling trip. On reading her near-hallucinatory experience most readers will either laugh or cringe with recognition. Lydia Goetze's account tells us that to test our will, to push our limits, is to gain emotional strength beyond what we had imagined possible.

Other tales of great physical strength are offered by Anne Dal Vera who pulled a sled with four other women on the Antarctic Women's Expedition (AWE) from the edge of the Antarctic to the South Pole, and Carolyn Kremers who describes her days in the Alaska Mountain Wilderness Classic, a one-hundred-sixty-mile race that fords eight rivers and crosses four mountain passes. But both stories are also about stopping, about acknowledging one's abilities in the face of incredible natural conditions, about the pain of giving up dreams and forging new ones.

Three pieces in this collection, those by Lucy Jane Bledsoe, Holly Morris and Gretchen Legler, are as much meditations on another person—distant, dead or gone—as on the activity at hand. But, I imagine, the one would never have happened without the other: it was the wind and snow, water and air that let the emotions emerge, become alive in the landscape, in the person seeking wholeness or solace outdoors.

Several stories take us physically and emotionally into new

landscapes of memory, desire and emotion. Interestingly, those from Clarice Dickess and Carolyn Kremers come from perhaps our last (American) frontier: Alaska. Another, from writer Ann Linnea, is about the initial stages of the circumnavigation of one of the largest lakes on this planet: Lake Superior. Everything in these stories is large: the landscape, the feats undertaken, the emotions encountered.

In sharing these stories, in bringing them together in this collection, I hope women and girls will read what I wasn't able to: stories that give them direction, a belief in themselves and a wilderness of adventure and play that is their own. And I hope that they will be empowered and inspired to cut loose, to do, and to discover another wilderness within themselves.

Susan Fox Rogers
High Falls, New York
February 1994

Solo

Lucy Jane Bledsoe

I STOOD ON THE RIM of a huge, perfectly formed bowl, deep with snow. I'd just skied over a pass that, according to my map, was 9,200 feet high. The peaks surrounding me were banked with snowfields that looked blue in the late afternoon High-Sierra light. Massive clouds, the color of pearls, swarmed around the peaks. And I knew exactly what I was—this being on skis in the marrow of wilderness—a human body and nothing more. That was one thing Elizabeth and I agreed on, even in the last couple years—that the goal is to reach that stripped down state where your cells know everything there is to know, where your feelings go so deep they become one simple force, where sorrow and joy become the same thing.

How I missed Elizabeth.

I cut the metal edges of my skis into the ice-crusted snow for balance and then reached into my pocket for a few yogurt peanuts. We'd always saved the yogurt peanuts to eat at the tops of passes, and nowhere else. Next, I checked to make sure the batteries in my avalanche beacon still had juice. What a joke, carrying a beacon on a solo trip. Who would pick up its high-frequency beeps if an avalanche buried me? I guess it was just habit.

Then I looked down into that steep bowl below me. Its snow pack fed a long drainage that in the spring would fan out into half a dozen streams. My destination was the bottom of that drainage. I planned to camp at High Meadow tonight and then ski out tomorrow morning. I scanned the slope for a safe route down. I figured it was about a five-hundred-foot drop.

"Yahooooo!" Elizabeth's voice hollered in my head. I could see her spirit lean forward with that open-mouthed grin of hers that looked more like a shout than a smile. She shoved her ski poles into the snow and flew off the mountain. Elizabeth would have taken what she called the crow's route, straight down. Her tight telemark turns would have made a long, neat squiggle in the snow all the way to the bottom of the bowl. In the meadow below she would glide to a luxurious stop, then purposely fall in a heap, exhausted from her ecstasy.

"Oh, Elizabeth," I said, missing her foolhardiness with a pain as sharp as this bitter wind. How I longed to lecture her right then: "Listen, girl, we've had over a foot of fresh snow in the last week. Got it? The snow pack is *weak*. Add to that the fact that this is a leeward slope on a gusty day."

By now she would have quit listening. Her face would be turned toward the valley, and I'd know she was already flying, dead center in that rapture of hers.

And yet, I would go on with my lecture: "And look at that cornice!" I'd point to the one about ten yards below me right now.

"What cornice?" she might ask, because it really was a small one and nothing subtle ever figured into Elizabeth's world.

"Elizabeth," I spoke out loud now. "This is a prime avalanche slope in prime avalanche conditions."

I think my voice was a mantra for her, the droning noise against which she took flight. My words of caution were her starting blocks. If she were here, this would have been her cue. Off she'd sail. I'd watch her back for a few moments and then realize that being stranded on a ridge top in the High Sierra in March, with a storm pending, was a greater risk than skiing an avalanche-prone slope. I'd be forced to follow.

The wind stormed over the pass, interrupting my thoughts and broadsiding me with so much force that I lost my balance and fell. I lay with my skis and legs tangled in the air above me, let my head fall back onto the snow and watched the clouds. They'd lost their luster and were becoming swarthy. The feeling of knowledge in my cells disappeared, and now I felt the opposite, as if I were all spirit, practically not here at all, like Elizabeth. How fast things changed at this elevation.

They found her car, of course. Who could miss it? Her bumper stickers were as loud as she was. This whole trip I'd been trying to imagine where her body might be. Deep in some crevasse. Buried in an avalanche. Or simply sitting in her camp somewhere, dead of exposure. I couldn't help wanting to believe that she had that shouting smile on her face, wherever she was, although even Elizabeth must have learned the meaning of fear in the moments before death. Or had she?

That they hadn't been able to find Elizabeth didn't surprise me in the least. She had always insisted on camping in the most remote places, hiking or skiing far off-trail, and changing her mind after the trip began so that even if she had told folks where she was going, it didn't matter. Perhaps in a month or two, when the snow melted, they would find her body.

Lying in the snow was a bad idea. I managed to get back on my feet and studied the slope again. The day wasn't getting any younger. My emotional state, as changeable as this mountain weather, cleared and the warmth colonized my cells again. I'd made this solo journey as a tribute to Elizabeth, and now I realized how this very moment, looking down at this perfect avalanche slope in the High Sierra, was the essence of Elizabeth. Here was her soul. She lived for this moment of risk. For the first time since we'd had our final falling out, I began to understand that I'd been as dependent on her for danger as she had been on me for safety.

Elizabeth, I think, knew this all along. She'd even tried to tell me that last trip of ours, but I'd been too angry to listen.

Elizabeth and I had been mountaineering partners, off and on, for almost twenty years. We began backpacking together when we were fifteen. I was the crazy one then, wild and daring, wanting to go farther, deeper, longer, faster, later or earlier.

But over the years there was a shift. I grew more cautious and Elizabeth grew more reckless. There were several years in there, when her recklessness had caught up with but not yet overtaken mine, that we were perfect partners. We could choose a campsite and make route decisions almost without talking. We shared the implicit understanding that courting the mountains was our first commitment and working as a team got us closer to those peaks.

I noticed her impatience for the first time on a hiking trip in the Brooks Range of Alaska, just a few months after her mother died. She wanted to take a short-cut and bushwhack some ten miles across a spur where we could join our trail again and save thirty miles.

I pointed to the map. "Elizabeth, that's a cliff. And there aren't enough landmarks to ensure we'd find the trail. What's the hurry, anyway?"

"Don't use my name," she snapped.

"What?" I must have looked hurt.

"The way you use my name is patronizing. I can read the map. We can scramble up those rocks."

"You mean that vertical cliff."

"Oh, geez," she said but gave in to me. We had several similar encounters that trip, but I attributed her impatience to the recent death of her mother, nothing more.

Over the years I watched this impatience grow into a hunger she couldn't satisfy. She took too many inappropriate lovers—a coke head, a sixteen year old, several corporate execs—and wanted each of them body and soul. She embraced new spiritual teachers and practices every year, each time with fast conviction. And yet even as she acquired new lovers and gurus, she remained fiercely loyal to a few of her oldest friends, including her brother Nathan and me. Elizabeth searched for the heart of wilderness in every part of her life.

Back then I thought that if she would just slow down she could discover what it was she so badly needed. Now I think that she hungered only for this moment I faced. That in a strange, almost ghoulish way, she got what she wanted—to see how far she could take a risk.

My choice now, to ski this prime avalanche slope or to turn around and ski out the three-day route I'd skied in on, was almost exactly like the one that precipitated Elizabeth's and my first all-out fight. We were circumnavigating Mount Adams in the state of Washington in late spring. Near the end of the trip, we reached a torrential river gushing out of the foot of a glacier. We spent an entire day, on my insistence and to Elizabeth's disgust, searching for a safe crossing. We never found one.

"Our choice," Elizabeth finally pointed out, "is backtracking five days, being home late and not completing the circumnavigation, or jumping the river, being home in two days and completing the circumnavigation." Her gray eyes looked like nails right then.

"You missed one option," I added. "One of us jumps, lands in the river and is washed downstream. The other goes home to tell her family."

"Oh, shit." She looked up at Mount Adams as if appealing for understanding, and I felt very small, cut out. I was in her way, had come between her and the mountain. And that, I knew, was the one sacrilege she wouldn't tolerate.

"Look," she deigned to explain. "Basically, there are two approaches to life. You can mire yourself in precautions as you endlessly try to outwit fate. Or, you can let her fly. There's risk either way. In the first scenario, you might—probably *will*—miss all that is good in life. In the second scenario, you get what you want, but you might not get it for as long as you want. Your choice."

I watched the chalky white glacial water as she hammered out her opinion. On either side of the river, a reddish moraine had built up, bereft of life. I longed for a forest then, the thick comfort of living things. I felt very alone with my cautious, fearful self. I also felt angry, used. I felt like that moraine, a pile of debris pushed aside by her forging glacier.

We did jump the stream, adrenaline carrying me across a much broader distance than my body could normally go. But nothing was ever the same between me and Elizabeth.

Another blast of icy wind, stronger still than the last one, blew me off my feet. I slid to within one yard of the cornice, my legs and skis once again a tangle. "Elizabeth!" I shouted. "I know you're out there! Quit pushing me, you goddamn wild woman."

Then, surprising myself I added, even louder still, "I love

you!" In spite of everything, Elizabeth was as good as these mountains, this wild, stormy sky. She was part of my wilderness. But that didn't mean I had to be crazy, now that she was dead, and go against all common sense and ski this slope.

I had an idea. I'd have to check the map, but I thought that if I backtracked just to the other side of this pass, I could go out the south fork drainage and still only lose a day. I could hitchhike to my car from there. It was a good plan. I'd always told my friends that my coming home late meant nothing more than I'd used good sense and changed my route. I had plenty of food and warm clothing.

I got to my feet, without sliding over the lip of the cornice, and skied back to the top of the ridge. The hard wind died down suddenly and now a gentle breeze brushed my face. I stopped at the top to take one last look at the bowl before retreating down the back, gentle side of the pass.

"Yahooooo!" Once again, I saw her spirit fly over the cornice and down the slope.

I remembered the night of our final fight, a year ago, when we were marooned in our tent. I was lying on my stomach, cooking freeze-dried honey-lime chicken on the stove just outside the tent door, my sleeping bag pulled up to my shoulders. Outside, the snow fell thickly in tiny flakes. We'd been stuck in this camp for twenty-four hours already. Elizabeth had a date the following night and wanted to ski out in the morning regardless of the weather. "It's only fifteen miles," she'd said.

"Fifteen miles in a white-out."

She shrugged, "We've skied this route before."

"You'd risk your life for a date?" I challenged.

"Yeah," she grinned, "if it's hot enough. And this one is. I mean, I'm not talking about OK sex, this is, oh, how can I even explain to you. . . . " She looked up to the ceiling of our tent, searching, as if the English language just didn't contain the words to make me understand.

"Elizabeth," I said calmly. "I know what hot sex is. And it's not worth dying in a blizzard for."

"Then," she said snatching off her wool cap. Her short, honey-colored hair was mashed against her head. "Then you *don't* know what hot sex is."

"Oh, fuck you!" I yelled. I was so tired of her constant mocking. "You're a goddamn lunatic!" I managed to pull on my boots and squeeze out of the tent without knocking over the pot of honey-lime chicken cooking on the stove. I stomped around outside in the blizzard for a few moments, fuming.

When I started shaking violently with cold, I returned. She had a novel propped on one knee and the last of our yogurt peanuts in a plastic bag between her legs. The honey-lime chicken bubbled away, most of the liquid boiled off. She wolfed down the yogurt peanuts one after another, munching loudly.

"What are you doing?" My voice was dry and accusing. "Those peanuts are for the pass tomorrow."

"I'm feeding the lunatic," she answered softly, faking innocence. "She's hungry." A bit of chewed up yogurt peanut spewed out of her mouth as she spoke. She held the bag out to me. "I think your lunatic may be hungry, too. Want some?"

"Oh, fuck you," I said again. And we were silent the rest of the evening. I lay awake all night reading short stories and looking forward to being rid of Elizabeth at the end of this journey.

By the next morning the sky had cleared and we skied out, Elizabeth happy to be heading back to the Bay Area in time for her hot date. Me, bitter. It was the last trip we took together. She called me occasionally after that, but neither of us suggested any trips. I went with other friends, she went alone. I dreaded the day when she would see our impasse as yet another unexplored territory she must venture into.

I did find some satisfaction in the fact that she didn't take another partner. Yet, in a way, I was even more jealous that she went solo, that she'd stretched to a place I didn't think I could stretch to.

When her brother called me two months ago to ask if I'd heard from Elizabeth, I knew instantly. He figured maybe an impromptu trip to L.A. Or that she was camped out at some new lover's apartment. "Nathan," I told him. "I don't think so." He waited silently for my explanation, and I could tell from his breathing that he knew too. I said, "She'd mentioned a trip in the Trinity Alps last time I talked to her."

"Who should I call?" Nathan asked dully. I hung up and went over to his apartment. We called the Forest Service, and they located her car within five hours. They gave up looking for her body after a week.

For a long time, all I could think was that I had been right and she had been wrong. She was dead, and still I wished I could continue our dispute, find some way of telling her "I told you so." Now, as I turned my back on the bowl, deep with snow, preparing to retreat back down the safe side of the pass, I realized just how great my jealousy had been. She was right. My lunatic *was* hungry.

Suddenly, I turned around again and faced the steep bowl. A pillow of fog nestled in the trees far below. Somewhere beyond was my car.

I dug my poles into the snow. I pushed slowly at first and then shoved off hard. I sailed out, directly over the lip of that cornice and landed squarely on my skis several feet below. I shot downhill, taking the crow's route, straight down. I wasn't a particularly good downhill skier, I'd never learned telemark turns, so I skied a straight, seemingly vertical line, amazed that I didn't fall. My feet vibrated as they stroked the long slope. My legs felt like springs, supple and responsive. My head roared. Everything was a white blur. I'd never skied so fast in my life.

Then I heard it. A bellowing that drowned out the rush of wind in my ears. I felt the entire mountain thundering under my feet. In the next split second, I saw powder snow billowing up fifty feet in the air. So this was it, I thought, feeling a strange, dead center calm. No one skied faster than a slab avalanche. And yet, as if I could, I crouched down lower, held my poles close to my body, allowed my legs to be even more elastic, and concentrated on the width between my skis.

Then the avalanche overtook me, careening down the slope to my right, missing me by about ten yards. The roar was deafening and the cloud of snow blinded me, but still I skied.

Elizabeth, I thought, perverse in the coolness of my mind, never raced an avalanche down a slope.

I came crashing into the flats of the meadow below the bowl and plunged into the snow, face first. Sharp pain splintered up my nose, across my jaw. I rolled over on my side and gingerly wiped the snow off my face with a wet mitten, touching my cheekbone and forehead. Nothing seemed to be broken, just mashed. I blinked hard to clear my eyes and finally saw the wreckage of the avalanche to my right; masses of snow that moments ago were as fluid as water were now as set as concrete. I could have been locked in that pile of snow, my beacon transmitting tiny beeps for some chance stranger to pick up. They would have had about thirty minutes, if I was lucky, to locate and dig me out. I stared and stared at that icy rubble as awed as if it were the remains of an ancient temple.

"Oh, God," I whispered.

My arms and legs felt paralyzed, but slowly I was able to move each limb, bending and straightening until it regained feeling. I rolled over in the snow and tried to get to my feet, but didn't yet have the strength.

I sensed Elizabeth nearby. "Did you see me?" I asked, still whispering.

Finally I wept, and as I did I thought I heard her laughing, that hard, wild woman laughter of hers. Then I realized it was my own laughter, in concert with my tears, shaking the very centers of my cells, wringing the sorrow out of my pores.

Where Bears Walk

Sherry Simpson

In the dream, I cower among tall grass, or beneath bushes, or behind trees. The place where I hide changes, but the terror never does. I hear the bear slavering and growling, its footsteps drumming the earth. It is looking for me. It sniffs the air, and I know it smells my fear. It will find me. Then it will tear me apart and eat me.

In the moment of discovery, as the bear rears high before descending on me, I always wake, my heart leaping against my chest as if it could abandon the rest of my leaden body to the kill. Sometimes, when at last I sleep again, the bear resumes stalking me through the night.

For years I could not enter the woods of Southeast Alaska without my heart flailing about like a crippled thrush, without dread persuading me that somewhere among the green twilight of trees, the great hunter hunted me. And yet, even though I have lived in Juneau since I was seven, never have I encountered a bear as more than a shadow fading away at the edges of some forest or beach. I have roamed through tidal flats and rainforest, alpine meadow and creekside brush, all the places where bears roam, and I have never been threatened by a bear. It is simply enough to know they are there, enlarged by lore every Alaskan cultivates.

I am a good student of such bear gossip. I could tell you about the hunter dragged off and partially eaten by a brown bear drawn to the sound of the man's deer call. I remember the neighbor boy chased down West Glacier trail by a black bear. There was the solitary camper missing in Glacier Bay, his death revealed by frames in his camera that captured the bear entering his camp. To believe in these tales of blood and flesh and teeth, to imagine them well, I had only to meet a man blinded by a brown bear he encountered as a seventeen-year-old hunter on a local creek. I saw the whole story in his face, a face rearranged into a topography of scars, and I wondered what he remembered of bears in his personal and enduring darkness.

Among shadows, things appear larger than they really are. I did not overcome my fear of bears until I smelled the dark, wild smell of bears on my hands, until I felt the slow wave of blood washing through a bear's veins, until I walked where bears walk.

LaVern Beier is not afraid of bears. The Alaska Department of Fish and Game calls him a technician for his proficiency in finding, trapping and tranquilizing mountain goats, wolves, wolverines and all manner of creatures that do not wish to be found, including the drugged brown bear slumped on the patch of stale snow before us. Vern is not just a technician, though. Something in Vern Beier makes me imagine he is part-bear himself, the offspring of one of those mythic matings between bear and woman that never led to any good for the bear. (As for the woman, who can say?) Perhaps it is Vern's wiry hair, the shagginess of his black beard, the economy and purpose in his stocky frame that make me think such things. More likely it is the steady brown eyes that see more than he ever says. But I detect the resemblance also in the rough but loving way he runs his hands through the thin spring pelt of this half-conscious bear, as if he knows her. Pretty bony, is all he says. Must have been a hard winter.

I am not looking at the bear's coffee-colored fur. I am looking at her teeth. My, what big teeth she has. Slobber webs canines the shade of scrimshaw and the size of a man's thumb. This bear galloped for more than ten minutes from the pursuing helicopter, her legs moving like pistons over ridges and up slopes, driving her across the alpine reaches of Admiralty Island. She did not hide; she ran. Even after Vern leaned through the copter's open door and sighted his rifle on her bounding rump, darting her twice with a tranquilizer potent enough to down an elephant, she ran and ran until the drug slammed into her and she did not get up. I make a promise to myself when I see that. I promise never again to fool myself into thinking a human can run from a bear.

Because I am in no danger at the moment, my sympathies lie entirely with the bear, though as a newspaper reporter writing an article about bear research, my job is to take notes, not to sympathize with anybody or anything. I understand the scientific rationale that volunteered this bear to be chased, prodded, poked, tagged, plucked, measured and collared with a radio transmitter that by a steady beep will describe her movements but never convey the true power of her motion. I have no trouble reconciling a personal fear of bears with a distant appreciation of them. But I don't tell anybody the real reason I asked for this story: so I can touch with my own hands what frightens me most.

Vern and his partner, wildlife biologist Kim Titus, are here on this mountaintop on an early July evening because they need data. It is not enough to know that a silver mine on Admiralty Island or too much clear-cut logging on neighboring Chichagof Island, means nothing good for bears. You must say it in a tangled dialect of science and bureaucracy, the way Kim says it in his cramped office at the Department of Fish and Game: "In theory the model will predict the capability of the habitat to support some given population of brown bears or some reduced population of bears, given certain developmental impacts." Out here under the naked sky, in the world of fish and game, he says it this way: "We're documenting the demise of the bears."

I have never been this close to a living bear. Her eyes flicker under half-closed lids. Does she see me? Does she dream of being scented out by strange and roaring creatures? Does her heart lunge in her chest? With each shuddering breath, she groans deeply, a sound laced with menace to my ear. "Is she snoring or growling?" I ask Vern, hoping my voice reveals nothing of the dizzy way blood spins through me.

"Probably both," he says without concern. Three times he has killed a charging bear in self-defense. He never sets his short-handled rifle with the custom stock out of reach. He is not afraid of bears, but he is not stupid.

Neither is Kim Titus. Fresh to Alaska from Maryland, he is a falconer and has spent several summers studying merlin in Denali National Park. He knows wild animals, and he knows science. But he is new to this particular project, and his lanky boyishness and his eagerness reinforce the quiet authority Vern wields here on this mountaintop.

Vern rearranges the bear, stretching out her legs and tilting her head so she can breathe more easily. He estimates her age at about six years old, a teenager in bear years, and her weight at about 280 pounds. "They come a lot bigger than this," he remarks. "They come a lot smaller than this. But she's big enough to kill you." Perhaps by the way I circle the sedated bear, leaning close, but not too close, he senses my nervous thrill. "Ever held a bear's leg before?" he asks. I'm not sure if he's provoking me or soothing me. He moves to her haunches and shifts a hind leg into my hands. I struggle to heft it as he draws blood from the tender groin. Each dark hair is ticked with white; skin shines palely through the sparse fur.

"Feel how warm her paws are," Vern says, laying the blood-filled syringe in the snow. I press my palm against the leathery pad. The curving ebony claws stretch longer than my little finger. Heat radiates into my skin. When I was eight, one of the fathers in our neighborhood killed a bear and stripped away its hide. His son showed me a naked bear paw that looked like a human hand with its bluish veins and knobby fingers. No wonder so many people regard the bear as a savage relation. The Inuit thought of bears as ancestors. The Lapps called the bear "old man with the fur garment." The Finns named him "golden friend." A Tlingit Indian who encountered a brown bear always spoke to it as if it were a person, addressing it in kinship terms. If a bear killed a Tlingit, the clan followed the social law of a life for a life; the Tlingit's family sent a hunting party to kill one of the bear's family.

Under my hands, this bear is a furnace, burning with life. Vern watches me, and when he sees the look on my face, he smiles a little.

When the helicopter lofts itself from the plain, the bear lifts her groggy head for a moment and peers after us. She looks clownish with a yellow and a white tag punched into each ear and a white leather radio collar circling her neck. We have stolen something from her.

In the helicopter, we soar around peaks still dappled with snow, dip into valleys, coast over alpine meadows. The evening sun drifts toward the horizon, where soon it will snag on the Chilkat Mountains. The slanting rays illuminate tufts of grass, beds of heather, purple lupine drooping with tight blooms. Beyond Admiralty Island, golden light spills across the rumpled waters of Chatham Strait. There is something not quite real, something dreamlike, in the way we float through this stained-glass light.

We look for bears. Long ago I learned to look for bears by noting their passage along the same routes I walked. The dense black pile of shit, deposited in the middle of Peterson Lake trail, the overturned clumps of Eagle River tidal marsh where tasty roots grew, or the eye-level scratch marks in the bark of a spruce tree near Montana Creek. I learned to look, and I learned to sing out to bears, to sing *Here I am, here I am, I'm walking through your forest.* Tonight, the helicopter signals our presence for us. The sign we seek in this fragile light is an explosion of fur and muscle across the alpine tundra.

This is the best time of year to search for bears from the air. Already this spring they have marched down to the tidelands to break their winter's fast with fresh sedges, savory horsetails, the stems of skunk cabbage still burrowed into wet, sucking earth. Once the alpine snowpack retreated, the bears trekked back to the mountain slopes to feast on another generation of greens. They mate here, in the open meadows. Just last week, as Vern and Kim collared a bear on Chichagof, a boar and sow delirious with lust accidently raced over a ridge directly at the men. In the confusion, as the men scrambled for their guns and the bears realized their mistake, no one was sure who yelled "Shit!" and who yelled "Shoot!" In the final moments, before a reckoning was required, the bears veered away, and everybody was happy.

Come midsummer, the bears of Admiralty will journey yet again to the coast to gorge on spawning salmon throwing themselves up streams. For dessert, the bears will nibble blueberries growing in avalanche chutes, and then they will return upcountry to den. A few bears never leave these elevations; they forego the meaty salmon and don't know what they're missing.

Admiralty Island is the Manhattan of bears, populated with one brown bear for each of the island's seventeen hundred square miles. In the Alaskan interior, where people call brown bears "grizzlies," though they are all of the same tribe, you will find, on average, a single bear in every fifteen square miles or so. There are more bears on this island than in the entire continental United States. The Tlingit Indians call Admiralty by the name *Kootznoowoo*, which means "Fortress of the Bears."

But Admiralty is not a haven, just a holdout. Trophy hunting, clear-cut logging and the constant press of civilization threaten bears even here. You can kill bears quickly, by shooting them, or slowly, by moving in with them. When the American West was bored through by railroads and pocked with towns, it took just fifty years to eliminate nearly all grizzly bears in those parts. Today, people fight with each other in places like Idaho over whether or not bears should be reintroduced to their former haunts, but I see little point in planting bears where they are not wanted. People will insist on seeing bears always as prey or predator. Life for a bear is more complex than that.

Flying high, swooping low, we spot several bears rummaging around the valleys and crowns of Mansfield Peninsula at the northern crook of Admiralty Island. Some escape with little more than a fright, for Kim and Vern seek females, especially sows with cubs. They want to know if Greens Creek Silver Mine pushes bear families into new ranges, rather like city families abandoning the neighborhood to a freeway. If the bears do strike out for more peaceful territory, who will they elbow out of the way? Or will they simply birth fewer young?

Near the head of Greens Creek Valley, the helicopter chases a three year old recently booted out on his own by his momma. The bear scrambles up a slope and skids down the other side. He rams into a wall of ice and snow and caroms off, regaining his feet to race away again. I suck in my breath, and Kim, noticing, says, "They're tough animals." The bear tears up a slope, and the pilot swings the copter around a rocky spur and along the ridge to meet the bear, who skids to a stop almost comically and reels around. Vern has already targeted it; he shoots and says calmly, "Dart's in." A minute later the bear sits down, seemingly perplexed, and falls over into the scree.

After we land, Vern prods the bear with his rifle barrel to make sure it's out. "Beautiful coat," Kim says, admiring the golden fur. The researchers quickly complete their routine, though they decide not to collar this young male. By now, Vern has tagged nearly two hundred brown bears, so he is efficient and smooth at this work. Kim uses a wicked-looking punch to tattoo a number into its black lip, and he smears the marks with indelible, fluorescent green dye. It is a curious sort of ritual, echoing the way Tlingit hunters marked bear skins with red ochre. If a modern hunter kills this blond bear in Gambier Bay, or at Oliver Inlet, or along the shores of Barlow Cove, the Department of Fish and Game will note the bear's fate in its big book of numbers.

It does not really bother Vern and Kim to think a hunter may kill the bears they mark. Theoretically, hunting regulations can always be changed to protect bear populations, although hunters and biologists will argue for hours about how to define a healthy bear population. But much has changed since 1950, when Alaska magazine reported that a Juneau federal judge had recently returned from a hunt with the cream-colored pelt of his 129th bear.

What angers the biologists most is clear-cut logging, especially in places like northeast Chichagof Island, where large tracts of old-growth timber are systematically shaved from Tongass National Forest and private lands. Bears rely on all kinds of terrain in their wandering lives, but a clearcut is not one of them. The problem is not only that logging squeezes bears into shrinking habitats. Logging roads lead hunters easily into the dense forests; garbage dumps lure bears into villages and logging camps where they are sometimes shot for their bad habits.

Officially, most of Admiralty is considered a national wilderness area, as if words were ever enough to create such a thing. But even here, bear hunting is legal on most of the island. Native corporations log their private lands as any other business would. Greens Creek Mine, though praised by environmentalists for its sensitivity, nevertheless has claimed a valley with a salmon stream and watershed. "The frontier is ending," Kim says. And Vern adds bitterly, "It stopped when they built the pipeline. We're not making brown bear habitat anymore. I don't know of any place where we're making it."

We descend into a wide bowl glimmering with a lake of melted snow. Six black-tailed deer, dainty as fairies, graze in a line along the ridge. Two bears shamble through this basin, one breaking into a half-hearted trot around the lake when it hears the helicopter whining. Vern darts the other bear, the larger of the two, thinking it is a female. When it shows no sign of slowing, Vern aims through the open helicopter door and shoots it again with a particularly effective drug called M99. One drop will kill a human, but it takes several cc's to down a bear.

With the tufted darts dangling from its hindquarters, the bear starts up a bluff knitted with twisted spruce and blueberry bushes. "All I can say is, you guys are going to have fun in there," the pilot says over the intercom.

"Yeah, it'll be great," Kim replies, peering out the window. "She can roll a long way in there." He's worried that the bear will pass out and fall before it reaches the top. The helicopter rises about twenty feet from the bluff as the bear steadily climbs, its passage revealed only by trembling brush. Suddenly the animal lunges from an opening below the helicopter and swipes at the skids, so close that the pilot jerks the craft away to avoid the bear's reach. "Did you see that!" Kim exclaims, and we all look at each other, laughing nervously. But really, it seems only slightly amusing to reflect that if rescuers were to find our crumpled helicopter at the bluff's foot, they would never know a bear had clawed it from the sky.

The bear does indeed fall senseless ten feet below the clifftop, but the brush holds it fast. The pilot lands the copter on the plateau so Kim and Vern can hoist rifles and a cargo net over

their shoulders and scramble down to the animal. The pilot maneuvers a hook over the net and hauls the limp bear out. A scale
on the net weighs the animal at 480 pounds.

It turns out to be a male, but Kim and Vern work him over
anyway. Kim straddles the boar with his long legs, then lies with
his face buried in fur as he stretches a measuring tape around its
girth. I resist making bear-hug jokes. A hunter sizing up the pelt
would call this an eight-foot bear. Vern estimates the animal at
about thirteen years old. A brown bear can live twenty years or
more in the wild, if it avoids disease, starvation, bigger bears,
men with guns and unexpected tumbles down cliffs.

Vern asks me to hold the bear's head while he uses pliers to
yank a small premolar tooth that will reveal the bear's age as
surely as my driver's license reports mine. I grasp the rounded
ears and pull, straining to lift the massive skull and to ignore the
half-open, reddened eyes. The snout is scarred, gnarly with
ridges and bumps. "Love bites," Vern calls them. You hear that
bears smell terrible—people who have survived being mauled re-
mark on the awful stench—but this early in the season, these
bears smell no stronger than my dogs.

When Vern finishes, I lower the bear's head and then sit
close, stroking the muzzle, admiring the nearness and smallness
of my hand next to the range of yellowed teeth. It is these teeth I
dream about, when I dream about bears. Teeth, and blood.
Some part of me connects the dreams to the dark passage from
childhood to adulthood, through rites of blood and sex and love
and loss, beyond that youthful time when we're attracted to dying because we don't believe in death. When I was a teenager, I
found both independence and discovery outdoors, in the places
where my friends and I hiked and camped. It was a way to escape
adult scrutiny, to go where we wanted to go. It was how we
stretched our new bodies as we walked and walked among enormous Sitka spruce and hemlock trees or scouted along the high-
tide line of rocky beaches for the proper place to build fires and
make camp.

There always came a time of night when we told bear stories
to scare ourselves, and then we told sex stories, to scare ourselves. But I was always the first to hear the bear's hoarse breath,
to smell the rank presence, to imagine what waited in the dark. I

was the one who worried that bears could smell us bleeding as only women bleed. I was the one who lay awake all night trembling, trying not to breathe, waiting to be rended, waiting to surrender.

I pass my hand over the bear's head, across thick, coarse fur. I can't help myself; I ask if a sedated bear has ever suddenly come to life. Vern tells about the time a biologist was nearly unmanned when a bear abruptly swung its head around and snapped. Everybody laughs, even me.

I smooth the black pelt, then ruffle it again. I'm taking liberties I haven't earned. I know that. Near the shoulder rests a tiny feather, creamy with tan stripes—from a grouse, I suppose. I lift it with my little finger and poke it into the coin pocket of my jeans.

As Vern and Kim finish collaring the boar, they notice a trio of bears rambling across a slope on the opposite curve of the basin. Through binoculars Vern sees a sow trailed by two tiny cubs—"cubs of the year," they're called. This is just the sort of family the researchers covet most for their mine study. Vern decides not to administer the antidote that would bring the drugged boar to its feet in minutes. The male was probably loitering in the basin with the darkest of intentions. Male bears are cannibalistic and will eat cubs, a fine reason for mothers to be so fierce. We leave the boar slumbering on the tundra and climb into the helicopter to hop across the valley.

As the copter begins tracking the sow, the cubs struggle to keep up, tumbling and falling, tripping over themselves. The mother slows to wait for them, then bursts into a gallop again. The cubs churn their short legs as fast as they can. I clench my teeth together when I see the way they glance blindly at the sky, not sure what they're running from. We circle, looping, twisting, hovering overhead. The bears slide down a gully. Vern hangs out the door, hair blowing wildly, takes aim, darts the mother in the rump. In a few minutes, as she begins mounting a rocky chute, she sags and then falls, hind legs splayed behind her.

The helicopter lands behind a ridge, and we creep over to the bears, whispering so we don't frighten the young. The cubs cling to their mother and watch our approach; only as we draw close do they retreat, turning back to look at us every few steps. They bawl in curious, wrenching croaks. A hundred feet away they clamber onto a rocky shelf and peer over the edge at us, and I try not to stare too hard back at them.

The men work quickly so the cubs do not wander off. Vern has a hard time finding a blood vein on the inside of the sow's hind leg, so when he does feel it, he asks me to mark the pulse with my finger while he readies the needle. Her blood surges in hesitant throbs against my skin. I think of the bear in her winter den, this faint beat offering comfort to the cubs while they, still barely formed, burrowed against her fur. Aristotle believed the mother bear licked her cubs into being, shaped them for the world.

The clean air chills. It's nearly ten at night, and the sun fades in a painterly way, coloring the sky in shades of salmon. The nearness of the honey-colored bear, the occasional squall of her cubs, the panorama that draws the eye beyond this green basin, across the straits—I try to saturate my memory with these details. A sense of beauty and loss pierces me as I struggle to tell myself something important, something lasting about this night, about how I have glimpsed the way bears live here, high above the world, and yet not nearly far enough away from roads, chainsaws, guns, helicopters. If this mountain top is wilderness, then it is wilderness that rubs so close to civilization that I can feel it fraying beneath my feet.

It is one of the oldest stories in the world, how the woman married the bear and gave him half-human, half-bear young. In the Haida version, her brothers killed her bear lover, of course, but the offspring lived to teach the people, to help them hunt, before returning to the bear world. It's been said that we kill what we both revere and dread. That is what myths do, turn something greater than ourselves into something human. I'm doing it right now.

It's a hard thing to know, that our weakness is that we hate what is stronger than us. And yet, without bears roaming through forests, climbing down from mountains, frightening us, what will we respect on this earth? What is left to remind us that while we stand in a world shadowed by myth, wilderness, death, we cannot master it, nor can we deny it?

When Vern finishes collaring the bear, he injects her with an antidote so she will rouse quickly and gather her cubs. He stands for a moment, looking down at the sow. She should be stirring. Kim gestures to me, and we pick our way back to the helicopter. I look back just once, to fix the still bear and those cubs in my mind. A few minutes later, Vern climbs into his seat. He doesn't say anything. I want to ask him about the bear, but I'm afraid to know. Sometimes, not often, but sometimes, things go wrong. Sometimes the drugs kill them, or hypothermia, or other bears. I'm afraid to know what could happen to the sow and her cubs. This is my weakness, that I'm afraid to know.

Sky translates itself into night as we fly homeward, across the peaks. We land on a mountain slope to recover the passenger door removed earlier so Vern could lean into the wind and track bears. Kim leads me to a nearby ridge and pauses at the edge of a trail. After a moment, I see what he wants me to see. Deep into the tundra, hollows dimple the path where, for centuries, bears have placed their feet in the same spot with every step. They wear their passage into the earth as they come down from the mountains and then return, season after season. I realize that there's another way to see bears—that a bear has nothing to do with us at all, that it lives wholly for itself and its kind, without any obligation to teach us a thing. The trail rises from the valley and disappears into dusk above us, and I feel no urge to step onto that trail myself.

When we return to the helicopter for the last short hop to Juneau, Kim and I look across Mansfield Peninsula, the only part of Admiralty not set aside as official wilderness. "This is beautiful, isn't it?" Kim says, almost helplessly. A moment later, he adds, "This is all scheduled for timber harvest." He starts to say something else, but he stops. Some things words can't do.

At home, in the dark, I hold my hands to my face. The smell of bear clings to me, not a stench, but a wild, pungent scent that I breathe again and again, as if I could draw it into myself. Perhaps those who are half-human, half-bear, smell like this. Perhaps they look like everybody else, but they are cloaked by a feral spirit. Perhaps they see things they don't say.

The scent evaporates by morning. The scrap of feather I

robbed from the bear's pelt disappears from my pocket. Anyway, it was so small. What remains is this: I still dream of bears, but in the dreams I watch. I don't run. I don't speak. The bears watch me, silent, waiting. I am not afraid of bears, I tell myself. I am not afraid.

Night Skates

Susanna Levin

When you live in the city, it's easy to feel trapped: either you're indoors, or you're on the street. Stepping out of an apartment building onto dirty pavement isn't usually described as "going outdoors."

This is especially true if, like me, you're the kind of person who thrives on outdoor sports, and particularly the so-called action sports, like skiing and rock climbing, where your life depends on your ability to control your body through the dimensions of time and space. The thrill-seeking city dweller has to *go to* the outdoors by car or by plane. And so the outdoors becomes a distant abstraction, a temptation, a source of self-torment.

I recently discovered that it's foolish to make such a distinction between the wild outdoors and the urban outdoors. In the process, I discovered an action sport that was made for the urban environment, for *my* urban environment—San Francisco. Now, I get my outdoor ya-yas, risking my neck and overloading my senses, in the ozone-choked air of city streets. I do it on skates, after dark.

Taking to the streets at night with an eclectic assortment of people on in-line skates (also known as Rollerblades), I experience time slowing down. I have always associated this sensation with playing in the great outdoors—dropping into a chute on skis, for example, or descending single track on a mountain bike. My ears and eyes plug directly into my motor neurons and go on high-level alert.

The night is the crucial element in this transformation. For high-speed nocturnal navigation on skates, visual processing is secondary to kinesthetics and proprioception: you rely on your body's sense of where you are and where you're going; you continuously react to terrain and gravity in an effort to remain upright and under control. Where you are on earth is much less important than where you are in space.

Of course, on earth I am in a city, yes, but it's also the country's premier paved ski resort, with an endless supply of double black-diamond runs and near-perfect conditions year-round.

Night skating didn't always strike me as a great idea. When I first started skating, I stuck to the relative safety of Golden Gate Park and broad daylight. It seemed like a winning combination. I'd heard about the night skate, and it sounded scary. The thought of contending with cars, trucks and potholes, not to mention the hills, seemed far beyond me. Skating from Golden Gate Park to downtown was just absurd: not only was there a three-hundred-foot elevation loss between here and there, but downtown had buses and taxis and Muni tracks and lost tourists, faking left and then turning right across three lanes of traffic. All of this, in the dark of the night.

Then one Sunday, at a local skate race in the Park, I met Jenny, a night skater who turned out to be a friend of an old friend. Jenny was a better skater than I was, but she wasn't *that* much better. Maybe it was just stupid competitiveness, but I figured if she could do the night skate, it wasn't a total impossibility. Besides, I immediately liked and trusted Jenny. She was enthusiastic and reassuring; she made the night skate sound like something fun, not some keep-up-or-die hammerfest around the city. I agreed to come out the following Tuesday night.

Of course, one better offer for Tuesday night and I would have bagged in a minute. But no excuses arose, and at seven on Tuesday I turned up at "skate central" in Golden Gate Park. It was an uncharacteristically warm, bright spring evening in San Francisco; both the fog and the wind had the night off. The days were lengthening, so it was still light when I arrived. A few skaters were already gathered and, to my enormous relief, Jenny was among them. As I rolled up, she was pulling a couple of lacrosse sticks and a ball from the back of her truck, and we started up a game of roller-lacrosse as we waited for more night riders.

I was immediately self-conscious. Roller-lacrosse was giving people the chance to demonstrate their ability to stop, turn on a dime and jump, while I could only roll around in wide-radius arcs, at a single speed.

Skaters, on ice or pavement, are divided into only two categories: the balanced and the unbalanced. Either you are in control of your edges, and you glide with effortless, elegant grace, or you are at their mercy, prone to intermittent spastic contortions when they betray you. I was unbalanced. If I didn't try anything too tricky, I could pass, but in fact, I was too worried about looking like a dork to experiment and learn to skate backwards and do quick spin-stops. As with many sports, to gain control, you have to be willing to give it up.

Skaters slowly turned up. At seven-thirty, there were seven of us. I recognized most faces from around the park, but Jenny and a local racer named Mike were the only two I knew by name. Judging from the preponderance of racing skates and the sinewy legs that sprouted from them, it was a hardcore group.

The group convened. "Where should we go?" someone asked.

"Downtown," another replied.

Although this would not always be the case, on this night there was no dissent.

"Which way?"

"Let's go Golden Gate."

Helmets were adjusted (I was the only person wearing knee pads, but everyone had wrists guards and most had helmets) and a few of us turned on flashing red lights that were attached to our helmets. (I had one of these. In fact, I had every piece of protection except a condom.)

We skated out of the park and onto Fulton Street. The pack was immediately in the road and, since the sidewalk was rough and cracked, I soon joined them. As we snaked through the streets north of Fulton, I felt surprisingly safe. There were hardly any cars, and the heft of a seven-skater pack seems to justify occupying the road. Connect the dots, and we're big as a truck.

I was a little concerned that we were going *up*hill. There is no way to get from the Park to downtown San Francisco without descending at least one monstrous hill. Every additional foot of altitude we gained, we were going to have to lose. This, I supposed, was the whole point.

Within a couple of minutes, we were at the top of Golden Gate Avenue, on Lone Mountain near the University of San Francisco. From there, Golden Gate runs east, away from the park, toward the federal architecture of the Civic Center and downtown. As is so often the case on skates, I began to appreciate nuances of this city's topography that had eluded me before. Only the Golden Gate hill isn't really a nuance: it's a fucking ski jump, plummeting over three hundred feet.

As the group assembled at the crest of the first steep section of the street, I didn't really have time to think about whether or not this was a very good idea, or even possible. Had I been by myself, however, I never would have dreamed of attempting it.

Mike, a shy, somewhat awkward guy in his early twenties, had some words of advice for me. Mike looked like he wouldn't be caught dead on a dance floor, but with skates on, he was a regular Nureyev. It was the Zen master's blend of skill and brevity that made me hang on his every word. "The lights are timed," he told me. "When this next one turns red, count to ten and then go."

"All the way to the bottom?" I asked.

"All the way. But cut it loose or you won't make it."

Whatever you say, Mike. I'm putting my life in your hands. The light turned, and Mike bowed his head, giving a slow nod for each integer. . . . nod eight, . . . nod nine, . . . "GO!" he yelled, and he went. Then I went, lemming-like. Mike got into a tuck and so did I. A guy named Chris shot past me, a light brown blur, but then no one else. Was everybody bombing this stretch, I suddenly wondered, or was I out front with the suicides while everybody else took the pro-life route?

The first light changed a few seconds before we reached it,

just as Mike predicted. Just to be on the safe side, Chris let out an authentic-sounding police siren whoop as we entered the intersection. (That sound would become the clarion call of the night skate, and my first few times out he fooled me about half the time. Every time Chris shot through an intersection, I'd turn around to see where the cops were.)

All my weight was in my feet. I remember looking down to see my skates tracking straight, taking comfort in their solidity. We hit that light at full speed, and then the next, and the next— with two heartbeats of apprehension verging on panic before each light blinked from red to green.

Below Divisadero, the street turns into a three-lane one-way. Mike, Chris and I occupied the right lane leaving plenty of room in the two remaining lanes for cars. I was faintly surprised that no one honked at us, but traffic was light, and we were moving faster than they were anyway.

It wasn't quite dark as we buzzed through the projects near Buchanan Street: the air was still rich with the purple light that lingers in the San Francisco sky after sunset on a bright day. A certain part of my brain was assigned to vigilance: watching the lights, listening for cars, scanning the ground for those built-in reflective lane markers, which at that speed were like little tombstones. Most of my consciousness, however, was awash in something much more potent than adrenalin: I was having the kind of rush you only get when you're doing something really fun, really stupid and illegal.

A Beastie Boys song came into my head. It was the perfect soundtrack: adolescent. Aggro. While screaming downhill on in-line skates at thirty miles an hour may not be an obvious time for insight, I was struck by my pleasure at behaving like an insubordinate thirteen-year-old. It was a Peter Pan thing, and I *was* flying.

We crossed six lanes of traffic on Van Ness, just beating the light, and blew by Star's, where I drink scotch in another life. As we descended into the piss of the Tenderloin, screaming past the crack dealers and prostitutes, I recognized the practical advantages of speed.

The Golden Gate rollercoaster finally bottomed out at Market Street, in the heart of downtown. Half the pack had fallen behind the lights, so we waited in silence for them to catch up. I figured out later that it had taken us five minutes, maybe less, to cover two miles: that's better than twenty-four miles per hour. It was now almost completely dark, and my self-consciousness of the roller-lacrosse game was gone. Yeah, I might not be able to skate backward, but I've always been good at speed.

We skated a mile or so to Embarcadero Center, a downtown, open-air shopping mall with numerous architectural invitations to skaters and skateboarders. One of these is a glass-walled, paved, spiral walkway in the center of a square courtyard. The walkway, which is about ten feet wide, does three rotations as it winds down from the third floor to ground level.

I had never done any trick skating, but out of sheer pack mindlessness, I followed everyone up the spiral.

Up is easy.

Down, however, calls for a series of tight turns at ever-accelerating speeds and, (the hard part), the ability to stop when centrifugal force flings you out at the bottom.

A guy named Nick went first. Tall and barrel-chested, with longish black hair feathering down his neck, Nick was the only skater that I suspected was older than me. But his style and his relish for radical jumps, said *pueri eternis*. Nick took the spiral fast, finishing with a skidding power-slide that stopped him just short of a group of wide-eyed tourists.

I watched a couple of other skaters do the spiral; a few zipped through it like Nick, others went more slowly; somebody grabbed the rail. It reminded me of wreaking havoc in another urban playground—lower Manhattan—when I was a kid visiting my cousin. We would slide down the escalator banisters and scale the aluminum sculptures that were Wall Street's public art.

No one was looking by the time I came down the spiral. I made it through the first loop okay, but then I got spooked by my speed. There was an opening in the railing onto the second floor, and I shot through it, only to discover I was heading straight for the plate-glass window of Ann Taylor.

I made a sharp right turn to miss the window, then applied the brake and skidded to a stop. No problem. I looked around and, comforted by the fact that no one had seen my dorky little detour, I got back on the spiral and rode the railing the rest of the way down.

We left the Embarcadero, and headed back uptown on Market Street, San Francisco's main drag and ugliest feature. It's a strange place to be at night—so strange, in fact, that nobody really seemed to notice a pack of skaters flying down the sidewalk and leaping over benches. Now and again someone would look at me through bleary eyes, and say, "Hey. . . ." I had the distinct feeling that they were not completely convinced I was really there.

Mike and Nick were leading, and after a few blocks they pulled up at the entrance to the Montgomery station of BART, San Francisco's subway.

"Let's do it." Chris said. Augie, a lean guy with dark skin and thick black hair, who'd been smiling since we left the park, suddenly got serious. "I'm not going," he said.

The others started down the stairs into the subway, then stopped. "C'mon man, let's go," Mike said.

Augie just skated off, saying he'd meet us at the exit. I followed down the stairs—taking them skater style: walking backward, holding the rail. I was not particularly psyched about our imminent transgression. Skaters have been banned from the streets in a few cities around the country, and this kind of sortie seemed just the thing to make trouble in this town.

It was about nine, and the BART station was empty. It didn't take long for me to see why we were here. In these quarter-mile-long underground walkways, with their linoleum smooth as butter, there's no resistance to our urethane wheels. It's like the Bonneville Speedway of skating—surreal, like the Utah salt flats at Bonneville, and irresistible for speed freaks. With just a few strokes I was flying through the fluorescence, whipping by ads for shoes and shopping centers.

As we neared the end of the first section of tunnel, a disembodied voice buzzed over a loudspeaker. "No skating in the station. Exit the station immediately. There is no skating in the station." The voice faded as we rolled down the next section of walkway, whizzing under a city block in about seven seconds. At the end of that stretch, a second loudspeaker hissed at us, this one a little more insistent: "No skates allowed in the station. Take off your skates or get out of the station."

There was something comical about blowing by these finger-wavers in their little booths, one after another, but I was relieved when we hopped on the escalator and headed out of the station. I didn't mind being bad, I realized, but I didn't want to get called on it.

I was trying to figure out whether skating in a BART station was a misdemeanor or not, when I understood why Augie stayed above ground. He was probably not an American citizen. Getting busted, even for a misdemeanor, could be catastrophic for him. When the rest of the group descended the stairs to skate another stretch in the next BART station, I skated the street above with Augie.

The pack emerged from the underground back at the Civic Center; from there, it's a long, steady climb on Market to Church Street, in the Castro district. The lead skaters formed a paceline, tucked in tightly one behind the other. Like cyclists, skaters can work together to cut the wind and increase their speed this way, but I hung back, unsure of my ability to stroke in synchrony.

At Church, we turned right and started zig-zagging through the streets of the Lower Haight, past the slacker cafes and night spots. The terrain suddenly got much steeper; again, we were on streets that I travel everyday but had never imagined skating. On a particularly steep stretch of Steiner Street, Augie skated up behind me and pushed me up the hill. My ego, which sometimes overvalues self-sufficiency, was tweaked, but my legs told me to be grateful.

When we turned left again, Page Street loomed monstrously between us and home. It was steep and five times the length of the stretch I'd just struggled up. All of a sudden, it felt way past my bedtime. Halfway up the first of three blocks of serious climbing, I realized how ill-suited the tools were to the purpose. When it's steep, you don't skate so much as run up the hill, in short choppy steps. In the space of three blocks, Chris and Mike had picked up about two-hundred yards on me; Jenny and Augie were not far behind them.

By the time we zigged back onto the relative flatness of upper

Haight Street, I was sucking wind big time. I chased the other four through Haight-Ashbury in overdrive, never quite getting my breath back. Once at the park, the group dispersed quickly; I hardly had time to say good-bye, and thanks. I skated the short distance home by myself.

When I arrived at my house, I was still breathing hard from the chase up Haight. It was after eleven, and tired as I was, sleep was out of the question. All the brain chemicals that had me pumped up like that were a long way from quieting down. But this wasn't the kind of feeling I have after a good long run in the park or even a bike ride on Mount Tam. This was a complete release. I felt like I had been to another planet, and maybe the night is another world, as different from daytime as country is from city.

In the months that followed, I became a regular on the night skate. I eagerly looked forward to Tuesday nights. Jenny, Mike and Augie were always there. Ingrid, a lifelong skater whom I'd always admired, started coming out again after the birth of her first child.

I looked forward to seeing all of them and to chasing them up and down hills and along the flats. More than that, though, I looked forward to being out in the night air, and visiting those parts of this city that in the daytime are sacrificed to tourists.

Our route often took us along Pier 39, where we'd stop and rest. The Golden Gate Bridge glowed in the distance, and beyond Alcatraz, the lights of Sausalito hovered just above the water. Boats floated by, and sea lions sprawled on the docks below. Big, blubbery sighs and random barks drifted up from the dark. Sometimes we'd go from there to Chinatown, where the pavement was always slick with something, maybe duck fat.

I started seeing the city differently. I began to know where it is quiet at night and where it hums; where it is cool and where the warm air lingers. Parts of town that I once avoided because they were congested or boring became my favorites because there's a hill that's just the right grade or fresh pavement or timed lights.

After I started skating the streets at night, I noticed I could go for weeks without feeling that desperate urge to escape the city. I still craved the solitude, quiet and timelessness that you have to get out of the city to get. But I didn't resent the fact that ninety percent of my life was spent on asphalt, because the pavement became my medium.

In fact, when I went to the mountains, I started telling people they should come to the city and skate with me. Of course, they looked at me as if I were suggesting a new career as a crash-test dummy. But I was caught up in the wild, glorious rush of it all; I was in that state where the danger was part of the thrill, but I hadn't yet learned real respect for it.

That all changed one night, some months after my first skate, when fourteen of us set our sights on the city skater's crowning achievement: Twin Peaks, San Francisco's eight-hundred-foot apex.

We left the park and went first to the beach, making for a brutally long climb from sea level. The road to the viewing area parking lot is so steep that in some stretches our locomotion was more like duckwalking than skating.

It was a spectacularly clear night, and the view from the top is 360 degrees: from the black Pacific, identifiable only by the twin-kling lights of ships in the distance, to the Golden Gate and its Bridge, to the Marin Headlands across the bay, to the pulsing lights of downtown, and east, to Oakland. That is San Francisco: an unending, glowing, buzz of life in one direction, and in the other, total darkness.

On top of Twin Peaks, I got to ask myself, again, a question I remember puzzling over when I was about six, at the top of a very tall tree. Why is it so damn easy to climb up to places from which you cannot get down?

The road that descends from the parking lot spirals around the perimeter of the mountain. As you descend the road, you start facing north, then west, south, and east. On the west side of the mountain, the air is cold, straight off the Pacific. On the city side, it's warm. Leaving aside these micro-climatic oddities, the trip down this completely unlit, poorly-paved road is a virtual free-fall. Compared to Twin Peaks, the spiral walkway at the Embarcadero Center was a merry-go-round. And here, there's no way to get off.

Keith, my guardian angel on this particular evening, skated with me. I kept my knees loose, to absorb unexpected ruts, and like a blind person, I followed Keith's instruction for each stretch of terrain:

"Around this bend, stand up and let the head wind slow you," he shouted. It slowed me.

Then, "Take a right at the bottom of this stretch for an uphill run-out." Worked like a charm.

With his help, I reached the bottom without incident, but as it turned out, I had precious little time to savor my accomplishment. We headed back to the park through the Sunset District, a basically flat section of town. There are a couple of big hills out there, but I didn't think we were near them. I was almost home and feeling pretty good, so I let down my guard.

I followed everyone down a block of 18th Avenue that has a slight downhill grade, but nothing major. I had a good head of steam as I entered the intersection, and I was over the lip onto the next block before I saw what lay ahead: the street suddenly got very steep—about the pitch of an escalator—and I was out of control instantly. I tried to do some slalom turns to lose speed, but I kept accelerating. In my peripheral vision, I could see houses and parked cars rushing by in blurry darkness. I went for my heel brake, but I was too late—it doesn't work at twenty miles an hour.

I looked up to see Ingrid, my skating idol, slaloming across the hill in front of me, completely in control. I shouted something, "Watch out," or "On your right," then I shot past her, almost taking her down. "Sorry!" I yelled back, feeling like the total idiot I was.

There was hardly time for self-deprecation though, as the emerging details of the next intersection revealed to me that I was in deep trouble: I had a stop sign. The cross-traffic didn't. There were headlights coming from the left. My only chance was to make a sharp right turn, going with the flow of traffic, and trying to stay close to the curb. Then I saw the train tracks, lying like twin vipers in the street.

I probably could have made the turn, but my brain overloaded and I bailed, taking a semi-controlled, hard, sliding fall onto my right side. My protective gear did its job: the wrist guards absorbed the brunt of the impact, and the plastic on my knee pads grated along the pavement. I could hear the hollow scraping of plastic on blacktop as my knee pad sacrificed its outer layer to save mine. My thigh wasn't so lucky.

I hopped up and onto the sidewalk quickly, helped by my momentum, which never really stopped. Humiliated and disgusted with myself, and hoping to minimize the attention given my fall, I made a big show of being okay. In fact, I was sure I hadn't broken anything, but my right thigh felt like chopped meat.

Keith skated over to see how I was, but my quick hop up and the lack of visible blood was convincing. The rest of the pack continued on, and I limp-rolled the final half mile home. The thrill comes from the risk, but sometimes the risk turns on you and bites.

The honeymoon was over; I couldn't sit comfortably for a week. After my road rash healed, I went through a period of overly cautious skating. I enjoyed myself a lot less and mourned the loss of the ignorant's euphoria. I took a second, minor fall a few weeks later precisely because I was being too cautious: while trying unnecessarily to scrub some speed with slalom turns, I hit a patch of wet pavement and went down.

On a more practical level, though, I worked on control. I learned to carve better slalom turns and to T-stop by dragging one foot behind me, which is more effective than the heel brake. Gradually, my new and improved skating ability revived both my nerve and my pleasure.

Meanwhile, the night skate started to grow, fed by the booming popularity of in-line skates. Fourteen skaters soon became thirty; then thirty ballooned to sixty and sixty mushroomed to one hundred forty. Dozens and dozens of skaters, not all of them very skilled, now hit the streets of San Francisco every Friday night. I join them occasionally.

For me, the allure of the skate is dimmed by sheer numbers—it's more of a parade than a sortie. What's worse is that to accommodate newcomers, the skate follows the same route every night. There's no more exploration, and to prevent massive carnage, the big hills, including Golden Gate Avenue and Twin Peaks, are out.

Fortunately, at about the same time, I discovered that if the terrain is radical enough, you can have a pretty good time in broad daylight. Jenny and Mike turned me on to the downhill terrain on Tunnel Road, in the hills above Oakland. The area has been deserted since the great blazes of '91, so the roads are mostly empty.

What this skate lacks in nocturnal otherworldliness, it makes up for in sheer, protracted, mind-numbing speed. It's about five miles up, and then five miles full-steam downhill. It's safe because with all the trees burned down, you can see ahead for oncoming cars or cyclists around every curve. Here, in this devastated area where wildfire levelled urban habitat, I found the city skater's paradise. I went there nearly every weekend during the winter.

When ski season rolled around, I noticed an extraordinary change in myself. When I went to the mountains to ski, I didn't feel the old streak of longing, the sense that every day I spent back in the city I was missing out on the best life had to offer. As long as I had Tunnel Road, I didn't have to wake up every single morning and talk myself out of blowing off work and heading for the hills.

This is a good thing, because for now I am where I am. And for now, I'll find the thrill of the outdoors where urethane meets pavement.

*A*AMAA DIDI

Jean Gould

A WOMAN WALKS BACK and forth, up and down over rice, drying it with her feet. Thin and barefoot, she holds an infant. Together they cannot weigh more than eighty pounds. At the Bagmati River near a Hindu temple, two bodies burn, tended by low caste men in rags. On the other side, women wash clothes on rocks, two men bathe, and a child drinks. Bagmati means "mouth of the tiger."

Elsewhere in Kathmandu, at Swayambhunath shrine, for example, Buddhists chant prayers to the motion of wheels while small monkeys chatter. A black goat wanders on the steep part of the domed *stupa*, or shrine, as a vendor plays a gentle melody on a wooden flute.

On unpaved streets, beggars with stumps for arms or legs sleep in dusty corners decorated with marigolds. Offering peanuts for sale in wicker baskets, women with gold teeth smoke cigarettes.

Before this month is out, this November, I will be the rice woman, the Hindu, the Buddhist, the monkey, that black goat. I will become the marigold, the river, the temple, and yes, even the wooden flute, the beggar. I will give myself over to flags of prayer called wind horses. And more. Much more.

Just now, of course, I do not know any of this. Just now, I am spending my first full day in Nepal, where I have come to celebrate my fiftieth birthday. Today, a witness, I am outside the high peaks and blue-purple skies enveloping this city. Predictably, societal contrasts energize me: whether you kill a man or a cow, you serve a jail sentence of eighteen years; there is no law regarding the murder of women.

Why have I come here? Why not? Although I feel somehow ageless, I am willing to acknowledge, indeed find it necessary to mark fifty years of living, to reward myself for having made it this far.

That night, I wake myself laughing, the taste of hot peppers and beer still on my tongue. Opening the French doors of my hotel room, I find the air heavy and fragrant in the walled-in courtyard. Bougainvillea, a lavender color only hours before, is now gray in the absence of light. Standing at the threshold, naked, I imagine rolling in the thick grass just beyond. The joy of all that has brought me to this place holds me as I dare to step outside.

At dawn the next morning, women and men huddle against the cold in doorways draped with flowers, as I leave Kathmandu for Pokara and the hills of Annapurna. The valley is fogged in. While the rusting van wobbles me over these ancient roadways, fruit bats large as opossums hang from pine trees. I am to spend ten days in the Annapurna range tuning up for two more weeks trekking in the Everest foothills.

I have joined a group of six others, mostly Americans, including one married couple. The others, two women and two men, have come alone, as I have. We are all white. As the sun rises and the day becomes warmer, we compare notes on training, expectations, nutrition, jobs. The woman who is to share my tent, Ellen from Missouri, smaller, younger, knows more than I do, and for once, that doesn't rankle me, as I note that her self-sufficiency parallels mine.

The journey is slow with frequent stops in villages I am told have no names. Everywhere, children's noses run. And it is striking to realize just how equally fathers share the caretaking of young children with such obvious pleasure. One carries an infant under his arm, swirls it around, places it on a table and then kisses it with abandon. A child of three or four tries to split wood with an axe under a father's gentle supervision. Fathers, uncles, even teenage boys hold, rock, or play with children as the treasures they are.

It is true that poverty, at least as it is defined by Westerners, is everywhere. Emaciated dogs roam the streets, their menacing ribs protruding such that it seems that the flesh must be inside and bones on the surface. If there are sewers at all, they run open in narrow ditches. In defense, some in our group speak about their possessions at home and their abundant lives. Some talk of "Saturday Night Live" and hairdryers and the Dallas Cowboys. When I sit on a dusty hillside and children cluster around me, I try out the hundred or so words of Nepali I have learned by tape. Ellen takes photographs of us playing tic-tac-toe. Later, a little girl with bright, almond eyes sits in my lap laughing when I ask her to sing, and I feel happier than I can remember, having abandoned myself to these moments. When the children ask for pens, for candy, for money, I ask them to draw in my journal while I sing "I'm a Little Teapot," and others touch my face and eyelashes and earrings and hair. My own nose runs. *Kitaab*, I say. Book. *Kalaakaara*, I say. Artist. I cannot think of the word for writer. But they are more interested in my children. *Ek*, I say, holding up one finger.

When we set out from Pokara the next day for our first climb, we are all anxious and full of energy from months of physical training and healthy food. Our *sirdar* or guide is Gelbu, an optimistic Sherpa who will stay with us both here and at Everest. Leaving the town, we zig-zag past cows, goats and women with huge straw baskets full of sticks and grasses on their backs. Already, with the pink of dawn in the hills, it is warm, and my skin is moist with sweat.

We all sprint enthusiastically for the first hour of the climb, although we are going almost straight uphill at a sharp angle. I am ashamed to admit to myself that I am competitive, as if this were a race with a prize at the end, but as quickly, I give up the notion of being first when I see that others, at least on this first day, are fitter, stronger, taking less water. There is only one who is older than I: Hans, a German, who climbed Kilimanjaro for his fiftieth birthday.

When we reach our campsite, the Sherpas have tea ready, our tents up, and warm water with which to wash. All day, walking on stones and rocks, one foot, then the next, there was little to see except the trunks of many tall trees. Here now, in this clearing at dusk, the terraced fields arrange themselves below us, geometrically perfect. The air is quiet and my body gives thanks for a day of strenuous activity as I stretch out my long legs, remove my boots, and drop my pack. An inchworm floats on its invisible string just next to me with only the gigantic Annapurna behind it, and what is small and what is big seem not so easy to know as they did this morning.

The dinner of rice and lentils, *daal bhat*, takes no getting used to; it is splendid from this first day on the mountain. I have brought dried apricots and trail mix in my pack as a supplement, but I am almost never hungry, except at meals. All of us, as instructed, try to drink as much liquid as we can, although we are only at about 7,500 feet. Hans, an engineer, trained for Kilimanjaro by running up and down twenty flights of stairs during his lunch hour. Already certain of dysentery, he carries a roll of toilet paper around his neck on a string and has the huge, sweet face of a Saint Bernard. The married couple is so exhausted they skip dinner and disappear into their tent.

That night in our sleeping bags, Ellen and I giggle at ourselves. Just lying down is a major gift, we say.

"I'm glad you hate football," I say.

"I think this is probably the last excitement in my life for a while," she says. "When I get back to St. Louis, I'm going to try to get pregnant." Both of us left husbands at home. Mine, in fact, is an ex-husband, the second one. We decide to make predictions about the trip, but fall asleep in the middle of our sentences in what is to become a pattern for the time ahead.

That night, I begin the first of many odd dreams, odd in the sense that even for the other-worldliness of dreams, the people and events seem out of place. The colors are wrong. The time sequence is at once too slow, too fast. There are tangential people from my convent childhood: a nun who let me play with her veil; a priest prying a communion wafer from the roof of my mouth. And then, miraculously, I am in a place with huge plumed birds of gold and green and red, flying on their backs or under my own power. I wake replenished, as if I'd devoured an additional meal during the night.

During the next few days we slip into a routine that offers many comforts, beginning with tea before dawn and ending with dinner and sleep at dusk. In between, we climb and stumble and soar among the hills and other wild things: great plants with exotic flowers whose names I do not need to know; birds with large fringed wingspans not unlike those in my dreams.

Ellen, Hans and I join with Ann, a woman from Washington just out of college, to form an agreeable foursome. Ellen, thirty-two, and Ann, twenty-one, are tiny, no more than five feet tall; Hans and I are huge by comparison, as well as old enough to be their parents. All of us notice that our clothes seem to be more wrinkled than that of the other three, and as time passes, we speak less and less about home. Age and size and clothing are somehow irrelevant. Even the fact that Ellen is Jewish and Hans German appears to be of no consequence. Eventually, we will discover that allowing ourselves to be captured by this present experience is what connects us: the surges of energy and their counterparts; an awareness of the pulse of muscles. Breath. Air. Water. And mountain. Always the challenges of the mountain.

One afternoon, when I stop in the woods to watch a tiny lizard-like creature slither among begonia-shaped leaves, my heart pounds beyond its rib cage, and I realize I have lost track of time. Others have been tired, taken altitude medication or antibiotics, but I have maintained myself on eight to ten liters of water a day. Ellen has dubbed me "best sleeper." But now I am overwhelmed with fatigue, and we are spread out on this trail full of boulders and soft mud, so that I see no one. I hum Souza's "Washington Post March" and perch myself on a smooth, flat rock. The leaves are nothing like begonias, I realize; they are too red, too big. As the lizard stops just aside of my boot, I imagine that our eyes meet. But it's more of a snake than a lizard as its feet have vanished and its skin shows an intricate yellow design. The red tongue darts in and out, beautiful against the yellow-green, and my heart rests and my breath comes more evenly as I am honored by this interaction, which in another time might have been frightening. From my pack, I retrieve the iodized water I have come to crave and am able to rise after a long drink. But my feet, uncooperative, develop a will of their own, taking one tiny step, then another in such utter slow motion that I am exasperated.

Kami, a young Sherpa, arrives and takes my pack. *Pani*? Water? he asks. Too tired to make my jaw speak, I nod. As he holds my arm and walks with me to the campsite, I am sure I will not be able to continue; I might be having a heart attack.

"How old you are?" he says in English.

"*Pachaas*," I say. Fifty.

"*Pachaas*? Fifty?" He is sixteen. Like the other Sherpas, he has called me *didi* or older sister; now he rolls his eyes and says, *aamaa didi*, mother/older sister. He never again lets me out of his sight. Strong and determined and oh-so independent in my real life, I love this kindness. My heart attack is gone.

When he deposits me at my tent with *chiya*, tea, the others are already at dinner, and I realize that it is nearly sunset as clouds gather over the greenness, over the heat of the day. Hot, thirsty, I sleep, wake up and know that this is, in fact, my real life, that whatever went on before is an island of some memory with only patches of truth in it.

"Electrolyte replacement," Kami says in perfect English as he pours orange liquid into my empty tea cup. In Nepali, I ask about his family and offer him some of the magic potion in my hand, although I know it is improper to drink from the same vessel. He brings food, but I am too tired to eat more than a bite of delicious, crisp *chappati*, flattened bread. Removing my boots, he tells me his family lives in the Khumbu, the Everest region, that he studied geography in school, that the best career is the army. I am lying down now; I am full of sleep; from the dinner tent there is music, singing. Kami will never join the army. "Too many guns," he says. I struggle to form the word non-violent on my lips, certain I know the Nepali word. His teeth are the whitest and most even I have ever seen.

The next morning, before beginning our descent, we have breakfast at what must be the top of the world. In fact, we are at only 9,000 feet, but the ancient terraces are so far below that we seem aloft here on this lovely expanse of earth higher, at least, than I have been thus far. Worried about malaria, the married couple talks about forming a chloroquine support group. Someone offers Muesli to mix with porridge. Fifty yards away, the porters and guides lie on the slope singing. From this clearing, the entire Annapurna range is gently visible as a pastel, while at my feet, tiny violet bluebells appear. I will not consider meditation until many months after this, but now I breathe deeply, more deeply than I can recall, folding this moment into my being.

Ellen tells me I'm over-tired; Hans takes my pack; even Ann who is usually at the front of the group on the trail, stays in the middle with me, while Kami brings up the rear. I feel better and better as we descend into the large, feathery ferns and giant white thistly-looking flowers growing spontaneously from the mountainside.

"Pay attention to your feet," Hans says, when I slip, as I point out a woodpecker overhead. The staccato of locusts greets us, like sleigh bells, I think. Ferns and thistles. Locusts and sleigh bells. Such contrasts. Now vultures circle low in the sky above us. Ellen says they're eagles. Ann sings "Taps." And I talk about tap dancing, while Kami rushes to pick me up when I fall crossing a stream. I try to explain what a guardian angel is, but he doesn't get it.

"Oh Didi, Aamaa didi," says Kami, bandaging my knee, disinfecting my leg. "You care take," he says. "You stop fall. You be happy."

"*Kushi*," I say. "Happy."

"Listen to him," says Ann, her blondness glowing around her like a mane.

"Yes. Listen. You can't afford to bleed here, to get wounded, infected." Ellen is angry with me.

But as we walk along narrow ledges, through sweet-smelling towns of more animals than humans, I am very happy. Kushi, I say only to myself this time. Even the roosters crow all day long around houses and millet fields.

Without bathrooms and hot water, Irving, my latest ex-husband, would be miserable here; he would not be as heartened by locusts or crows as I am. Nor would he embrace unwashed children so freely or try to teach them the hokey-pokey. And I find tears, just a few, on my cheeks now as I take in the poinsettia bushes and wish for a minute or two that he could be as charmed as I am by the depth of color and precision in nature. Lower and lower, the mountains crumble in bits around us, shape themselves into houses, walls, more rocky trails. They carry us from town to town, are trod upon by water buffalo, sacred cows, pigs, sheep, and even chickens. Many in our group complain of sore knees as we descend, but I have less trouble than with climbing and know again that I can manage this trip. The challenges of physical exertion erase everything else from the mind, clear the senses, maximize the body's capability, so that nothing matters except a boot on the path and then the next boot, like a mantra.

The lodge where we stay overnight in Pokara rests adjacent to the calmest lake on earth. Around it, spider webs grace the trees like layered pueblos, and perfectly beautiful, perfectly wild cactuses grow. One man, Paul from Santa Fe, claims he didn't know we would be camping so much of the time and wants to go home, and I'm reminded once again that the lunatic fringe is usually not me. Poor Paul. He is not really a lunatic at all, only a very nice dentist who likes to wear clean clothes every day.

When we fly back to Kathmandu, we are joined by two older women, older even than I: one a physician from California, the other the director of a UNICEF-related program in Britain. The physician looks very frail, and I can't imagine her with a backpack. Both are witty and pleasant and eager to get going. The rest of us, willing to admit sore muscles, are pleased for a day without hiking boots and backpacks. Half the group is sick with intestinal problems. Ann is out on the street looking to buy hashish, which she claims will cure everyone, but has no luck. Ellen calls home to tell her husband she is still alive; I send a postcard to Irving. As usual, Hans is out taking photographs. The familiarity of the city and its music and smells and inhabitants hold me in a remarkable safety, and my leg heals itself.

It is early in the morning when we fly to Lukla at 9,000 feet in a twin-engine plane that lands uphill on a two-hundred-yard pebbled runway. This time, we wear many-layered, heavy clothes with hats and gloves; as soon as I take my first steps, my lungs protest the thin air. Ellen is ready with her Diamox, which she was smart enough to begin taking in Kathmandu.

The air is different here, colder, thinner. The terrain is

greener and more angular. From Lukla to our campsite, we hike along the Dudh Kosi River, brilliant aqua water bubbling over rocks. Freezing to the fingers, the water tastes pure and ebullient as it slides down my throat before I can remember I am not to drink unpurified water here, just as I am not supposed to bleed. Only Hans watches and exhorts me to vomit.

Back and forth, across and down and up we go, quieter than at Annapurna, as if indeed there were something sacred here. Of the Sherpas, only Gelbu has accompanied us; the rest of the crew are new to us. And the yaks carrying our heavy gear are also new. But already, another young man looking oddly like Kami approaches me.

"Tashi," he says. "You Aamaa didi?"

I try to point out that there are other aamaas, other didis among us, but the two who joined us in the city have already fallen behind. I am angry with myself for thinking Kami and Tashi look alike, angry I have turned out to be the worst kind of bigot, when Tashi announces in Nepali that he is actually the brother of Kami, an older brother. He has already heard about the aamaa didi, he says, taking my pack.

"I am very strong," I tell him.

"Ah yes," he says, throwing the load over one shoulder with ease. "Very strong lady."

I do not question that he knows of me. Communications are speedy, and news is transmitted before it has a chance to get old. The two new women, the older women, for example, are two hours behind, we have heard.

And this day, too, passes quickly, as well as the next, while we make our way along ledges and river beds, gasping at the perspectives each new step presents, spreading ourselves confidently across the expanse we cover. Temperatures span fifty degrees in one day. At night, I crawl deep inside my sleeping bag, wearing all my clothes, and find dreams where glowing creatures come alive and speak to me of truth. I wake assured that all the important questions are being answered. When my heart pounds as it did at Annapurna, I have no fear, but when my legs shake, Paul, the dentist, takes my pulse and claims it's too high: 98. I take another Diamox and tell everyone we are all safe here. But just before Namche, a dead yak lies feet up on the side of the trail, and seconds later a man, carried on the back of a Sherpa, his legs dragging, is also dead.

Perhaps it is at that moment, although I think now it was more an accumulation of moments, that I begin to see that this is a survival experience, not an adventure in the way I usually describe such things. Sent to a convent as a child, neutralized at a Quaker boarding school, married and divorced twice, raising a child on my own, selling my first novel to the first publisher that saw it—those things, and others, were adventures. This climbing, this Nepal, is of a different order.

Even Hans, with whom I am walking, remarks on his own shallow breathing. We give each other our water bottles, and I take out the dried apricots. This time, Tashi takes one, as well as a sip of my water.

"This is worse than Africa," says Hans. He is very nearly transformed in the sunlight into that lovely yellow lizard-snake at Annapurna.

"You'll be OK," I say.

"They've just found four bodies, three Japanese, one American farther up," an Australian tells us as he descends. "Eight liters of water a day," he says. "Maybe twelve. Makes all the difference."

"Thank you very much for the good news," says Hans.

Unused to the heavy German accent, Tashi giggles whenever Hans speaks.

"My pleasure," says the Australian, gliding past us.

At Namche Bazaar, the trading center for Tibetans and Nepalis alike, we stop for a day or two to acclimatize. In the mornings now, I can see my breath. Some of our group wash their clothes and hang the laundry out to dry on tent ropes. Two wash their hair every single day. I buy a bracelet of coral beads for two rupees, thirty cents. Ellen and I give offerings at a monastery and drink our first yak-butter tea, which she insists is better than anything she's ever had. Even the potatoes here are not ordinary, but taste sweet and powerful. On market day, wrapped in the skins of animals, families come to trade and wander among the freshly butchered yaks and sheep. A goat's head sits atop a hand-woven blanket.

In May 1953, when Edmund Hillary and Tenzing Norgay

reached the summit of Everest, I was fourteen. Two years before, my father died after a long illness, and I'd been sent away again, this time to a Quaker boarding school where blue jeans were allowed only on Saturdays. We lived in a world without radio and television, full of strict rules we resented and longings we were not yet able to identify. Regularly refusing to draw the earthworm or memorize geometry theorems, I may have been difficult. That first year, I walked from room to room outside on rain gutters, four flights off the ground.

At 12,000 feet now, in the Everest foothills, I cross a long but narrow suspension bridge that spans the Dudh Kosi a hundred feet below. Feet apart, I sway while others scream out for me to stop.

"Oh Didi, Aamaa," says Tashi. "You, you such a devil dare."

"Oh *baabu*," I call him, despite his seventeen years. Father. "You, you such a worry wart."

"What is worry wart?" The bridge still rocks us.

"Is opposite of devil dare."

"What is opposite?"

"Up, down. Right, left. Hot, cold. Big, small," I say in Nepali.

He laughs, and I see that he is teasing me and has known all along the Western colloquialisms.

A day later in Thame, we leave the two older women behind; they are too sick with dysentery to continue. Others have serious trouble sleeping. In fact, the two older women, as I like to call them, are only a few years older than I am.

Thame, at about 13,000 feet, is the westernmost valley of the Khumbu, nestled among fir forests. At a cliffside monastery, I find myself chanting with monks before dawn. Only Hans and Ellen accompany me. That same day, Ann and I take the easy route to Kunde, stopping at the hospital, built by Hillary just above the town, where a nurse asks if we have come for treatment.

Arriving before the others, we find Tashi's family with whom we are to spend the night. The old grandmother brings us popcorn and, of all things, Coca Cola, which she drinks along with us, while giving up her place by the fire. Because there is no ventilation, the room fills with smoke, blackening Ann's face and making us both cough. During the night, we all sleep on the floor together in the room designated for worship, but the higher altitudes and cold weather make us tired and irritable. When one person doesn't burn her toilet paper as instructed, another tells Gelbu, our sirdar, and we have a group meeting about it. Ann is ill, and we have to leave her with Tashi's family; she attributes it to yesterday's Coke and popcorn.

I'm not sure when it is I stop washing my face or changing my clothes. But it has become so cold that even in a down sleeping bag, even wearing many layers of thermal clothing, I never stop shivering. Before bed, we line up for hot water in bottles to tuck into our parkas. Ellen and I wrap ourselves in a foil sheet designed for combatting hypothermia. Nevertheless, each night as I lie in the thin air and listen to the gentle bells of yaks on the hills by our tents, I am swept into spectacular dreams. I fly over these very mountains or run up their sides, the energetic boulders nudging my feet. Or I sway long sways on suspension bridges amid the songs of huge birds and the eyes of musk deer. And there is nothing else.

Each morning after a breakfast of fruit and oatmeal, we pack up and start climbing at increasingly sharper angles. Bent over, we are nearly above the tree line now, although we need no special equipment. Everest looms in the distance, and as international marathon runners sail through our ranks heading for Namche, the fact that we are halfway from the summit, still in the foothills really, raises again the question of what is close and what is far away, what is small and what is large. Snow crystals drift on the air like prayer flags.

"Colder than usual," says Gelbu.

"Right," says the dentist, who reminds us that we have forgotten Thanksgiving. Despite himself, he has met every challenge so far.

The truth is that we speak less and less, since the proper words have vanished. We are, after all, walking in the heavens now with only the changing profiles of mountains and the colors of white day and burning twilight. Still, I regard the scruffy faces and hollow eyes of my comrades and wonder what it is that drives each of us.

My fingers are stiff. In teahouses, the butter tea warms us, and stoves with no ventilation seem to spew less indoor smoke than before. When my nose runs, I lick the goop or leave it to form ice on my lip. And just when I think there is only wilderness, a Buddhist convent juts out from the mountain, and we are treated to yak stew.

But truly it is the air and color that feed me, as well as the constant cheer of Tashi, who never balks at carrying my pack or offering his hand. Having been one who takes delight in small pleasures, I am astounded nonetheless by my own good humor and flexibility.

My father was fifty when he died. I do not even think of it until we are at the highest point of our trek, Dingboche, a traditional Sherpa village of yak herders at about 15,000 feet. An accountant from that part of the Midwest where there are no hills, he was not at all athletic and would never have chosen to be here.

Today again, I am the last one to reach the campsite, and the others cheer as Tashi and I arrive. Because of deforestation, we use kerosene only for cooking and thus have never been able to really warm ourselves. Tashi mimics my exaggerated stagger, my rush for tea.

I am beginning to realize the differences between what is difficult and what is dangerous. I double the altitude medication. Arlene Blum trained by walking up steep hills with sixty pounds of bricks in her pack or by running five to ten hilly miles a day. All but two of us are now wishing we had trained better. I had not heard of the stairmaster. I had walked five to ten miles a day over medium terrain. I played tennis. I should have done more.

The meal of daal bhat I have grown to love tastes bitter that night, and the others annoy me with their own travails, sprains, bruises and stomach aches. My voice speaks harshly. I drink more tea. With knitted brows, Ellen brings me hot water for my sleeping bag, and in an unusual gesture, Tashi comes by to say goodnight.

The next morning, I know that I will never leave this place. Gelbu arrives with a first aid kit. My layers are peeled off for the stethoscope, and the heavy odors of an unwashed body comfort me. How good to be warm, alive. Modesty and clean clothes are part of a life I had long ago left behind.

The dentist removes his thermometer from my mouth. "One hundred and two point five," he says.

"Pleurisy," says Hans.

"Pneumonia." This from the married couple in unison.

"Promise you won't leave me," I say to Ellen.

But the tents are down, the gear packed, the porters on their way. Barechested, I lean against a tree while Ellen tries to fit me in my old clothes and an embarrassed Hans takes pictures of mountains. The others have gone.

"You can wait here with Tashi for helicopter," says Gelbu. "Or you can try to walk down. Or yak will carry you. Don't worry. Is easy."

I envision my lanky body with its long arms and legs over the back of a five-foot Sherpa or possibly on a yak descending these steep slopes. I imagine waiting for a helicopter here in this place. "I can walk," I say.

Someone dresses me. Another pulls my hiking boots on over the stiff woolen socks and laces them up. Ellen rolls up my sleeping bag and then whips out a camera.

"This is a great picture," she says grinning.

Stop, I mean to say, but my throat has closed and no sound comes out.

"Don't you want a picture of yourself dying?" she protests.

And in spite of it all, we laugh. Hans, Ellen, me, and even Gelbu and Tashi. Even when they try to pull me to my feet and I wobble, we laugh. I am too weak to contemplate anything else.

Snow makes for a grim day, and all the colors are muted. But my legs work, pulling my reluctant feet along with them. Tashi takes one hand and Ellen the other. "Aamaa," says Tashi with his brother's white even teeth. "Didi, devil dare, we help you."

A hacking cough assaults my ribs, battering places whose names I cannot recall. I am unable to stop shaking. One foot. Stop. Another foot. Stop. I make no effort to speak, but the mountain carries me again, as it has lifted me throughout these weeks. I am unable to point to them or to their silences as we walk, but I am mindful that great beauty gives much sustenance and energy, even as my own body grows heavier.

At a *bhatti* we stop, and I lie down while the others eat outdoors. A Sherpa woman with her bright wool apron holds my head in her lap and spoons butter tea and something tasting of lemon into my mouth. There is magic here, I decide, but when I cough up her kindness along with something bright red Tashi says is blood, I am frightened. The woman rubs a small piece of turquoise over my head and cheeks and neck, and my tears fall into the crook of her arm.

Walking again, the crew is behind us, all of them singing now. Hans takes Ellen's place by my side. And Ann, fully recovered, she says, rejoins the group. The old grandmother cured her with herbs and potato soup. Someone else read her stories in Tibetan.

That night, in my sleeping bag, I am held for warmth by the others in shifts. Or is that only my dream? No. Tashi and Gelbu. Ellen and Ann. Everyone crushes against my shaking bones in front of a kerosene stove they keep going until dawn. Even the two older women are here. The Sherpas sing; the Westerners play word games. I am both inside and outside my body now. This cannot be such a terrible way to leave this life.

But I do not die. The woman from California, the physician, the frail, older woman gives me penicillin with sugar from her hand. And this is the last day of our journey.

Back in Kathmandu two days later, a mirror reflects a dark chiseled face I do not recognize. I refuse hospital care and sleep for a very long time in a hotel room with Ann and Ellen and Hans. We are all very thin. The rest of our group are scattered in other places in the city or have left for Bangkok or Delhi. Gelbu and Tashi and the crew are already on another trek.

As luck would have it, the four of us have several more days here, and joined together by the bonds peril creates, we celebrate our endurance and friendship with good food and drink, as people do everywhere. But here, in this bustling Asian city, daily life with its predictable rhythms seems ordinary and passionless. In our addiction to the dangers of survival at high altitude, we have temporarily painted the rest of the world without color.

Within the year, Ellen will have her baby; Hans will quit his job and retire; Ann will start law school; and I will remarry my old husband, my second old husband.

Just now, in this hotel room, after a day of biking to the old town, Bhaktapur, and a visit to a Tibetan refugee rug factory, we lie on the floor, heads together, bodies like the spokes on a wheel.

"You made the fastest recovery from pneumonia in history," says Ellen.

"I'll never be the same," says Ann.

"I don't think I had pneumonia."

"This has been the best time I've ever had," says Hans.

And I know that after this night I will be more whole than I have been. In fact, I do have pneumonia which will take weeks to disperse. Also, I have the hands of those who cared for me so kindly that long night imprinted on my body, the arms of those who let me lean on them on my descent, and the assurance that nature affirms, clarifies, as well as challenges.

I am visited that night by dark chiseled faces in my scattered dreams, my own faces with questions only those who live among mountains can answer. What marks, for example, the line between survival and abundance? When does a stone become a rock, a rock become a mountain? How can one hold peaks and valleys in the same thought?

WOLF

Gretchen Legler

I AM DEER HUNTING, twenty feet up in an icy popple tree that is covered with frozen rain. My hands ache. The wind burns my face. I feel the unmasked skin around my eyes pucker and crack. All my senses are alert for movement in the woods. A leaf sails down to the ground, startling me. A woodpecker lands on a branch within my reach and pokes at a tree limb, rat-tat-tat. The sound echoes in the frozen air. Farther away, four fat gray-and-brown grouse fly into another popple tree and walk their way like penguins to the top branch.

My husband Craig and I walked in here in the darkness, in the black-gray light just before dawn, not using flashlights but letting our eyes get accustomed to the dimness. We moved slowly, heating up fast in our heavy clothes as we lifted our knees high in the snow. I climbed this tree, hand over hand, hoisting myself with my rifle and my backpack, up, up onto this safe, sturdy limb. For awhile, all I heard was the beating of my own heart and my labored breathing. But then everything became silent. Silent. The cold started taking away my heat, my breath, and ice crystals began to form on the outside of my scarf.

I am waiting for a deer in this silence and I am fighting the darkness: my darkness, an anxious terror that comes from inside of me, like black hands groping, whenever I am not occupied with an immediate task, whenever I am waiting. I am fighting the darkness that comes whenever I am still and whenever I allow myself to think about my sister Ally, who is dead, who died when she was twenty-three, who killed herself by taking an overdose of antidepressants. Suspended in the quiet, twenty feet above the earth, looking out over the red brush, golden grass and yellow tamaracks of a northern Minnesota woods, I am pulled into darkness.

She hears noise like wind blowing. She hears no one talking. She hears silence surrounding Ally's death. Her father, her mother, her brothers, not talking, not talking about Ally. "No use in opening old wounds," her mother says. "We have finished grieving." She sees colors, mostly yellow, behind her eyes. She sees that everything in her life now has something to do with Ally's death. If someone asked her now, "Do you love anyone?" she would say, "Yes, Ally." She feels as if she is floating. She wants to crawl into the grave with her sister. Darkness fights with light. Darkness fights with clear, sharp pain. She pushes the darkness away, shakes her head. It comes on anyway.

Ally tried to tell the truth is what Ally did wrong: the truth about their family. And in this one way, Ally was fearless, careless, wide open. Ally couldn't lie anymore, couldn't keep it all in, couldn't be quiet, would not become silent. "We're not a normal family," Ally said, "Can't you see?" Ally tried to make her hear, wanted her to see, but, like the others, she did not listen to her sister. "You're forgetting everything," she told Ally. "What about the hikes up Millcreek Canyon? The trips to the zoo? Hearing Mom read us Moby Dick, *all gathered up around her on the couch? What about traveling to Australia? Be thankful," she told Ally. "You love to make trouble, don't you?"*

She thought then that her sister was angry, or maybe crazy, that what she needed was three months alone in the woods, a course in mountain climbing, something to shake her up, make her believe in herself. She thought then that her sister was imagining things. Ally wrote her letters: "Face it, Gretchen," she said, "Mother is an alcoholic." She wrote back: "You can't say that. You can't say that about your mother." Ally wrote her more letters: "Forget it, Gretchen, for our father there is no forgiveness." She wrote back: "Why do you fight with him? You only make it worse."

She starts to cry. She thinks, Ally knew. Ally knew we are all fucked up. What she knows now, what she sees and understands, what Ally tried to tell her, sits like a stone in her chest, held there by guilt and pain. In this vicious grayness she thinks she sees answers. Rule number one: you must pay attention. You cannot ignore anything, or someone will die. She sees her life every day as a terrible struggle against forces that drown out peace and smother light. Forces that make things fall apart. Her center holds not by miracle or luck, but by sheer force of will. She thinks, I will not go mad.

This blackness is always inches away from her heels and her back. Anything, any slip, and it can swallow her. Constant vigilance is necessary. Pushing forward is necessary. If she lets it pull her backward she will fall, dark earth closing up around her and her falling, falling, pulled down and down by darkness, looking around, confused, her hair like tangled tree roots curving around her face, filling her mouth, her eyes, her ears. . . .

She pulls up from this dream, whether she is in a duck blind, in a fishing boat or in a tall popple waiting for deer, by imagining herself rising up out of the earth, springing forth, gasping, with dark rivulets of dirt coming off of her and dirt clods flying.

At home, she springs up in bed, twisted with sheets and wet with sweat yelling, "Ally! Ally!"

In front of me, the sun has begun to rise, spreading orange light over everything in the woods, and I pull the visor of my parka hood down to shade my eyes. I am back into some light, back into what seems to me more real: me sitting in a popple tree that is slick with frozen rain.

Behind me and to my right I see grayness moving. All the animals except some birds are shades of gray or brown in the woods. Easier not to be seen. I think I am seeing a fawn with spots, which is unlikely but not impossible in November. The gray shape glides through the willow and brown grass. A long nose. Two dark eyes. A thick neck. A straight back.

A coyote.

Or a wolf.

It trots, paws lanky and loose, making noise in the grass. Swish. Swish. Leaves collapse under its wide feet. It has no idea I am above it looking down. No idea. I want to make it acknowledge me. I want to say, "Hey, wolf!" But I wait. I am quiet and amazed. I want to see if I can see how it would be if I was not here. I imagine myself here and not here, seeing but not watching.

The wolf heads out into the open grassland between the popples and the woods. It stops beneath me. I could jump down on it, drop my orange glove on its yellow-gray back. I want it to know I am here. I want to see its wolf eyes. It turns around and goes back into the woods, gracefully, as it came.

When I see Craig at noon I tell him about the wolf. He has been sitting across a clearing from me in a tall tree. I keep track of him by looking for his orange parka. When he climbs down I do too and we meet on the logging road near his tree. "I saw a wolf or a coyote," I say.

Craig takes me gently by the shoulders, a bunch of the fabric of my hunting parka in each mitten. "You saw a wolf?" he repeats.

"Or a coyote."

"Either way, you're lucky," he says. "Either way." For both of us, to see any animal in the woods—a chickadee, a black moose, a deer, even to hear a mouse scurrying beneath dry leaves—is to join with some part of a wilder world, a world we are self-conscious travelers in.

"It had a long tail," I say, stretching out my arms. "I'm sure it was a wolf."

"How big?" he asks.

"This tall," I say, my hand at my waist.

"It was a wolf," he says. We walk out of the woods, feeling diminished and uplifted. It is a gift to see a wolf. We walk in the rain to the van where we will have some soup and coffee and take a nap.

As we take off our mittens and coats and unload our guns, another hunter drives up in a black pickup truck. While his wife waits in the truck, he comes over to talk to us. He's wearing an orange sweatshirt and a cigarette dangles from his lip, his hands are thrust deep into the pockets of his blue jeans.

"Get anything?"

I had. A small buck. I had killed it and cleaned it and put a piece of its liver on the highest branch of a bush. For a hawk. Or a goddess.

"I see you did." He eyeballs the deer on the ground by our car.

"It's small," I say. It is small. Tiny, really. Its horns are only as big as nipples. We feel lucky. Even this tiny deer will give us meat to eat for most of the winter, and its hide will cover our feet in soft slippers.

"It'll be good to eat," he says.

"We saw a wolf," Craig says. He is smiling, excited.

"Those timber wolves," the man says. "There're two packs here now—a pack of eight and a pack of ten. They really cut into the deer herd." The man shakes his head. "I live right by here." He points to the north. "Christ, you hear 'em howl at night. It sends shivers up my back." He shivers. "I haven't seen a deer all day."

"Yeah," we say. We don't want to tell him we have seen plenty of deer besides the one I shot. We saw four, their tall white tails zig-zagging through the brush. And in the quiet tamarack, I saw a horse-sized buck who, before I could get my rifle off my shoulder and untangled from my parka hood string, got up in slow motion and bounded away.

"They oughta just pack those wolves up and send 'em back to Washington," he says, "where they belong."

Some noise fills her head. There is a voice saying, "Be Quiet." There is a person with a pillow smothering her impulse to say to this man in the most vulgar language, "Fuck you asshole. You're the one we should pack up and send to Washington." There is a lot of noise in her brain. A lot of violence going on. It feels to her like water just let go from a dam crashing through a small culvert. It is a whoozing. A pressure. She loses her sense of place and time. She rises above herself in her blaze-orange jacket and above this man and Craig. She is above the woods where she can see wolves and deer in the trees and brush. Along with the voice that says, "Quiet," and the smothering pillow, there is another voice and to her it sounds like Ally's, soft and insistent: "You can't ignore this. You must speak to this ignorance. You must speak to this cruelty. You must say something."

She thinks she owes her this. She owes it to Ally to learn this lesson. If it is all she can do for her now, she will learn this lesson. She will learn to speak. She will learn to say something real. But she can't talk. Her words are frozen. She thinks if she said what is in her heart something terrible would happen. Something would break or snap, in her, in this man who she so wants to speak to. Someone would get angry.

The man leaves, spinning the wheels of his black pickup truck on the frozen ground. I ask Craig if we should have said something.

"I didn't want to tell him about all the deer," he says. Neither did I. Because then, the next morning the man would be in our spot, maybe in my tree. "But about the wolves," I say. "Right," Craig says. "They aren't our deer. On the other hand, what is a wolf? It could be about economy. If you live out here and try to get a living from the land and a wolf is eating your cattle, it's hard to think about natural order."

"That's not what we're talking about. Cattle, I mean. He lives in the city, that man," I say.

"You're right," Craig says.

I vow that the next time someone talks to me about wolves, or any animal, in the same way as the man in the orange sweat-shirt, I will say something. Something. Anything. "They aren't our deer," I will say. "They are the wolves' deer first."

At the end of the weekend, Craig and I drive to meet his aunt, Bea, and her husband, Bob, in Roseau, Minnesota. They are headed to St. George, Utah for the winter. We want to say good-bye and have some dinner. Craig turns on the heat, and we speed along while the heavy smell of wet wool fills our van.

Bob reminds me of my father and of my grandfather too. He is German, knows the value of a dollar, lines up his wrenches in order of size on the wall behind his workbench. He has gray hair and a thin gray mustache, like my grandfather, Frederick Wilhelm Legler, and like my father too. But he is also unlike these men I know. My favorite picture of Bob is a snapshot of him squeezed into a tiny go-cart, a red Shriner's fez tilting on his head, waving at the camera. This ignoble frivolity is something my father, and his father, would never stoop to. Because of this, I like Bob and I trust him.

We settle in around a table at the Holiday Inn. "Let us pray," Bob says, and reaches out his hand for mine. I reach out mine for Craig's and he does the same to his aunt. We form a circle, and Bob and Bea bow their heads and close their eyes. I never pray like this. I watch everyone else while they close their eyes and move their lips, and I wonder what they are really thinking. I have never believed in this kind of god. ". . . For all of this we are truly grateful, Amen," Bob says. We clink our cocktail glasses together.

Craig and Bob start talking about football. Craig does not watch football, but this is something he can talk about with Bob.

"Gee, how about those Vikings?" Craig says.

"How did that Walker boy do?" Bob asks.

Bea's eyes go back and forth between the men as if she is watching a ping-pong ball bounce between two players. She breaks in. "Can I interrupt this conversation?" For her, this is what women are supposed to do; keep men civilized, keep them from talking about football.

"OK," Craig says.

"How are the girls?" She means Craig's daughters, who live with their mother, Craig's first wife, in Rochester, Minnesota.

"Fine," he says. This is the end of their conversation. Craig is irritated with his aunt for breaking in.

Then I tell Bob, "We saw a wolf." There is a pause and I smile, waiting for him to tell me how wonderful this is, how lucky I am to have met one of these elusive beings, one of these mysterious, marginal creatures.

"I've seen timber wolves while up in a deer stand," he says. I am still smiling, waiting to compare stories with him about their beauty. My heart is wide open.

"But I could never get a bead on 'em," he says. "Never was lucky enough to kill one from a deer stand."

My food is dry in my mouth.

"But I got one in Canada once," he says. "Bea won't let me spread it out on the living room floor. She thinks it doesn't go with the carpet or the couch." He laughs and winks at Bea, and she rolls her eyes.

I remember the wolf skin now, rolled up and stuck among boxes of Christmas ornaments and gardening trowels. The summer before, when I'd gone into the basement to clean walleyes in the sink, I had seen it, pulled it out of the box, and stroked the yellow-gray fur. I had laughed. It was ludicrous, really. The big yellow glass eyes, the pathetic pale-pink plastic tongue and the sinister, snarling lips curling back over plastic fangs.

"So, you killed that one?" I ask, my voice steady and cold. I had imagined, somehow, that he had got it at a garage sale or that it had been given to him by a friend.

He tells us he was fishing in the winter, and everyone was shooting the wolves. I want to know the whole story.

"Everyone?" I ask.

He says, "In the late afternoon the wolves would come out onto the ice of the lake and cavort—you know, jump around and chase each other. Man, it was some sight to see, those wolves, some gray and some black, just playing like that." Bob makes a dancing motion with his arms and shoulders. "So, I just went out one evening, and I got me one between the lake and the shore. I shot it." Bob holds up his arms as if he is holding a rifle. "Wham!"

"Was it legal then to shoot wolves?" I ask. "You know, they're an endangered species now."

He laughs. "Everyone was doing it."

Her face fades, her smile melting away like hot wax. Her body curls up around her heart. She is shrinking. She is looking through the scope of a rifle, the thin cross hairs centered on a wolf. She hears a crack, sees the wolf's body fall in a spasm into the grass, and just as it goes down, it turns its clear yellow eyes to her and she shudders. In those eyes she sees some kind of misery, some kind of knowledge of betrayal, and she feels a nauseating guilt fill her up. If she could only speak, she thinks, if only she had spoken, if only she had listened, it would have all been different. She rises up again and hovers over this dinner table. She sees four people trying to engage clumsily and fiercely in some kind of love. She sees a

*woman among these four who is glowing red with fear and anger. She
starts to remember things. Images go past as if on a speeding filmstrip.
Sounds blur together in one long moan. She is reading Ally's journal
from the week before her sister died. "I can't talk to anyone," Ally
wrote. "I try to talk to Eddie, but he doesn't understand, and I can't talk
to Gretty either. They see death differently than I do." She is letting her
anger pulse through her veins like acid, like poison. Christmas 1984:
Ally wrote, desperate, that she took their Mother's glass and poured the
white wine in it down the kitchen sink. Fall 1984: Ally wrote that she
couldn't work and take her medication too. It set her heart skittering,
beating wildly. She had to spend hours every day at the gym to counter
the side-effects. She went to their mother and father for money. "He told
me he won't pay for school unless I go full time. There are certain responsibilities you must take on as an adult, he says." Ally wrote, "I
went to them for help and I felt betrayed."*

*The noise in her head is getting louder. Things are spinning. There
is chaos in her head. Someone is holding her back and someone is pushing her forward. "Quiet," one voice says. "Go ahead," the other voice
says. The second is Ally's voice. Everything is thin now and dangerous.
She is entering dark territory. Something is ready to shatter. She knows
she could blow up this tenuous gathering. Her words could be like dyna-
mite. She already has wounded everyone at this table, so fragile is the
crust of their relationship. She wants to explain something to Bob, to
have it make sense. She wants to speak. Why kill such a beautiful animal for nothing, she wants to ask him. Not to eat, not to feed your body,
but to take its skin and fold it into a box in a dank basement? Why hate a
wolf for eating a deer? Why murder a wolf for trying to live the only
way it knows how?*

"The wolves and the deer are all God's creatures," I say, my
voice urgent and shaking, trying to speak to Bob in a way I think
he will understand.

"Na," he shakes his head. Craig is watching me nervously.

"They're not our deer," I say, my voice more firm. "They're
not *your* deer."

·

The more she talks the less the pressure, the softer the noise, the closer she gets to light. She feels as if she is swimming up through dark earth toward sun rays on the surface, her hair flowing down her back in thick strands, her legs kicking, her hands pushing and pulling the earth around her in muddy swirls.

"They're not *our* deer," I say again. I lay my fork on the table.

"The wolves have ruined mucho hunting spots for me," he says.

"We can go to the grocery store. The wolves can't," I say. Hunting is a privilege for me, not a right, not a necessity. I choose it. I will not starve if I don't shoot a deer one fall. I have no claim to the deer in the woods, to the tiny buck I shot this year. When I hunt I am a stranger, a visitor, leaving my circle and entering another, entering the circle of wolves and deer, where I have a duty to walk quietly and respectfully, as much as I can, honoring them both. I would not shoot a wolf to save myself a deer. I want Bob to know all of this, to understand.

"They're a plague. Best thing to do is get rid of them," Bob says of the wolves.

Words are collecting within her. The voice of Ally is in her, and the face of the wolf. They say, together, "You must speak to this." Ally tried to tell a truth and no one listened. "Look, look at how it is all wrong," she wrote. "It's not my fault," she wrote. "It's not my fault that I'm so crazy. Look around you, what we grew up with." Ally spoke into dark clouds, into thick mist. No one heard her, or if they heard they twisted her words. They preferred silence to her truth. No more. No more silence. She owes it to Ally, she thinks, to learn this lesson, to do this one thing. To speak, and then to live.

A voice is growing in her. The voice rises from her belly into her throat and when it comes out it sounds to her like a long, ragged howl. It feels to her like her guts are being ripped from within her. "Wrong," she says. "Wroooong."

•

I am out of any darkness now, and I am not floating. The backs of my legs feel the hard seat of my chair. What I say does not sound like a howl to Craig and Bob and Bea. I say, looking at the steak on my plate, the half-eaten vegetables, "It's funny why a deer is worth killing and saving to eat and a wolf is worth killing for nothing, not meat, not anything but meanness." I look at Bob, straight in the eye, and say again, "Not anything but meanness."

STONES ALL AROUND,

AN ABUNDANCE OF WATER, OF BUSHES,

OF BIRDS

Deborah Abbott

for Chris Adams, who brought me back to the water

I AM LYING NAKED, warm and drowsy in my sleeping bag, half
caught in a dream, when I am startled awake by a small bird that
alights on the back of my head. For an instant I am still, and the
bird is still and then, even before there is an urge to breathe, the
bird has flown noisily into the thicket in which I am ensconced.

I open my eyes. It is just light. The river has fallen in the
hours I have been sleeping so that it is close, but not so close as
when I curled up beside it, under the expanse of night sky, and
let its waters murmur in my ears. I draw my body out of the bag,
gasp at the chill, and walk gingerly across the sand. I squat and
pee. The warm stream washes over my vulva and, with a rush of
pleasure, I shiver.

I look at my body, tawny from these days on the river, at
my arms, thick and achy from hours of handling the enormous
wooden oars, at my blistered palms, at my breasts, clustered
against my chest, at my soft belly. Finally I look at my legs: the
left one supporting me as I squat, and the right one, frail as the
twigs around me, sagging under the weight of the birds.

I look out at the water and see myself rising up from my

haunches, running the few yards to the riverbank, scrambling up the large stone that lies below and diving into the still space of its eddy. Like the bird on my head, my mind is startled by this image, takes sudden flight. I cannot run. I will not run, ever, except fleetingly, in dreams.

My mind settles itself quickly onto that which can be done, which must be done. I consider the plan for the day. I am responsible for building the fire this morning, for organizing breakfast and for securing a massive load of gear onto my raft. Before I leave this place to take on these tasks, I reach for a small, cool stone. I draw it back, fling it outward. The strength of my arm propels it faster than any legs could run. It lights on the water once, twice, skipping, then sinks with a plop near the farthest shore.

I return to my sleeping site, rummage through my pack and find my clothes. I pull on my bathing suit, still damp, and my soft khaki shorts. I smile, knowing Kate, my lover back in Santa Cruz, would be pleased to see me now, so casually buttoning my shorts. It was she who managed, with her tender insistence, to get me into shorts for the first time in twenty years.

I lace up the boot on my left foot. As I'm ripping at the velcro on my brace, ready to slip my right leg in, I am struck by the sound of the tearing. I think: torn. This is how I am. My body is able. My body is not. I touch down like the bird, and then I am away. For a moment I am the rock nestled among others on the riverbank. Then I am hurled to the opposite shore. I occupy both places. I belong in neither place.

Last evening I hiked to the farthest point on the beach, so my walk to the kitchen site is long. I gather twigs for the fire and a rusty can, bottle caps, a bit of shredded webbing. My thoughts are like litter, cluttering my mind's landscape. I realize that the hardest part of this trip is not in the physical strength, endurance, nor skill required in rafting, but in finding a place for myself, a place to make camp. The company for which I am volunteering organizes trips for people with different needs. On this particular trip there are five rafts. Five guides: four able-bodied guides and myself. Four attendants and five participants: two paraplegics, one quadriplegic, a deaf woman named T.J. and a girl with cerebral palsy. I am both disabled and a guide.

The day spreads before me. I make the fire. T.J. joins me, gathers more sticks to feed the flame. We haul water up from the river, signing with our free hands and giggling because, with my limp, I slosh half of the bucket onto my feet. Back at the fire I boil the water, brew coffee. I set the griddle out over the flame and cook french toast. The attendants have dressed the other participants, tended to bladders and bowels, and brought the wheelchair users, with a great deal of effort and humor, to the kitchen area. Marta, the quad, and I greet each other. I sit beside her on an overturned bailing bucket, give her sips of coffee, bits of french toast dripping with syrup. She makes faces, tells me my coffee tastes like river sludge, that I'm making a mess of her new Patagonia jacket. We laugh. In that moment of laughter, like the bird, I land. We are two disabled women enjoying the morning.

An instant later, I take wing. I am down on the boats with the other guides, loading gear, fastening purple ribbons of webbing around Marta's chair, my brace, our supplies. I am scrambling over the load, cinching the tether with the full weight of my body. In these moments and all morning as I negotiate rapids, row through the calm stretches, I am indistinguishable from the other guides. I fit into the able-bodied world more than the disabled.

I go back and forth between worlds all day. I think that the hawk crisscrossing the gorge above me, hour after hour, is looking for more than food. It is searching for a place to come down, for a nest.

Marta calls to me. I look for the nearest large rock and pull hard on the oars, pivoting into its downstream eddy. Marta's body is slipping. I lift her into my arms and settle her into a more stable position. I return to the oars. By bracing my legs and pulling with the combined strength of my arms and belly, I break through the turbulent eddy fence back into the current.

An hour later, our party is stopping to scout a rapid, which involves walking through thigh-high water, climbing a steep bank and walking a half mile downstream along a narrow, rocky path. From there there will be a sort of aerial view of the tricky whitewater we are approaching. The four other guides make a bridge for me to walk along since my one strong leg and one weak one cannot hold me up in water this swift and deep. When we reach the shore, one of the guides carries me piggyback up the bank. At the top, another gives me her arm. We walk behind until finally I tell her to go on without me. Even with her support, my leg has given out.

I sit in the hot sun, watching the guide disappear around the bend. I look down at Marta, the other disabled participants, and their helpers. Marta catches my eye and nods her head, which is her way of waving. I wave back, raising my arm and wagging my hand. T.J. signs, "Stuck there?" I make a stab at my throat with two fingers, then a fist which I shake up and down. "Stuck. Yes. Stuck here."

Then I draw my knees up to my chin, put my face down and cry. It is a relief to be crying; my body has been holding these tears all day. At first I am crying out of anger, anger at my body for its limitations. Then I am crying out of sheer loneliness. I am the hawk weary of its solitary circling, wanting company, a place to claim as home.

I am neither in the boats, nor at the lookout with the other guides. I am somewhere in between. Amphibian: the one who passes between water and land. The one who occupies the border. I am on the faultline looking into the abyss. I am the fence-sitter. The bridge. I am the woman who straddles the gap. Like the light-skinned black who can "pass." The lesbian who can slip in and out of the closet. I am the disabled woman with access to able-bodied privileges but without inclusion in either world in any predictable, solid way. I live on the outskirts, the fringes, the edge.

I sit on the embankment for a long time. After a while, there are no tears left to cry. I hear something stirring beside me. I lift my head. A young rattlesnake crosses the path with a lopsided motion, as though it has not yet learned to glide. It reminds me of myself moving unevenly yet gracefully through space.

I smile. There are stones all around, an abundance of water, of bushes, of birds. In this moment, my solitude dissolves. I am part of this place, peaceful and content. My kinship is here, with the snake. My community is here, with the population of stones. I have no need of any other.

The guide who led me up the path is the first to reappear around the bend. She has brought a sprig of wild mint, which she presents to me as a bouquet. I put my nose into its center and breathe in. She squats beside me, clears a space on the ground and draws a map of the rapid I will be navigating. We discuss the various routes, the risks involved in each. I am distracted by the sharp, good smell of her body, by the two sturdy legs on which she leans. When she finishes, I have memorized my course down the rapid, the curve of her strong right thigh. She rises, gives me her hand and pulls me to my feet. We walk toward the boats, toward Marta, T.J. and the others, arm in arm.

A CITY GIRL DISCOVERS THE FOREST

Gabrielle Daniels

A walk in the woods

I<small>T'S USUALLY EARLY</small> afternoon when I take a walk. Today I've been up since about eight. I've been writing since nine-thirty. I've eaten lunch. I want the meal to circulate in my body rather than lie like stones slowly melting in my stomach during a siesta. I slide into my don't-stop-green Sportos, take up the walking stick leaning near the door and head up the trail.

Actually, many trails wind around Hedgebrook Farm, a women writers' colony, my home for two months. Some are large enough for a little truck, some are simple footpaths. I am fascinated by the little heap of stones which appear here and there. I am unsure whether they are pointing out a new path, or how much farther on this path there is to go.

It's a semblance of wilderness here; there are six cottages and the farmhouse where we meet for dinner and other activities. Grasses and secondary growth encroach, seemingly waiting for their chance, then the woods begin. The nearer one gets to the property line, several long thin silvery wires broken at times simply by the weight of a bush, one hears cars a few hundred yards away on Washington's 525, and closer, the activity of neighbors, sawing, shouting, or even shooting on the next lot, as it is also deer hunting season. I have yet to see a deer, although some of the other writers have seen them. They have watched each other behind the barriers of wood and curiosity, glass and fear. It is safe here and there are no guns.

Right now, I feel like a deer. I can't believe that the quiet is so safe. Sunlight peers through the trees. I lean on my third leg, the piebald walking stick. Hearing tree frogs call to each other, I am startled. I strain my ears for an enemy that never appears. A yellowed leaf spirals and flutters to my feet like Mary Poppins' umbrella.

Spider webs flatten against my face like veils. I take off my glasses, dry wipe my face, dust my hair for creepy crawlies, and brush my shoulders. But a dragonfly takes dead aim between my chest and lands, attracted by the vivid red in my pullover. It has been a long time since I've had this kind of attention; I frantically shoo it away. When I was a child, my boyfriends and I called them mosquito hawks, because they fed on mosquitoes, the carriers of disease. Diseases that existed long before we were born: such as yellow fever, *vomito,* the New Orleans scourge. Seeing a mosquito hawk is a pleasure; they have disappeared even from the open spaces in the suburbs, like the doodle bugs and ladybugs that we'd let crawl all over our hands. We watched caterpillars munching on poinsettias, sucking milk, green lizards and if we were lucky, small snakes. We wished for a real hurricane, so the levees would "bust" and we'd see the water moccasins and even a gator.

Only certain insects have survived in the cities. Flies. Ants. Moths. Cockroaches. The most hardy. Mostly scavengers. Pests.

The mosquito hawk gets the message. It has dropped down on some tetchy animal—me. It flies high, takes a ninety-degree turn toward the berry patch and disappears.

Mushrooms have sprouted everywhere since the rain arrived, in many sizes, shapes and colors. A gigantic white mushroom looms from under a bush. It must be a toadstool, but it is as big as an child's wagon wheel, with a thick stem. Enough for Holly, our house manager, to brew several bowls of soup, if it is not poisonous. Several mushroom patches are already turning brown, fading back into the dead soil, ready for another episode of rain. I think it is like playing hopscotch, studying the ground, self-consciously avoiding where they grow. Where I least expect, I nearly mash one growing defiantly purple and bumpy and alone in the middle of the trail.

There has been some logging and clearing for firewood for the cottage dwellers, with little caches curing, stacked in the open and covered with plastic. During the storms, some trees have blown down, or are on their way to the ground. They lean as if defying gravity, hoping that something like a nearby tree will break their fall. *Catch her, catch her.* Dead trees wear little orange ties about them as if dressed nattily for death, though their roots still cling tenaciously to the soil. Some look naked and sad, their stark boughs reaching out in the air, *why, why?* The stumps are another story: happy, teeming condominiums. If it isn't lichen spreading on the stump, it will be insects chewing through the bark, weeds choking the roots.

The trail, strewn with fading, wet leaves and fallen branches, crunches or slides under my feet. The sound scares off a blue heron, the first I've ever seen in the wild, which spreads its magnificent wings and alights on a nearby bough, watching me. I sit on a rock beside Green Pond. Unlike the manmade waterfall and its pond, this pool doesn't drain off. It is very still and black as yin with a burgeoning coverlet of algae, leaves, pollen and some kind of bog clover. The heron gazes, disapprovingly I think, over his shoulder at me. He wants me to leave. This was his pond. I am his predator and I could hurt him at age six or thirty-six. He will not come down closer for me. He will groom himself and wait for me to leave. I watch the stillness of the pond, the reflection of the trees framing it. A snapshot will not do justice to this picture. The air is fresh; I breathe in and the trees breathe out; the lungs of the earth.

While driving from California on Highway 1, I remember encountering large-bed trucks, sometimes one behind the other, hauling sweet-smelling, fresh-cut timber to the mill like a funeral cortege. I imagined the sap still running like blood in my veins, shocked. Their cousins, other trees, lined the highway. *What did they think?* Pieces of bark and pine needles flew off by the wayside. Some thudded on my windshield, then caught in my wipers. Hawks above me flew from branch to branch as if fleeing from a sight.

Then, in Oregon I saw a timber graveyard. I was astounded. Like many photographs and documentaries I had seen of concentration camp victims, the logs were stacked. There were acres and acres of what was left of trees, denuded of leaves, branches, families of animals, the hum of wasps. Some appeared in various stages of rot. Bark had dropped off in places, exposing what I call the real skin of the wood; it looked speckled and discolored as if, separated from the soil, it had been poisoned. It is one thing to see a dead tree surrounded by its living cousins, and another to see a dead tree surrounded by its dead cousins. Men in their forklifts next to these poor giants resembled sinister Lilliputians. *Remember,* a random thought courses, *they need a job, too; they are just doing their job.* But I don't believe it. On the other side of the road, rising over more logs like a chapel presiding on a hill, lay mills, their relentless engines chuffing smoke into the sky.

And yet, in the little stove in Owl Cottage, I burn wood. Everyday, I haul logs up the small hill and, alternately, starter: newspaper or pine cones or small pieces of wood. This is the only heat in the cottage. And so I keep warm, feeding the flames. Making a fire, like writing, is an art, too. It's hard work to keep it stoked. I hate to waste kindling. Sometimes I let the kettle boil on the stove. Watching it, I thought it took about twenty minutes to bring it to a boil at two hundred degrees. The time was probably less. I live in a cottage framed in warm-colored wood. An owl sitting on a branch is carved above the hobbit windows. Sometimes I hear the beams and pillars creaking and settling and humming, and not just at night. The whole house is yet alive. The public radio announcer warns that much of the air pollution in Seattle and its environs is caused by wood-burning stoves. This morning, I open the stove door to find the sap from one of the logs is boiling, bubbling, popping. When I return from the bathhouse, the chimney puffs a greeting.

It is night

I've washed the empty lunch containers, placed them in the basket, folded the colorful paper tote in which I pack my breakfast when the after-dinner talk fades. The basket waits while I put on my coat, my Sportos if it has rained, then pick it up with the cottage key and the beam flashlight. I can't trust the good fortune of living in the country. How you can leave your cottage, your car unlocked, the windows wide open and challenging. I tried it once or twice until my thoughts hyperventilated. I worry because I have always lived in the city. I am a person who scratches her driver's license number on what little she possesses; who was robbed while a student; who leaves the lights blazing and the TV talking when I am gone at night. Whether I'm going into downtown Langley, or going to the farmhouse at night, I'll lock the door.

It is dark around four in the afternoon, as October has somersaulted into November as gently as scattering leaves. Less than a month to go at this writing retreat. A storm is buffeting the island, but it is mostly the wind; the rain hasn't yet arrived. The trees are swaying with a *whoom, whoom!* I sweep the flashlight in a protective arc every few paces. I chose it at the Price Club because the packaging promised that the flashlight would be seen from two miles away. I pass the avenue where the bathhouse, the pump room and the wood pile lie. H's cottage is illuminated, but her porch light is off. All my antennae are up, *he could be behind any bush, the next tree* though every vestige of common sense insists, *there's no one there.* Everything is rustling, twisting and bowing. The wind parts my unbuttoned coat like a knee between my legs; it flaps. I look up. The darkness reveals not trees but boughs like shadowy, many-headed Hydras. They could fall on me, their fantastic weight crushing me flat, to death. I feel like running, but I think, *if I run, I'll panic, and if I panic....* I take a deep breath as the wind swallows my face, whips my hair. Ahead in their corral, the goats Ozzie and Harriet hear my feet crunching towards them and begin to baa and bray: *open our barn, let us in and feed us for the night!*

He was black and heavy-set. Younger and a few inches taller. Ugly and dangerous as a beaten dog. He had crept out of the bushes to rape me.

It was about ten at night. I was twenty-four. I had stayed late in Palo Alto to see a movie. Impatient for the connecting bus running on Story Road, I had started walking toward my mother's home in East San Jose. Time and again, nearing another bus stop, I would look back to see if the bus was approaching. Ahead was a well-lit gas station; I would soon pass a shoe store, a car stereo store and the new Chinese-Vietnamese restaurant.

I remember passing a parked car and some bushes. They were neat and trim, but high, serving as a kind of fence from the next property. I wasn't unduly cautious; I was preoccupied. The antennae had gone to sleep. I was on a busy thoroughfare. Then I heard something: a crackle. I turned and there he was, almost upon me, his hammy arms raised to execute what turned out to be an empty chokehold.

He was more surprised than I was, in that split second, that his quarry would turn and stare him down and not scream or cower. He turned tail and ran. He wore a white T-shirt against the cold night. I watched him run the entire distance I had come, from the intersection of King and Story.

I didn't mention this to my mother much less report the incident to the police. As usual, she fussed at me for coming home late; I was a grown, responsible young woman now. I had to wake up early the next morning to go to work. But it's your business, she said, if you want to *plockay* around looking to get hit on the head!

Where can you go to walk alone in a city? Not even Golden Gate Park, I thought. When I lived in San Francisco, when I couldn't sleep and didn't want to go home, I would take a bus that ran all night, like the 22 Fillmore or the 24 Divisadero, and ride from Potrero Hill to the Marina Green or from Pacific Heights to Bernal Heights. From foghorns to a clear, unimpeded view of downtown. No one would hurt me. Sometimes I talked with the driver. I watched bleary-eyed people board for the midnight shift. Most of the time, I looked out at the quiet streets, the winking neon, and I thought.

I lay down in my socks and nightgown and drew the covers around me. That night I left the light on. I fought for sleep because my legs seemed to tremble. But nothing had happened. Nothing.

One Saturday morning, while waiting for a bus on the same street, in broad daylight, I saw my would-be attacker again. I didn't look him in the eyes. I don't remember who sat down first. But I could barely mask my revulsion when I recognized him. A perfect student for Eldridge Cleaver, who, two years later in 1980, in the *San Francisco Chronicle,* would again instruct young black men on how to size up black women for rape, though he called it seduction.

His hair wasn't combed. The knots stood high and as tight as peppercorns. He smelled. It looked as if he wore the same T-shirt—now I noticed it was dirty—and dark trousers. Maybe they were jeans. *Wild, blue/black, poverty black, dirt under his nails black. Boy.* He was no man. I stood up and, as coolly as I could, took the two steps toward the bus stop sign to examine the schedule, which seemed to blur. Fortunately, other strangers were present, also waiting. But then, I thought, that was no guarantee of safety. *Where did he live? Did he eat? Who was his mama? How long had he been doing this?* The bus rumbled forward on time. I made sure I was first. I paid my fare and sat near the driver, surreptitiously, fearfully, waited for him to board. He didn't. I looked down at an empty bench as the bus pulled away from the curb.

I ask J, one of the other women writers: "Can you wait and walk with me back to the cabins? I'm a city girl," I say smiling, nervousness tugging the corners of my lips. "I'm not used to all these bushes." She giggles. "Sure," she says. "I love your flash-light."

It is the late eighties, more than ten years later. I flick on the evening news after grabbing a bite out of the refrigerator. Shocked, I believe I see my would-be attacker yet one more time, manacled for his arraignment. He has made the six o'clock news on all four major stations, the front page of the *Mercury News,* page two or three of the *Chronicle* and *Examiner* and the news in Japan. He has raped and murdered a Japanese exchange student. She was last seen at a bus stop in the Rose Garden section of San Jose.

Relief sweeps over me. He was caught. I think, *I'm glad it wasn't me.*

I remember the Rose Garden section of San Jose as just that, a garden. It is one of the older areas of the city and the planners took time and effort to create and maintain beauty alongside the homes. These are not your usual tract homes, but are custom-built. Some homes are almost mansions. It is a quiet neighborhood: newly married couples versus families versus older couples. Children go to a spacious park to rip and run and scream. It contains a lot of old, grandfatherly trees—oaks, palms and willows—and generous shrubbery that can hide a child in a game, your cat in an adventure and an animal ready to spring.

With the first identifying stain of skin color beamed in via satellite, the unenlightened among the Japanese will see him as a criminal. The terror of dark skin will again be confirmed. On second look, they will measure his face, that forehead, and see an animal, out of the forest, out of the jungle. But first and always, the color.

The girl probably believed she was in a safe neighborhood— that is, a white neighborhood. She had travelled in her native land relatively unmolested. She trusted the shading of those trees and shrubs. I never can.

Home in the heart
I am looking back, imagining the place where my father's family lived. Bay St. Louis, Mississippi, in the thirties and forties had thick woods, open drainage ditches, black children with fluffy brown hair and red skin, and graveyards within the city limits. I imagine my great-grandfather (who was still years from being bedridden and smelling of sores and medicine) standing tall in the sunshine, admiring his troop of grandchildren, one of whom is my father. Perhaps one of his grown children, slamming the car door, pauses long enough to give thanks that he is still with them.

Even then, silent, terrible things were perpetrated at night, when the long shadows of white men vied with those of the trees, the only witnesses. My great-grandfather well knew the alternatives. He could speak out and die on a tree or drown in a river or shut up, bow his head and live.

But he bore with it, as I was told by my father when I was thirteen, sitting with him on a swing, wearing a brown dress "in mourning" and on my second and last visit as a young adult. He taught his black neighbors and their children how to read so one day they could vote, and lived until 1967 at the age of eighty-nine. That was his answer to the whites.

In my father's youth, these incidents in his grandfather's life may not have fully touched him. Later, however, he recaptured them in his own mosaic about what it meant to be black and a man. But a visit to Bay St. Louis must have seemed like a vacation to the boy who worked selling newsprint or shining shoes, giving his few pennies to his mother, enduring white customers who rubbed his head for luck. Away from New Orleans, the days must have seemed longer, bearable, happier. My father and his siblings, cousins or summer friends must have romped in the very old but green woods and marshes, caught catfish and craw-fish in the nearby waters with just a pole and a line amid beards of Spanish moss. They may have visited the store to get a few staples for Grandma, and seen the old black men sitting quietly, contemplating their shrunken world on stoops or on chairs with a board across their withered legs as they played checkers. At night, perhaps tired of hearing grown-up talk they could not yet comprehend and unafraid of roaming in the dark with no flash-light or lantern or streetlights above, the children would sneak off, play hide-and-go-seek among the colored people's head-stones with no compunction that ha'nts were going to rise up in indignation at being so disturbed. I wouldn't be surprised if this had been a ready opportunity for the ancestors to wander in and out of the children's skin and bones, at least one more time, blood coursing like urgent sap in veins, an errant breeze brushing scratched elbows, skinned knees, runny noses and sticky faces like a kiss.

Visits like these confirmed the idea of place for my father. From Bay St. Louis, he could plot the meaning of his own life. You started from here, you do not have to live like this, but you can go forward. Going home, for black Southerners just lately relocated—or was it dislocated—to cities like Chicago, San

Francisco, or New York, meant more than just a visit. Home meant rejuvenation, renewal, healing and appreciation of the place where their fathers and mothers were born. To go home was to begin to understand, to witness, to take their places on the family tree. It took the place, for many of us, of going all the way home to Africa.

The South, whether rural or urban, where our parents and grandparents came from, was almost always rough and timeless, beautiful and cruel. It was pristine in a child's eye, shockingly dirty and crumbling in an adult view. Big and spacious as a child, surprisingly small and cramped as an adult. Year by year the woods dwindled, roads marched in, swamps were filled and new homes built on the flats in the eye of the next hurricane. The rough edges were smoothed, homogenized, tamed. Did my father forget how great it was to have a shoving match in cool loam on a hot day? That soil full of our ancestors' blood, our sweat, our selves. We, the original people. So said *Time* magazine with a cover story about evolution. The cover depicted Adam and Eve as black people. (This issue disappeared quickly off the newsstands at my local Safeway.) "He made a man *out the dirt*," I remember some preacher shouting long ago about the Creation; whether from the TV or radio, I couldn't tell. He pronounced it "doit" like someone transplanted from Brooklyn. "And you know that dirt, when you hold it in your hand, and you smell it, so fresh and clean, just as black as you." Would my father taste wild mint, then drink from a stream instead of a water fountain? How different it must have tasted, from the one marked "colored." Was this an alternative for him? I imagine he would withdraw, straighten his suit and tie, say he was just a kid. A puddle is a puddle. It's a new day now. One could never live that way again. He's grown up.

My eyelids hood, then close. I can see a figure at the screen door: my great-grandmother in a voluminous, but faded apron, peering into the dark. "Heyyyy you! You boys! Chil'ren! Come on, and stop ripping and running like you some kind of wild Indians! It's getting late! You-all ain young savages! Come on, come on in here!"

•

In East San Jose, near Ocala Avenue and Berona Way, across the street from Reid-Hillview Airport, behind the public library, there once was an open field.

It encompassed an entire city block. The planners could have extended the subdivision, but apparently there were big plans for this open field, which did not develop until my junior year in high school.

Until then, the surrounding neighborhood took the field for granted. Like the mountain range beyond, it turned green, high with weeds and other growth in the fall and winter, and with the spring and summer became golden brown and brittle. The grass was mowed in the summer, and against the cracked adobe-like soil, it resembled dry spaghetti. In the winter, school-age children took delighted shortcuts through the squishy muck. Adventurous mothers would *boot up,* bend over and forage for wild dandelion greens, poke salad and other greens and onions. The women pointed them out for those who ventured past and didn't know their uses, or who thought the women were crazy for bending over what looked like weeds as diligent as farm workers in such a wild-looking place.

Then, without warning, the field was roped off. The bulldozers arrived. The soil flew in all directions as they made little hills and valleys, and paved a new shortcut. Destroyed were that year's, and all subsequent years' patches of dandelion greens and onions.

The open field is now Ocala Park. It was carpeted with rolls and rolls of new weedless lawn laid from up hill to down dale. Young trees were planted. In one corner, there is a baseball diamond for Little League. The bathrooms can be freshly painted one day, and within twelve hours, covered with graffiti. At another corner, there is a center named for a Chicano community leader, with teeter-totters, swings and a sandbox.

But some mothers won't allow their children to play in the grass, afraid they would come up with a needle stuck in their hands. Drug deals are sometimes made in Ocala Park under hills, down dales, at night. Such a wild-looking place, after all.

•

While still in her twenties, S, a preceptor in a wilderness program, brought a troop of black city children, mostly twelve to fifteen year olds, to camp out for several days in the woods.

She laughs now when she talks about it. She had volunteered for the job. For many of the children, it was their first time in the wilds. Initially, she noted, they were terrified and fearful of their surroundings. Then, days later, as they began to grow accustomed to the forest and were increasingly sure that the trees and creatures were not going to attack them, the children engaged in destructive behavior, like starting small fires and vandalizing trees, signs or other property. "They couldn't trust being in the woods," she said. "They didn't know how to respond in a positive way, so they reacted in the only way they knew. I felt that they were noisy inside as well as outside, and that they didn't know how to enjoy being quiet."

Eventually, as an experiment, she decided to teach some of the children meditation. This idea appeared to work. On the whole, they became more receptive, respectful and orderly. By the time the camping session ended, they were calmer, relaxed and sorry to leave the woods.

"I sometimes wonder whether they were able to take the meditation back with them and use it," she said, wistfully. "They really needed it."

For several years, after I had left home for college, a neighborhood friend began to take my brothers and sister camping with his own children. My mother, separated from my stepfather for about three or four years, welcomed these excursions. She was free, alone in the house, away from children, at least during the weekends. Apparently, the children enjoyed it as well.

But of my three younger siblings, only J, the baby of the family, has returned to the woods, to go fishing with his buddies. "More likely, drinking," my mother says. But I'd like to think that over a couple of poles, they wouldn't talk much. They are concentrating, hushed, not looking at each other, occasionally gazing or staring off at the green surroundings. The planes from Reid-Hillview Airport, often flying too low over the neighborhood, the blinding, often stinging sunlight, my mother's loud fussing, and ghetto blasters and boom boxes pouring out the latest rap, the noise within and without, are as distant as the first and last waves made by a pebble thrown into the water.

Sometimes, I think black people forget that we once were an agrarian people. That for seventy-five or eighty years, we lived mostly on the land. That our most vivid cultural memories, even from the time before slavery, spring from our connection to the land. That we celebrated the harvest and believed in our own hands. That we often joined with the other original people, the Native Americans, whose respect for the land mirrored our own. *Runago, runago.* That we have always fought for our claim to this land, through hunger and debt. That when we continued on the land, the spirits continued to live with and within us.

And yet we try in the cities. The Fillmore District, where I spent my first two years in California, is now in the last stages of "redevelopment" and is almost unrecognizable to me. There, at the age of seven, I fell in love with real quarter-pound burgers and the busy, jooking bars. I saw the Ice Capades at the Winterland before the hippies flocked to concerts there. Today, the remaining black citizens, mostly elderly, fight in vain to keep the community gardens in two colorful blocks, incongruous to the surrounding highrises and condos marching from Pacific Heights.

I like to think Green Pond is shaped like a heart. It may be closer in shape to a distended kidney. Its carpet has separated and moved over to the left; later, the next morning, it will have journeyed over to the right. The direction of the wind, the amount of rainfall acts like a current. The rain plinks into the water, creating little gas bubbles that sit neatly on the surface and soundlessly pop. I think of tadpoles hatching, sucking in the bubbles, eating on skimming insects. Like the overflowing rivers on the mainland during this wild November in Washington, it is growing larger.

.

Before I left California for Hedgebrook, Cheryl said, "Feel green. Think of nothing but green. Visualize it. It is a sacred color. Wear green close to your skin. Breathe it. Let the green heal your heart."

Back from breakfast in Langley, I walk up the hill to Owl Cottage. The wind has died, I anchor my umbrella against my chest. It is raining steadily. I take small steps, the ground is soaked, and it sounds like water squeezed reluctantly out of a sponge. *Squinch, squinch.* It's easy to say it's because I've eaten a full meal. However, my period has drained me again of blood and oxygen. I've been inordinately tired; the worst day was Thursday. I am in the boonies, I tell myself, I have no health care until I return to work at Stanford in mid-December. Get well. Suddenly I don't want to go back to the cottage, not just yet. Now I don't need a bus. *Get your walking stick,* I think, *and let's go to Green Pond. I've never seen it in the rain.*

But in taking those small steps, I see the forest for the first time. Previously, when I left the forest, I always felt as if I had missed or overlooked something. There was too much to take in; waves of information from my senses seemed jumbled and sometimes unfriendly. I wondered whether I was hurrying through, identifying sights as if they were separate from the habitat. Now, I am overcome. I look up and around me. The trees are heavy with moisture; their canopies gaze down quietly, their trunks stand like the bare legs of grownups. Except for the downpour, the only sound is the croak of a tree frog hidden in a tangle.

> *Lush breath*
> *and strength*
> *in species*
> *Heavy with birth*
> *and rebirth*
> *and rebirth,*

I once wrote these lines as a love poem to B describing myself as a teeming forest. I cannot fight the tightness in my throat. It is all there for me, I am not missing a detail: vulnerable, majestic, restorative. *Cry, because it is beautiful* and the tears roll down and dry on my face as the clouds weep, because they have to. The wilderness is in me.

I attend a night class on shamanism, spirituality and magic in writing. The woman instructor dims the lights except for a lighted candle. Our assignment is to close our eyes and picture ourselves as a tree, our roots splaying into the earth. She plays a cassette recording of the shaman's drumming.

My eyes close, I feel myself sway, however imperceptibly, much like someone about to swoon. I grip with my toes this side of reality. Then the vision opens for me. I am a brown girl—and green. My feet dig into the black soil; I become the tree, its young trunk grows into my vagina, branches into my belly, my lungs, my breasts and my heart. I raise my hands, like boughs, and I grow and I grow and I grow and I grow. Upwards and outwards. My face smiles among the leaves, my hair has never been so long and so thick, climbing towards the sun, and I grow and I grow and I grow.

"Wait!" I say to myself. I am not supposed to go up, but down. I stop growing, I pull myself down, down, into the darkness, the cool, damp roots, and I find it is not so interesting, not so wonderful, as growing and reaching. So I climb and still I climb, higher and higher, thickening and spreading and growing higher and happier.

I've been looking for Hedgebrook's spirit tree. It is a tree that is twisted and seems to have a knot in its middle and is located on the map between Cedar and Owl Cottages. Like rock formations and trees that look vaguely like famous people or the shape of one of the fifty states, I am looking for the tree that resembles my surgical scar. When the surgeons cut me to remove the fibroids from my uterus, they didn't think to ask whether I had the kind of skin that causes sewn flesh to pucker and twist like mashed bubbles from a child learning to blow chewing gum.

I've been drawn to the spirit tree's cousins. They are the pieces of trees I've burned, the kind with bumps, knots and hollows and twists, dead lichen or other tree fungi, and strange hieroglyphs where the bark separates from the wood. They are different, interesting. At home, I purposely buy deformed vegetables, like tomatoes or eggplants, I find in the supermarket. I think it's magical to eat something so imperfect from a processed world. A gift.

I want to stand under the twisted magic of that tree and hear only the wind. I want to close my eyes and remember the night I lay naked and asked to be healed in the sound of drums, when indefinable warmth coursed from my heart to my scar and back again—the two hearts of a woman, I've learned. And another night, in a vision when the bear crashed out of the woods and gently licked the sole of my foot (and I felt the tingles on my right foot even days later), and turned and went away, dragging all of the woods—twigs, leaves, horns, sap mixed with defecation and feathers among others—sticking to its furry backside.

The forest as desire
The forest is only what we choose to see, out of our fears and myths. Most of the time, it is dim and unknown. We hear the keening of hawks and eagles, the buzzing of cicadas mating, and we think there is danger. We attack without reason. When it is chopped or scythed down, when it is finally prone and overcome and cleared, there is nothing left but rotting stumps, space and dead leaves scattering on the wind. Generations are cut off, heredity and possibility for difference and change stand still for the sake of control. And so, where was the monster, after all? Where does it reside? Did it ever live among these boughs, these leaves? And the axes are turned in yet another direction. There, and there, and there. The endlessness, the open-mouthed voraciousness of the chase to *subdue.* Between court orders, let them sneak in and cut and haul the beautiful ones away. Despite periodic complaints, let the train of tank cars full of chemicals fall into the river, choking the fish, turning the clear blue waters into a smoky green, which mocks us. When can we finally congratulate the prince for slaying the dragon?

.

The black woman as wilderness. Unlike Sojourner Truth, however, the forest is forcibly trained, like bad nappy hair processed into good straight hair, until one tree looks like another. Every tree, like every black woman, is different, full of an intimate magic. We dare to name ourselves. Cypress, redwood, sycamore, chestnut, yucca, willow. Eartha, Andrewnetta, Oletha, Syrtiller, Mattiwilda. Straightened, dreadlocks, permanents, fades, jheri curls, finger waves, French braid, Afros, dooky braids. My name for the overnight braids that stuck out of my head, making my brothers and sister laugh: *Medusa,* after the mythological woman who turned men into stone, whose beautiful hair was turned into one mass of hissing snakes. And yet in the morning, my hair rises out of my braids from the coaxing of the comb into my seventies' natural hair: soft, thick and high.

I forego one Thanksgiving with my family to go hiking with a lover and share mooseburgers and salad. I am too honest, wide open and twenty. I've lost my virginity only three months ago, but not to this man. Even he is not the prince.

It is an unseasonably warm, shining day for November, about 60 degrees, so that I don't have to wear a heavy parka, just a long cardigan sweater over a shirt and some jeans and wafflestompers. We make small talk and laugh, walking steadily for at least an hour. He points out the trail to the beach. I'm sorry we've come too late to take the whole day to hike. The sodas chink in my backpack. Other hikers pass us on the trail before he takes my hand, pulls me into some scrub and kisses me quickly, urgently, in hot little nips and nibbles. I drop the pack. I've half-expected this, but still I am surprised by his sudden lust. He is seized with desire. This is not just a nature walk. He wants me. (What is it about the woods that turns men on? Is it the fresh air? The snap of twigs underfoot? Or should I let the beast out of his mannered enchantment?)

I find I like being surprised, at least by him. I want to coo. I respond, my arms about his neck, and he presses gently against me, dry fucking, my back against a tree trunk. I close my eyes, feel myself moisten my panties, thrust my hips forward. After a few minutes of this, he watches me, without any prompting, as I unzip his pants.

He spreads out a blanket and we strip, well away, well hidden by trees and bush from the main trails. The cool air hits my skin like an astringent; my nipples rise. He is waiting, his head propped by his jacket. His skin is healthy, pink, "flesh-colored" like a Band-Aid, generously hairy in the places white men usually are. He is balding and clean-shaven. He is not like the white man who, when I was sixteen, followed me nearly all the way home in a pink, late-model Thunderbird, asking me if I wanted a ride and not taking no for an answer. Frightened, averting my face at intervals, I nevertheless memorized the license number. He was very pale, like biscuit dough, fat and wore sunglasses.

My lover and I met on a massage table in a workshop. For a long time, we gave each other massages, stretching over three hours in length, and were not sexual. The center to which we both belonged—he was the caretaker—frowned on overt sexual contact. We touched and hugged each other. It was delicious. We went away—to soft, nonthreatening places in our minds, sometimes out of our bodies—and came back under coaxing fingers amid piped-in Paul Horn, sitar, and koto music and the oil scent of frangipani or coconut or pine and even chocolate.

Finally, when we joined, sex was realistically affectionate between us; there was passion without violence. We were both looking for someone, somewhere else, and on the way, we found each other. There was much enjoyment. We were able to sweat and explore each other in a Swedish sauna, dive into the cold pool and later fall asleep in each other's arms.

Today, he squeezes a breast, brushes a finger against my lips. I take it, bite playfully, and let go as he fucks me rhythmically, faster. He looms over me, my leg is over his shoulder. Deeper. I take his face in my hands. We kiss as if swallowing water. Deeply.

Suddenly, there is a clack, clack high above us; my eyes widen in disbelief. We are not sure this is a Forest Service helicopter; there's no discernable emblem on the whirlybird's door. My lover stops, shielding me. His cock, still inside me, grows flaccid; it will slip out on its own accord. "Should we dress?" I whisper. He squeezes my hand, waits. We giggle nervously, shake our heads, look away from each other. The copter hovers a few more seconds, then veers off.

Suddenly, it is cold. We can't do it anymore. We dress slowly and head out of the thick brush, shaking the blanket between us. We drink cola quietly, lean against a steep hill, watch the trees and, furtively, each other. "Do you want to go?" he asks. We return to the center to make the mooseburgers, try sex again at my house. We are nervous again, as anxious as ever, even in the dark. No such luck.

Nettles

W and I stand quietly in a cathedral of redwood trees behind Green Pond the morning after rain. I have asked her to take pictures of me in the forest, walking towards the pond. It is here, she says, that she does her little ceremonies of stones and prayers. It is dim, but green and fresh here. The moist soil sinks under my feet, leaving a size ten canyon. I think of Melusine, of Marie Laveau and where they may have kept their secret places.

"What a beautiful darkness," I say, in hushed tones, looking skyward, and then I stop. Voices seem like such a sacrilege here.

But W starts up after a long pause: "How can we reconcile white and black? Light . . . and dark?"

I prod the ground with my walking stick and turn over the dirt, rich in peat. "Well, politics is only part of it." I turn away from her, not because she is white, little and lithe, with dark Celtic hair and sharp planed features, a lesbian, and one of my favorite writers here. It is the stand of trees that informs me, the old ones without voices.

"Remember Star Wars, the Star Wars trilogy?" I say. "Light and dark were not as they were supposed to be. Skywalker could have been Darth Vader. He could have easily gone over into the evil darkness. He always had the potential for evil inside him. He had to wrestle with the evil darkness to become a warrior, not give into it." I thought of the deer S and I had seen one night after dinner. In the dark it had frozen at the danger of our approach, so we nearly walked past it without even seeing it. There were no antlers on this creature, so it might have been a young male as well as a doe. I came close to it with my flashlight, and it bounded away and looked back. Elated at my discovery, I trained the light on it again, but really into its large eyes. Immediately I was sorry. It leaped and darted off. It could not know me, even if I had held out a block of salt. It couldn't fathom I would not be "evil" and rob it of life.

"Light and dark are four-sided, not two-sided," I resume. "In our bodies, tumors can grow and they can be benign or malignant; we make babies—healthy or deformed—in the womb. *But everything happens in the dark.* Black skin does not necessarily mean black deeds, but that's what most people think. Black people are careful of white people because they can and will carry out evil things. Whites can call *evil* good, perfect, pure and beneficial. Darkness has power for good as well as for evil." It is partly cloudy above in the break of the trees, with a patch of blue. "Once everyone realizes this of each other, realizes this *within* themselves, then the politics will work."

Later, we visit a little swamp which has renewed itself during the frequent rains. There is a hum to the place, like an organic engine. It is a riot of shades of green and death as the roots, tree trunks and tendrils drink, leach from each other, nourish themselves, grow all over and all the way out and rot. The tree frogs call out to each other, birds interrupt their conversations. Brown, dark water in which a floating branch or stick could become, at second look, a snake. The murkiness of the unknown stirred up, until the clouds of silt present a vision. The Everglades. The Amazon. Insects must be climbing out from under a few hundred leaves or fissures. I snap a picture of the ruins of a gigantic, fantastic, shiny-wet, old tree; it is squishy against my waterproof shoes and that word, *primeval,* comes to mind.

Going a different way home, it rains again. We walk, stop for cover, and walk again, stop. Drops collect in my jheried hair, paste W's to her pale skin.

When you are searching for something or someone, go off the beaten path. This is the lesson I learned (again) when I found the twisted tree. It stands off the path towards Green Pond just as the map said. What it didn't say was that it stood half hidden from view and that to see it, you must stop the moving picture of your life in order to notice this scene.

I was examining another tree off the path to the pond to take a picture of it. It was interesting but ugly and forlorn looking because it had been either burned and or had its limbs sheared off by fire or lightning. I couldn't get any closer because the foliage was so thick. On the way back to the path, one of my rings slipped off my finger into the grass. I reached down to retrieve it and almost dropped the ring because I felt as if my thumb and forefinger had been burned on a stove.

I looked down, bewildered. Grass can't burn, I thought. "Nawwww!" I said aloud. Maybe there is a bug down there. So I bent to make sure and again, felt that burning sensation.

"Nettles," I finally concluded. So these were nettles growing lickety-split and willy-nilly towards the cleared road. I remembered the fairy story of the wild swans. How a princess named Elisa had to crush these plants into flax fiber with her feet and then weave the fiber into shirts for her brother princes who had been turned into giant swans. All eleven of them. Elisa's princess hands and feet were constantly reddened and inflamed. She could not stop weaving and she could not speak, on pain of her brothers' deaths. The eleventh prince wept tears onto her hands, and the blisters magically healed. At the end of the ordeal the eleventh prince still had a wing where an arm should have been at the moment of transformation, because she had no more nettles for the last sleeve.

I straightened, rubbing my hands. I looked out at nothing. And then I saw something. Quickly, I gained the path and strode down a few feet. Now I was at the crossroads and saw a scant opening in the trees at my left. There was another path, slim, only faintly discernable because it was thick with nettles. I stood crushing the nettles into the mud and then wound very slowly around still another large stump lying next to a living tree.

Of course, it looked nothing like the drawing. It looked like two brown arms not wanting to let go and pausing at about ten years' breath to separate from each other and then joyfully embrace once more. It had a thick, bushy head which swayed gently in the breeze a few hundred feet above me.

I felt honored, a rush of happiness at the achievement. I half-climbed onto the remains of stump shaped like a lap and touched the shift where the two arms began. I didn't think that perhaps it was filled with leaves and a bug or two, that my fingernails would turn blue-gray with dirt. After a moment, I began to cry. Not loudly, not out of grief, but out of feeling released and washed. At the same time, an eagle opened his wings over me and seemed to call down a blessing.

PAJARITOS

Terri de la Peña

THE WINTRY BREEZE lightly brushes the tips of the sycamore against the overhead window. Awakening, we snuggle under blue flannel sheets, listening to morning sounds: the rustling of spotted doves on the roof, the twittering of yellow-rumped warblers among the sprawling branches, the mellifluous serenade of a neighborhood mockingbird. In the bedroom, the resident *pajaritos* wake, too. Maxwell the cockatiel shrilly responds to the mockingbird's song, while Pepper the parakeet begins to chirp. In this ersatz aviary, it is impossible to sleep late.

This morning is no time for sleeping. We are off to the Malibu Lagoon to see and photograph other pajaritos, not only the indigenous ones, but also the shorebirds and ducks that migrate to California waters. Unlike their human counterparts, bird migrants are more or less welcome in this once golden state, swooping in each winter for a temporary stay.

We pull on jeans, sweatshirts and jackets, down coffee and bagels, pack some snacks, grab the camera, binoculars and field guide, and head north on the Pacific Coast Highway. The chilly air and overcast sky are typical of a December morning. Keeping warm in the car, I sip my coffee and entertain Gloria with my impersonation of the resident Bodega Bay ornithologist in Alfred Hitchcock's *The Birds*. She was a stereotypical character, British and butch in a beret and tweeds. Years before I came out, I saw that film and somehow identified her as a dyke, though the sexual chemistry between "birds" Tippi Hedren and Suzanne Pleshette seemed more authentically lesbian. Since then, being a dyke and being a birder have seemed synonymous, though when *we* bird, we wear Gap or Eddie Bauer gear, *not* tweed.

Along the drive, among the flocks of California and Western gulls, we spot squadrons of brown pelicans, like modern-day pterodactyls, flying low over the ocean. Hungry cormorants loiter in the Gladstone's 4 Fish parking lot, and solitary kestrels, the smallest American falcons, scan for prey while perched on utility poles. These pajaritos may have never heard the expression, "the early bird catches the worm," yet they abide by that instinctively. In order for us not to be disappointed, we have to be "early birds," too. Birds can be notoriously elusive at mid-day.

Beneath a fragrant grove of eucalyptus trees, we park off the highway and trek through the chain-link gates of the Malibu Lagoon State Beach. The cold weather and low tide explain why we have the place almost to ourselves. There are a couple of die-hard joggers along the beach, but the brushy areas surrounding the Lagoon and its inlets remain ours to explore.

Before meeting Gloria, I had never been to the Malibu Lagoon. I'd only driven by, not particularly curious about what wonders lay beyond its posted sign. Though I had grown up with pets, parakeets among them, I had been uninvolved with animals or wildlife, much less birds, for many years. Not particularly nature-conscious, I tended to keep to myself, reading or writing, living in my head more than in the great outdoors. When we began dating, I realized with some embarrassment that despite my life-long proximity to the Pacific, I had limited knowledge of its geography and none of any local birds beyond gulls and pelicans. I did not even realize the Lagoon is a sanctuary for the feathered crowd. Loving a birder means loving her birds, too—all birds, for that matter—and I have grown to cherish our Lagoon expeditions, sometimes with the local Audubon Society, more often alone together. Eager to expand our knowledge of the area, we have even taken a weekend course on the history and geography of the Santa Monica Mountains, which included investigating tidal pools and observing shorebirds at the Lagoon.

Watching pajaritos in this natural habitat has evoked my strong connection to Southern California. When the region was Spanish territory, Francisco Marquez and Ysidro Reyes, my paternal grandmother's forebears, settled in Santa Monica Canyon and northward toward Topanga. Malibu Lagoon, currently surrounded by prime beachfront property, lies slightly northwest of that land granted to the Marquez-Reyes families by the Mexican government in 1828.

Nearly three hundred years prior to that, Juan Rodríguez Cabrillo had sailed the Pacific and taken possession of California for Spain. He first encountered the native population, the Chumash people, when he landed in Southern California on October 10, 1542. Viewing their numerous *tomols*—plank canoes—Cabrillo called their village "Pueblo de las Canoas." Local historians who have studied the navigational references in the summary of Cabrillo's log, written by Juan Paez in the sixteenth century, assert the present-day Lagoon and its state beach embody the site of that village. Archaeologists have discovered deep midden deposits at the Lagoon, proving its continuous occupation for thousands of years. The Chumash name for the site was "Humaliwo," the probable origin of the word "Malibu."

Far into the Santa Monica Mountains, Malibu Creek originates, bubbling and gurgling in a winding fashion until it empties into the Lagoon and its inlets. Archaeologists have found evidence that the creek banks served as pathways for the Chumash of Humaliwo to travel toward the mountains and for the inland Chumash to journey to the Lagoon to barter for fish.

Because of its proximity to both mountains and ocean, the Lagoon is home not only to a variety of birds, but also to several types of plants. These include sand verbena, beach primrose, beach morning glory, marsh rosemary, reeds, California buckwheat and several types of sage. At least once a year, the local chapter of the California Native Plant Society converges at the Lagoon, not only intent on weeding out intrusive vegetation, but also on preventing fire hazards. This year's heavy rainfall has increased all forms of vegetation. On noting the overgrown sage lining the paths, I joke about our being "bushwhackers." Gloria laughs at the double-entendre.

Seconds after we approach the picnic area on our way to the Lagoon, we spot a Black phoebe on one of the outdoor tables. The phoebe is a member of the flycatcher family. A chunky, mostly black bird with white at its belly and outer tail feathers, the phoebe prefers shady areas near water, often stationing itself on a large rock to catch insects as they whiz by. This one scampers along the table top before uttering "fee-bee, fee-bee," and flying off.

We are disappointed to miss a glimpse of the resident red-winged blackbird. With magnificent scarlet "epaulets," he usually acts as a sentry, frequenting the reeds at the saltwater marsh near the entrance to the park, issuing his loud territorial call, "ok-a-lee!" to whomever he observes. However, we cannot avoid the ubiquitous coots with their slate bodies and pale bills, croaking and poking through the mud-lined inlets, and the comically quacking mallards swimming with their mates.

Binoculars ready, we move toward one of the plank bridges over the closest inlet. In spring, barn and cliff swallows build conical mud nests on the underside of the bridges; this late in the year, only their abandoned homes remain. We spy a lone Northern shoveler, one of the many who come to the Lagoon from the Pacific Northwest each winter. Green-headed with chestnut-and-white plumage, the shoveler is so named because of his blunt black bill which he uses adeptly for "shoveling" through the mud and water while feeding.

In the bird world, the males tend to be flamboyant, the females drab. I find my feminist sensibilities aquiver at this injustice, yet I remind myself that nature has equipped the out-numbered males to attract the females, not vice versa. And, though I have read about whole colonies of lesbian seagulls, I have not been lucky enough to spot any at the Lagoon or else-where. They supposedly exist on the Channel Islands, off the coast of Santa Barbara.

Floating by is a green-winged teal, its chestnut head deco-rated with a bold emerald slash. With the overcast sky mirrored in the water, the duck's colors seem even more brilliant. Ducks enjoy the marshy edges of the Lagoon. Soon the teal is joined by some plump black-and-white buffleheads, migrants from British Columbia. Nearby we see elegant Western grebes, their white necks bobbing underwater now and then, and their smaller relatives, the brownish pied-billed grebes, paddling adjacent.

Shorebirds are more difficult to identify. Unlike the ducks, these birds often have less variation in color. Curlews and whimbrels like to stay by the inlets, patiently searching the mud for insects. Both are tall sandpipers with curved-under bills. The curlew is larger, its coloring mottled with hints of cinnamon and buff, its bill much longer. The whimbrel has a paler bill, a striped crown and grey-brown markings. Their descriptions may seem distinct, yet differentiating between them, especially with their seasonal plumage, can be troublesome.

Smaller sandpipers are even more of a challenge. They scramble beside the incoming tide in their quest for beach insects. A new birder can get dizzy trying to follow them. I recognize sanderlings in their light grey-and-white winter plumage, rushing in flocks along the shoreline. Their frantic actions remind me of the Keystone Cops.

Killdeer, robin-sized members of the plover family, occupy the area by the last plank bridge, closest to the Pacific. The tan-and-white birds have two striking black breast-bands. If a predator approaches a nesting site, the female feigns injury, dragging her wings and tail in a distracting maneuver. On witnessing this protective behavior, one cannot help but marvel at the mother killdeer's courage.

For some moments, we watch the hyperactive sanderlings on the beach before deciding to head to one of the narrow land strips. On our way there, we pause quietly on a bridge to observe a green heron perched on driftwood. It searches the water intently, its yellow eyes mesmerized. This sleek chestnut-and-green bird is an excellent fisher, biding its time. Gloria focuses her camera on it and memorializes the moment. Beyond the heron, she also photographs two American avocets, trim and graceful in their black-and-white winter plumage. One balances itself on one leg while the other feeds efficiently.

Turning away from the inlets, we trek toward the bank beside the Lagoon itself, inhaling the pungent scent of sage along the path. While Gloria begins to stalk likely subjects with her zoom lens, I plop down on a pile of rocks, binoculars around my neck, content to relax and watch the bird activity around me. For some seconds, I watch a Heermann's gull flying low before it expertly lands. This dark grey gull with a red bill breeds on the Channel Islands and winters on the coast. The only one here so far, it stands out among the large flocks of white-and-grey Western and California gulls.

After a while, I notice the gulls, grebes and ducks keeping away from a stark, leafless tree overhanging the mouth of the Lagoon. Only the pelicans and the double-crested cormorants remain stationed nearby. I recognize a tell-tale shape on the top branch. Through my binoculars, I stare at a young peregrine falcon, probably the offspring of a pair reintroduced to the wild. Its youth is apparent from its brown rather than slate gray markings and its streaked rather than barred breast. Veteran birders tend to be unexcited about spotting a peregrine, but this is my first up-close look at one. I am awestruck by its piercing eyes, its innate dignity. Only its head moves as it scans the terrain below for prey. No wonder the pajaritos are giving it a wide berth.

Months ago, Gloria and I were equally excited when a merlin falcon swooped over our heads while we were birding in British Columbia. I motion her toward the peregrine and she aims her zoom lens for just the right angle. The falcon seems oblivious of her and remains motionless for the rest of our time there.

We spend hours at the Lagoon, she photographing, I day-dreaming about describing the site in my novel-in-progress. Side by side, we silently watch the shorebirds' frenzied antics, the Anna's hummingbirds' aerial acrobatics, the belted kingfisher hovering over the Lagoon, the great blue heron majestically preening on the opposite shore. Sometimes we "pish" (make sounds to attract birds) like the best of 'em, but usually we do not "twitch" (rush from one bird to another). For us, birding is serene, not competitive. We would rather enjoy their presence than keep lists of how many pajaritos glimpsed in a day or weekend. We are simply happy to have seen them at all.

Although the Coast Highway is walking distance away, we hardly hear the traffic because the Pacific's stirrings and the gulls' cries blot out the noise. While Gloria continues photographing, I close my eyes and imagine Humaliwo. Instead of the curving highway separating the Santa Monica Mountains from the ocean, centuries ago there were wide expanses of undisturbed land covered with chia bushes, yucca and sage, which the Chumash burned for ceremonial purposes. There were no stately eucalyptus, no scrawny palm trees then; both were introduced at the turn of the 19th century. Where Malibu Creek empties into the Lagoon and from there to the ocean, the domed willow-and-tule dwellings of the villagers stood, no doubt surrounded by fleets of canoes. And the indigenous birds—gulls, pelicans, cormorants, herons and peregrines, whose descendants we admire through binoculars—shared the bounty of the Lagoon with the Chumash people.

I am not one for romanticizing the past, yet I shiver to think one of the first encounters between Spanish conquistadors and native Californians occurred at this site, Homaliwo, Pueblo de las Canoas. The Chumash are nearly extinct, their numbers having dwindled because of diseases introduced by the Spanish, forced enslavement by Catholic missionaries, intermarriage, and the racism of all California settlers. I know from old-time family tales that the land-grant owners, *mestizos* themselves, shared guilt in abusing the native population. Reluctant to ponder that, I open my eyes abruptly. In a moment, Gloria runs out of film and sits beside me.

I take her hand and hold it. She has introduced me to the serenity of this place, this accessible haven from personal stress and the never-ending injustices of racism, sexism and homophobia. Off the highway near the water, we can temporarily leave behind our daily lives and witness together the transforming face of nature: the high or low tides, the diversity of plant life, the shy cottontails peering beneath creosote bushes, the ever-changing bird population from ruddy turnstones to black skimmers, soras to swallows.

Yet the problems of the world inevitably intrude here. After rainstorms, we see drain spill-off polluting the Lagoon's waters. Styrofoam cups, plastic bags and condoms trash the beach where shorebirds gather. Near the famed Malibu Colony, homeless men camp at the Lagoon's boundaries, spreading their meager possessions on the beach much as long-ago traders displayed their wares. For always, at the site of Humaliwo, among the repetitive "kee-yah" calls of the gulls and the characteristic rattle of the kingfisher, I remember the original Chumash inhabitants and, with bitterness, the genocide of that long-ago native people.

We cannot recreate the past. We do have the power, however, to safeguard the future of the Malibu Lagoon and other places like it, by respecting and protecting their history, beauty and resources. Birding at the Lagoon has taught us to appreciate life more by observing how fragile it can be, not only for us, but for all inhabitants of this planet.

Birding has taught us to love—not only the enormous varieties of birds who share our skies and space—but also ourselves—and each another.

As I rewrite this in fall 1993, the landscape surrounding the Malibu Lagoon has changed drastically. On November 2, the Mexican Day of the Dead, the Santa Monica Mountains erupted into flames. Santa Ana winds swooped through Topanga and Malibu Canyons, fueling the deadly inferno. From my upstairs apartment in the city, I could see tongues of flame licking rugged ridges, outlining their destruction against the darkened sky. Chaparral and introduced vegetation such as eucalyptus trees burned like matchsticks, igniting hilltop homes. Television news crews broadcasted live from the highway bridge bordering the Lagoon. I watched my screen in horror as flying embers whizzed past familiar landmarks, places I had recently described in my manuscript. Palm trees and overgrown sagebrush on the fringes of the Pacific were ablaze.

For days, the hot, windy air was thick with ashes; grey flakes covered cars and patios. I scanned newspaper maps showing the fire had skipped along the edges of the Lagoon, and wished the media coverage had been more specific. Reporters focused on property damage rather than on environmental devastation. And I wondered what had become of the shorebirds and ducks, the first wave of avian migrants?

Miles from the Lagoon, I tried to console myself. The Santa Monica Mountains have been consumed by fire hundreds of times in the approximately 11,500 years since the last ice age. The chaparral, the area's dominant vegetation, already is sprouting. Landslides caused by winter storms are likely to occur, yet by spring, the hills beyond the Lagoon will be covered with fire poppies, penstemons and mariposa lilies. Closer to the water, barn and cliff swallows will reoccupy the mud nests, hummingbirds will flutter among the coastal sage. The charred landscape, the troubled waters, will become distant memories, transformed by the turbulent life cycle of the region.

Gloria and I will return to a rejuvenated Lagoon to seek different pajaritos. And as we stand on its shifting shores, we will cherish it even more.

MOUNTAIN BIKING AND

THE PLEASURES OF BALANCE

Marti Stephen

LOOKING BACK OVER my metamorphosis into a mountain biker, I realize that sometimes, in order to achieve balance, you have to go to extremes. In my case, it took a love for the extreme, the passionate and even the epic, to sign up to race twenty miles of fire roads and single-track (narrow, one-bike trails) in drizzling rain and through snowbanks at the summit of a mountain. But I didn't see it as extreme then, I saw it as initiation, and I had a powerful, though vague, longing to be on the other side of an experience I'd never had before.

My memories of my life-long cycling odyssey begin at age seven or eight and center around two things: a bike borrowed from the boys across the street, and the infallible sense that I could learn this new physical skill. Now I know that some girls were lucky enough to learn from other girls, but in my neighborhood there were no girls riding bikes, and I had to approach the very font of physical prowess—a boy.

I repeated the ritual of turning to men for knowledge about cycling at least two more times before owning balance completely for myself in my mid-30s. But after those first years on the bike—when I felt I could learn anything—I lost my childlike trust in my body, my sense of balance, and my place in the sporting world. The rediscovery of that trust, which I made on a touring bike in my mid-20s, is now made substantial every time I line up for a mountain bike race.

After the boy next door, my second tutor in the world of the wheel was a bike racer—an architecture student who was my boyfriend and who had a passion for the history, the cliquishness, the working-class values and the outlandishness of road racing in these United States (as opposed to Europe, where it is as well understood as football is here). I was in my 20s then, and he reintroduced me to the bike. At the time, mountain biking was in its infancy, and while I was vaguely aware of it, I was busy worshipping male role models and discovering that the brutal physical requirements of road racing were far beyond my fitness level. As a little girl, I'd had a nonathletic childhood and had been brought up, as many girls were, to avoid risk. I'd also developed a case of self-loathing during numerous failures in co-ed kickball games, recess hours and p.e. classes. In road riding terms, I felt permanently o.t.b. (off-the-back, a term used to describe the rider who can't keep up with the pack). At the time, I adored the idea of road racing so much that I couldn't even speak about my own racing aspirations above a whisper. So my dreams, born somewhere deep within me and diametrically opposed to anything I had dared in a long, long time, took control of my soul.

As I moved beyond that transitional boyfriend and into my own halting self-discovery as a racer, I discovered other women racers (what a blessing) and, on a particularly memorable century ride in the Santa Ynez Valley of California, another boyfriend. He became another guide on my bicycle quest, and probably the last male tutor I would ever need. He lived at the base of Mt. Tamalpais in Marin County, California, a mountain named after a woman and a location famous as the birthplace of mountain biking. He took my road bike elitism (carefully copied from the old boy school) and rubbed it in the dirt. It was the beginning of the lesson that would eventually set me free.

Oh, he made me suffer. Four-hour-long, bone-jarring rides that were approximately half uphill and half downhill, each presenting a completely different set of obstacles. My only real taskmaster was the incline of the earth, and she was the only real audience, too. Bless her, she was impartial, and her challenges made me fitter than I had ever been. We made an unspoken bargain: as long as I would honor the suffering, she would make me fit.

This bargain with the dirt was a cold one. I honored it sometimes while shrinking from the effort required, sometimes in the exhilaration of strength. I kept my side of it in violent gusts of wind that blew me off my bike on the tops of ridges and I broke it on fine, sunny days when the challenge—particularly the challenge of balance—made me wither in self-disgust and stay close to the hearth instead of close to the heart. But I would keep it again on mild rides and wild ones. I remember one in particular where hip-deep water at a stream crossing nearly washed away my bike. But as long as I came back, Nature extended the terms, and I grew fitter. Fit enough, in fact, to race mountain bikes.

I agreed to the challenge with my eyes shut and with the hope that the experience would be alchemical—that the base metal of a rider would finally, gloriously, be turned into the gold of a racer. Since I held such a simple, grandiose view of racing, no such thing would happen, but there were transformative moments, nonetheless.

I arrived at the race with the man who had conducted my studies in mountain biking so far, and he was about to relinquish his mentorship as I discovered the wealth of support I felt from other women—my competitors. I remember how I expected him to be all-knowing in regards to pre-race jitters, and how I followed his example of reading a book before the warm-up of my race, and how I nearly missed the start of my own race because I was slavishly not looking out for myself. (Obvious enough, but I was expecting absolute knowledge from this man.)

My race rode off without me—it seems hilarious in the retelling—and I was forced to chase the field. But I caught them and even passed a number of riders—solidly—while climbing. I was instantly in an elated, anaerobic state (which anyone will tell you is not always elated) and flew up the mountain for the first several miles. Both the will and the ability to go on at this level seemed to be on a slow-drip transfusion into my veins. I'd never felt more at home or more centered. Neither, in my perception, has the presence of trees and clouds and dirt seemed more immediate to me—or closer to my marrow.

I met several memorable women along the way. When I was forced in the second mile to stop at a bottleneck clogged with racers and wipe my wet, mud-spattered glasses, the first one stepped off the sidelines. She said, "Here, let me wipe them for you. I have watched this race for years, and I've never had the guts to do what you're doing."

During the first half of the race, I had kept company with another woman rider. In the years since then I've forgotten her name, but I remember how we paced one another; how we passed men together (who unkindly joked that they were useless if women were passing them); how we looked out for each other as we tipped over in the snowbanks, waiting for the other—the competitor—to get back on her bike. As the climb changed to a descent halfway through the race, and the drizzle to a steady rain, I could no longer see the track or stay upright. She could do both, and I had to relinquish her company.

Left on my own and growing increasingly colder in what were really hypothermic conditions, my friend Mother Nature and I did a dance down the mountainside.

On the way down, my long-sought-after ideal of racing revealed that sport isn't always about competition—sometimes it's about compassion. As I descended, about three quarters of the way through the race, I found a racer from the longer elite event sitting near the stone stairstep section, holding his face in his hands. His group was crashing and hopping down the steps while he was immobilized by the mud in his eyes. The technical demands of riding in this section were so consuming that no one noticed him—but I was walking. I gave him a water bottle to wash out his eyes, and he called me an angel. Given the contrast between my solo act of kindness and the obliviousness of others to his plight, I half believed that my intervention was heavenly.

I threaded past the sections of the descent that were too technical for me, and as the rain stopped, I was on my bike again for the final quarter of the race. At a broad stream crossing, I picked up another woman competitor, who came charging from behind. My numbness gave way to that elevated, anaerobic dance again, and spectators began to reappear and shout that the finish was only two miles away, and then one, and then around the next bend. When the finish banner appeared, it was suspended over the end of a quagmire filled with peanut-butter mud. I moved into place beside my latest traveling companion, and 250 meters away from the conclusion of my first epic, I heard my name being shouted by the woman I'd climbed the first half of the course with. "Go Marti, go!" It was like the trumpet blast of real angels, and I got out of my saddle and sprinted to the finish line, determined to expend any energy I hadn't already squandered on this spending spree of exertion. My latest partner responded, and then faltered—either giving up or just plain losing—but it didn't matter what she did, because for me the last four hours of experience were being distilled into one final outburst of love for being in a human body, trying to find its limits.

And then it was over, and it was so remarkably concluded that real time seemed to come back with a thwack, and I couldn't imagine riding my bike out of the muck in the staging area that I had just sprinted through. Someone handed me an electrolyte drink, and its chemicals tasted dry. I made my way back to my boyfriend's car, unlocked the door and promptly sat down on his fastidiously kept upholstery in all my muddy glory. I was no longer captive to a male sport, I had found my own kingdom of balance—with a little nudge from the wild side. In it reigned the feminine aspects of both mountain biking and competition.

I found the feminine in mountain biking because I realized that the ability to balance requires the quality of yielding and of working with something rather than against it—if you fight gravity, it will conquer you; if you work with it, it will grant you balance. The struggle to find this quality often means leaning to extremes. In my case, it meant the extremes of worshipping the concept of racing and then psyching myself out of ever attaining it. In my first mountain bike race, I also discovered the feminine quality of competition when I realized that for me, competing meant striving *with* people to surpass myself, rather than striving *against* them—the idea of competitors as community.

Since that race, I would like to say that I have kept both that balance and that spirit alive in a little shrine in my heart—but I haven't. I've lost the path and rediscovered it. Led others to it, and then failed to follow it myself. Owned it and then completely squandered it. But it has always called to me, and in my own way, I have always kept its value in mind. Finally, I think I have surrendered to it, and it's no longer a matter of will for me to train and ride—it's a simple matter of breathing the air I was meant to breathe.

THE BEDOUINS OF NEVADA:

FIVE WOMEN SNOWBOARD THE FIRST

DESCENT OF WHEELER PEAK

Kathleen Gasperini

WE CALL OURSELVES "Bedouins" simply because the ascent trail we forged our first day up the mountain truly did look like the trail of wanderers, switch-backing haphazardly across the snowy fields and jutting off into various directions. We got lost—more than once—despite topographical help from Ranger Andy at the Wheeler Peak Ranger Station that morning and months of studying the route up the mountain ourselves. But due to our heavy packs with snowboards strapped to the outside, we had to stop and rest more often, take an easier route, and twist our way through thick brush to avoid low-hung boughs that our snowboards would undoubtedly snag. These were factors we hadn't counted on when studying the topos from the comfort of our homes earlier that year.

But it didn't deter us from our mission: to snowboard the first descent of Wheeler Peak in Nevada. After more than a year of planning, including phone calls to ranger stations, researching climbable peaks, and mapping the ascent route of the peak we had chosen, heavy packs and pine trees weren't about to stop us. Besides, we were a team of determined women, starting with the leaders—Kathlee Martin and Bonnie Learey—who are extreme snowboarders and founders of an organization called Team Artemis, a group of women snowboard mountaineers. Other team members included Greta Gaines, the sole female entry of the '92 World Extreme Snowboard Championships in Valdez, Alaska, photographer Mary Siebert, extreme snowboarder and instructor Caroline Falkenburg, and myself. All of us had done our fair share of mountaineering, climbing peaks, and camping for days at a time. But only Kathlee, Bonnie, and Caroline had done it in the winter months—and with snowboards strapped to their backs. But, they said, after "bagging" one peak, it became addictive, and soon they found themselves seeking terrain to ride outside of ski resorts, away from crowds and into pristine wilderness.

What was most unique about Team Artemis wasn't the peaks they rode in the backcountry so much as the fact that it was *women* who were riding these peaks. With women comprising about ten percent of the snowboarding population, it's rare enough to see women snowboarders at resorts, to say nothing about women in the backcountry. But Team Artemis meant to change all that.

"We'll get women out here," Bonnie had told me over the phone last January when we first discussed riding Wheeler. "They just need role models, to see that other women are doing it. Women don't need heroes, they just need us."

Wheeler Peak wouldn't make us heroes, but it would give us an intense gratification in four days time. That's why Bonnie and Kathlee had chosen it. "It'll take two days to get to basecamp, a morning for the peak ascent, then we'll have at least a full afternoon for some major rides...and maybe we can do it a few times...if the weather's good...," they said, overlapping each other in excitement. It sounded incredibly challenging, but fun and worth considering. The rest of the group agreed. Wheeler Peak, with its perfect slopes for riding and unique location smack dab in the middle of a Nevada desert, was for women. Here we would discover what we could actually do on our own.

•

It did only take two days to reach basecamp, despite our zig-zag route up the mountain, and we pitched camp by late afternoon on flat ground amidst a grove of bristlecone pines. From there, we could see the humble peak of Wheeler—a flat pinnacle rising just above a floating cumulus. It looked like a fairly simple day hike to the summit. But without chairlifts, porters to help haul gear or a warm lodge, life's small traumas (like dredging poop pits) became time consuming. By the time we were prepared for the summit bid the next morning, snowboarding down had taken a back seat to: A) melting snow, B) loading packs, C) adjusting crampons and D) sinking ice axes into faces that were far steeper than they seemed to be the evening before.

Although our packs were lighter for the summit bid, we had another set of traumas during the final ascent. First, the pitch was steeper than the lower sections of the mountain and each step required a jab with the ice axe and a kick-step with our crampons. Combined with the effects of altitude, our pace slowed. What we thought would be a three-hour summit bid, turned into a five-hour challenge.

But after a quick lunch of turkey sandwiches, cookies and energy bars, we switchbacked up the final three hundred feet to the summit. While we sat at the top to rest and look down at the desert floor 10,200 feet below, snowboarding seemed almost anticlimactic. We'd gone through so much to get to this point. But the anticlimactic feeling didn't last long, in fact, only as long as it took me to plunk down my pack and watch Bonnie carving the first tracks on this smooth, white mountain face.

With her right knee tucked neatly into her left—alpine style—she rode the mountain with flare, spraying fat waves down the mountain's featureless face after riding off the summit cornice for a bit of added speed. We couldn't help but scream hysterically with excitement while Bonnie rode the mountain with a new-found energy; riding like she did at every mountain resort, with a style, grace and unforgettable beauty that was solely hers.

In turn, we each interpreted the mountain in a personal way. Kathlee vaulted down her chosen line like an avalanche—her unruly red hair the only thing visible in the waves of heavy snow spraying up from her board. Caroline performed one graceful carve after another—gaining mach speed—while a long, blond braid swished quietly from side to side. Mary chose a wickedly steep, narrow ridge about seven hundred feet long and loaded with icy snow. It was a run, she said, "that would truly capture what were doing up here." Greta hit jumps: cornices, snow-covered rocks, anything that would launch her into the heated air of the late afternoon spring season. I chose a run for safety and satisfaction: soft bowls of corn snow just below the peak. Only snowboarding can give the feeling of floating, uninhibitedly. And riding on new terrain, with my board an extension of my body, it was a rush so powerful, so feminine, I felt like a creature of nature.

We were soaked that night back at camp, but our spirits soared. Talk was fast and filled with exciting, breathless tales of our first descent. As we sat finishing a dinner of stroganoff, herbal tea and apple Fig Newtons, we went from discussing our most recent adventure, to the fortitude required for a hanging belay on the Nose of Half Dome, which *somehow* led to the emotional forti-tude required by country singers (*Coal Miner's Daughter*, Loretta Lynn in particular). Only women would compare snowboarding and rock climbing to country singing, we were sure. Maybe it was the mountain air or the warm tea in our bellies that led to such uninhibited conversation. As we settled into our sleeping bags, we looked forward to tomorrow's rides and another night-time conversation like this one.

The next day was more of the same: sweet tracks in big bowls. But we also found chutes and trees shots five hundred feet lower, which were tighter and more challenging, keeping us on edge. As our friendship grew, so did our riding. Miraculously, we became less inhibited and our styles reflected this as we flew off lips landing backward and spinning forward, then carving huge arcs in new-found bowls. We'd scream wildly, passion-ately, then shed our clothes down to our jog bras for the climb back up for more runs.

These feelings continued into dinner time. After a strange

meal of whiskey-soaked venison sandwiches (thanks to Greta and Mary), pasta and veggies, we sang loudly. And for our last night under the stars of Nevada at more than ten thousand feet, we popped two bottles of wine that we'd actually hauled up the mountains. It was then, while watching the North Star first appear in the desert sky, that Kathlee explained our purpose on this Peak.

"You know you guys, the rad stuff is out. It's the *hidden* agenda that's really in," she said. "Like what we've been through—testing our skills in the mountains—and where we're at right now with ourselves. Remember this feeling."

"You mean the stuff besides our snowboarding success?" I asked.

"Yeah."

"Like our evening conversations? Like the struggle of the ascent? Like untangling snarled hair from tree boughs and mistakenly peeing on our snowboard boots at night? And..."

"Yeah, yeah, that and *more*," she said.

She was right. The hidden agenda between five women snowboarders in the mountains was different. It meant camaraderie without pretenses or unrealistic expectations of our abilities. It meant shared baby steps to the summit that we could handle and no machismo about riding the raddest line. Despite the hardcore nature of the adventure, this first descent was almost...easy. And it was reflected in our snowboarding style, which became startlingly natural and flowing as well.

By the time we loaded our packs on each other's backs the morning of the last day, it was nine and the snow was already soft from a creepy Nevada heat wave. Every few steps, someone would sink to their hips in slush and we'd have to help them out of another sucking hole. But, by late afternoon we reached the road that lead to the ranger station. Within two hours, we were gulping Bonnie's homemade brew and sitting on the tailgate of her Toyota.

Perhaps it was the beer or the corn chips and salsa we'd found under Greta's car seat that made us loquacious that late afternoon at the ranger station. But whatever the reason, there was a mutual respect and understanding in our circle—a tapestry of emotions that could have blanketed the flat top of Wheeler Peak. It didn't come from "conquering" the summit, or even riding the toughest chutes and bowls. It came from us: from the hidden agenda we'd found within each other.

*E*NDURANCE ON THE ICE:

THE AMERICAN WOMEN'S ANTARCTIC

EXPEDITION

Anne Dal Vera

Editor's Note: This account is of the American Women's Antarctic Expedition (AWE) to the South Pole. The four women involved in the expedition included expedition leader Ann Bancroft, mountaineer Sue Giller, ultra-marathoner Sunniva Sorby, and the author of this piece, Anne Dal Vera. Their goal was to traverse the Antarctic from near Hercules Inlet to McMurdo Sound, pulling all of their supplies on sleds, without the help of dogs or motorized equipment. The expedition left on November 9, 1992, and reached the South Pole on January 14, 1993, where, for many reasons, the women decided to end their trip. Anne Dal Vera's account takes us into the day-to-day life of such an expedition and reveals the many reasons—personal, scientific, and political—for undertaking such a challenge.

THE COLD WIND STUNG my face as I pulled a 185-pound sled over the ice at eighty-five degrees south latitude in Antarctica. The temperature was zero degrees. I cursed the wind as I bent to pull against it, then turning, I saw the *perihelion*, a rainbow around the sun. It filled the sky with the brilliance of thousands of particles of ice reflecting the light. *Sun dogs*, or false suns, shone on either side of the sun, and a band of white light stretched horizontally around the sky.

It was November 20, day twelve of the American Women's Antarctic Expedition (AWE). I was enjoying this spectacular scene with three other women—Ann Bancroft, Sue Giller and Sunniva Sorby—as we skied and pulled sleds with our food and equipment from the edge of Antarctica to the South Pole— 678 miles, the distance from Denver to the Mexico border. Our sixty-seven day undertaking was a challenge in every respect: physical, emotional, spiritual, mental and financial.

We began this expedition by flying one third of the way around the world—first, from St. Paul, Minnesota, then due south to the tip of South America and on to Antarctica. After several hours of sorting gear, we flew by Twin Otter plane to the edge of the continent at eighty degrees south, near Hercules Inlet, on the Edith Ronne ice shelf. We started skiing on November 9, nine days later than we had hoped to begin our journey, and we knew we needed to make up the lost time if we wanted to arrive at the Pole by our target date of January 1. In spite of the schedule, we planned to work up to a full day of sled pulling.

Our routine was much the same each day. Above all, we needed to stay warm and avoid getting injured, so we developed efficient systems to keep ourselves well-fed and happy.

We camped in two tents, two women in each tent, changing tent partners every eight days. This gave us the opportunity to get to know each other better and to keep good communication in the group.

A typical day unfolded something like this. We woke up at six a.m. and one woman in each tent lit the stove and boiled water for hot chocolate or mocha java. She then got her mittens, socks and hat down from the drying rack and cared for her feet, taping on moleskin to prevent blisters, or foam pads to relieve tendonitis. As she cooked breakfast, her tent partner got up and prepared for the day. We ate as much hashbrowns and cheese and sausage (or oatmeal with cherries) as we could. Then we put on sunscreen, sunglasses, layers of pile clothes, wind pants, wind jacket, socks, boots, gloves, mittens and a down jacket. Dressing was a difficult task in a small tent with an overstuffed stomach!

Emerging from the tent at eight, we packed our stuff sacks of food, clothes and equipment into the sled, laying the sleeping bag and its waterproof cover on top. We greeted the two women from the other tent and asked how they were as we rolled up the

tents and slid them into the sleds. Sue gave us the magnetic bearing for the day, to keep us heading south. Finally, we buckled
ourselves into the harnesses of our sleds, adjusted our compasses,
and skied off in single file.

The first two and a half hours of travel were measured by the
steady progress of the sun from our left shoulders toward our
backs. I usually needed to warm up a bit before pulling hard. The
first break was very welcome, as Sue and I were almost always
starved. We sat on our sleds and drank hot water and ate gorp,
cookies, cheese sticks and crackers. After a few minutes of talk
and rest, the cold seeped into our bodies and we knew we had to
move on. We reluctantly took off our down coats and swung our
hands to warm them. Then we skied for two more hours. One of
us led by sighting on a distant spot of bright light or a shadow
and following the compass bearing. We took turns leading, enjoying the feeling of discovery and freedom and the exertion of
pulling hard and making the first tracks. Those who were following could occasionally let their minds wander or take photos.
When the terrain wasn't too challenging, I tried to remember the
words to songs of struggle of people in other places and times.

We skied hard like this for up to ten hours a day, with a break
every two hours. At the end of the day, around 8:30 in the evening, we set up the two tents. One woman in each tent started
dinner while the other finished securing the tent and sleds for the
night. She also piled up a stack of snow blocks by each door of
the tent, which we later melted for our water.

Dinner was a creative endeavor: beans and rice, or mac and
cheese, or pasta with sausage and tomato sauce. We often had
soup and grilled-cheese sandwiches for an appetizer. I made apple crisp a couple of times. Sometimes we baked oat scones, bis-
cuits, cornbread or gingerbread. We had quite a bit of variety in
our food, which prevented most cravings. Usually one of us
cooked while the other relaxed or wrote in her journal. Our tents
functioned as bedroom, living room, dining room and kitchen—
all in the space of a double bed plus four feet. In the constant
wind, the tent fly flapped in a staccato rhythm, making communication with the other team members difficult, if not impossible.

Melting snow for the next day's breakfast and thermos

bottles was the last task of the day. On cold nights we took a hot water bottle to bed. But often the solar radiation in the tent at night was enough to keep us quite warm, as we had twenty-four hours of sunlight. November at the South Pole is actually summer, so sometimes we even had to unzip our sleeping bags to cool off! If we were efficient, we managed to get seven hours of sleep before the alarm went off signalling the start of another day.

These efficient daily systems were developed during four and a half years of planning and training. We skied together as a team in Yellowstone, Northern Canada, and across Greenland, testing equipment and ourselves. During our 1992 traverse of Greenland in April and May the temperatures were much colder than the conditions we found in Antarctica. Temperatures in the Antarctic ranged from twenty-three degrees to negative twenty-two degrees with the most common temperature being zero. In Greenland, we had some nights that measured forty degrees below zero. I woke up one night and debated about whether to do sit-ups in my sleeping bag or fire up the stove to make hot chocolate. I opted for hot chocolate with a lump of butter. It warmed me right up. We also had a three-day storm in Greenland that threatened to bury us in our tents. The wind-packed surface of the snow was three feet higher after that storm. Since Antarctica receives less than two inches of precipitation a year, we didn't get much new snow, but the wind was a constant companion.

As expedition leader, Ann Bancroft kept track of the "big picture" of the project. Sue Giller was expedition navigator, while Sunniva Sorby made sure we kept the correct procedures for the research that was done and kept record of our use of medications in the first aid kit. My role was expedition food planner. I worked with a dietician to plan the food and obtain donations of everything from bacon and butter to beans, dried cherries and pasta. I continued to make sure we ate well on the expedition.

For Ann, the past four and a half years had been a constant push of letter writing, phone calls, and meetings to work out the myriad details necessary for a nearly million-dollar expedition. She had a wonderful sense of humor, a big dream and the desire and determination to achieve her goal. It was on the 1986 dogsled journey to the North Pole with the Steger expedition (where she was the only woman), that she was smitten with love for polar regions. She brought together over two hundred volunteers to work together and form the American Women's Antarctic Expedition Foundation. Ann also selected the other members of the team from women recommended through the mountaineering and dogsledding communities.

Every three days in Antarctica, Ann set up our radio antenna, which was stretched between four skis. She called Mo (Morag Howell), a radio expert at the Patriot Hills base in Antarctica, who would relay our position and information to Carrie Bancroft, Ann's sister who was located in Punta Arenas, Chile. Carrie would call or FAX the information to the AWE office in St. Paul, Minnesota. That way we could keep educators, kids, sponsors and friends up to date on our progress and condition. We longed to send messages to our loved ones. Sometimes we would send them in code: "To Arnold: *Truly, Madly, Deeply.*"

The long hours of hard work to make forward progress and maintain our health required all of our energy. Still, I missed Martha and Peggy, two very significant women in my life. I would think of them as I skied during the day, composing letters that never were written. We did send out letters on December 11, at our resupply, and from the South Pole after January 14. We received letters as a plane flew by on January 8. Those letters from Martha, Peggy, and other friends were precious, a real connection with life in the world I had left behind.

After eight to ten hours of pulling sleds, we were quite anxious to find out how far we had gone that day and how far we had to go to reach the Pole. Each night Sue warmed the batteries (by slipping the battery pack inside her shirt) and turned on the Trimble Global Positioning System (GPS) unit to get our position. The "magic box" would receive signals from four satellites and give us our latitude, longitude and elevation. Sue plotted our position on the map and computed the miles per day we needed to travel to reach the South Pole and traverse the continent to McMurdo Sound. As a veteran of twenty years climbing in the world's highest peaks, Sue knew the importance of efficiency. She obtained the majority of the equipment for the expedition through donations from manufacturers. She had an eye for detail, whether it was making sure that a tent could withstand high winds or insisting that we follow our compass bearing accurately as we skied.

While the AWE expedition was not a scientific expedition, the fact that it was the first women's expedition to attempt a ski traverse of Antarctica did provide research opportunities. Scientists asked how the cold, isolation and constant sunlight would affect us as women. We donated our spit, blood, and thoughts to the research. Psychological research consisted of filling out a "Daily Questionnaire." It was meant to be a quick record of our feelings, stress levels and coping mechanisms. The time it took to fill out the questionnaire was directly related to how tired and stressed out I was. This tiresome task also gave us a way to reflect on the day and consider how we were doing individually. The results of the data has shown that we had a more consultative decision-making process than mixed or all-male expedition teams. We also listed "concern for a fellow team member" as our most frequent source of stress. This concern did not result in a loss of productivity, however. Our positive moods were correlated to the number of miles we skied; the further we went, the better we felt about the day.

Every three weeks we spit into test tubes for chronobiologic research. Imagine sleeping in a desert and trying to spit first thing in the morning. Ann thought she would gag. It was just as bad trying to ski into the wind and spit. A definite change was seen in the levels of cortisol and melatonin in our saliva from samples taken in Minnesota and those taken in Antarctica. Cortisol and melatonin are two chemicals that are not fully understood, but it is felt that the levels of these chemicals affect our emotional response to long periods of daylight and darkness. This study established the effectiveness of saliva samples and will make future studies possible among a greater population who live in Arctic areas year round. It is also a non-invasive method of research. Efforts to correlate the AWE psychological and chronobiologic research are still being made.

Sunniva Sorby coordinated the research on the expedition. At thirty-one, she was the youngest member. Although Sunniva joined the team only three weeks before we left the U.S., she put her life in order quickly and embarked on this grand adventure with her whole mind, body and spirit. Her cheerfulness in spite of illness and injury was remarkable. Sunniva had muscle spasms in her neck for the first week, then she came down with bronchitis. When that cleared up, she got tendinitis in her feet and sprained an ankle. She remained determined to continue on, and became aware of new lessons in dealing with pain.

Holidays brought an opportunity to celebrate and renew our spirits. Sue turned forty-six on November 15. We sang "Happy Birthday" and had a little party with balloons and magic candles on gingerbread cake—all of us in one small tent! On Christmas, Santa visited us from the North Pole, pulling a sled loaded with goodies. Stockings hung by our air vents were filled with small treats and we cooked scrambled eggs with cheese and peppers for a special breakfast.

As I spend time in wilderness, I develop a strong attachment to the land. Antarctica is an incredibly beautiful place. Although we didn't go where the penguins live, we saw snow sculptures of dolphins leaping into the frozen air. And, we were blessed with an ever-changing landscape as the wind sculpted the snow into unique wave-like shapes called *sastrugi*. Quite often we would pull our sleds, creaking and groaning, over six to eight inch ridges of snow.

From December 29 to January 2, we wound our way through and around six-foot sastrugi, drawing on all the resources we had: route-finding skills, mental focus and the ability to anticipate the momentum of a fully loaded sled. One day when visibility was low I remember saying to myself, "Keep your head up and ski by feel." It was rather like skiing in the moonlight in Colorado except the terrain was much more choppy.

One of my most memorable experiences took place on the winter solstice, December 21, at eighty-six degrees south latitude. The sun was high all day and night, and it was warm in the tent that night. As the sun circled around us, it cast shadows—first right, then forward, then left—providing us with different scenes as we skied. The dark shadows of skiers and snow formations reminded me of the crisp reality of my being, and I was very glad to be alive, breathing the purest air on the planet.

The wind blew in our faces every day. Some days it was hard to pull against the wind, as it scattered crystals of snow and ice into the air. We protected our faces with a "Harrison beak"—a pile and nylon covering for the nose and cheeks—glacier glasses and a neck gator. In general, our fingers and toes stayed quite warm.

Sue, Ann and I all got minor frostbite on our thighs from opening the side zippers of our wind pants for ventilation and from having to "drop trousers" to pee so often. We learned to go very quickly!

We successfully avoided getting hypothermia by staying warm and dry even in the cold wind. I did manage to overheat one day. I was wearing too many layers on my legs and began to sweat. After some time I felt nauseated and weak. Sue said, "You must have heat exhaustion." I took off some layers and skied slowly to stabilize my temperature. For a few days I felt as if I were constantly on the edge of being too hot or too cold.

As we got closer to the South Pole (which is 9,300 feet above sea level) we breathed heavily in the thin, dry, cold air. We all began to hack and cough. Sunniva's bronchitis recurred. The snow had been deposited in several layers, and as we added our weight to the snowpack, it suddenly settled with a thunderous roar. The first time this happened we all stood in shock, our knees shaking. Each of us had her own fears associated with the rumble and movement of the snow. Ann remembered the opening of a lead or the buildup of a pressure ridge in the Arctic Ocean. Sue felt the collapse of a snow bridge across a crevasse. Sunniva was sure it was an earthquake. And I looked up for an avalanche. Fortunately, we were on very flat terrain, over land, and Sue had navigated us around the crevasses. So we were in no real danger. As time went on, I began to look forward to the rumbling sounds and the feel of snow settling. The release of tension in the snowpack, or "snow orgasms" as I called them, were unpredictable and somehow magical.

Many days as I toiled to pull my sled over cold hard sastrugi, I asked, "Why am I doing this?" I came to realize that there were many reasons. Although I had taught cross-country skiing for fourteen years and led year-round outdoor trips for the past ten years, I was now ready for a personal challenge. I am an experiential educator. I ask people to take risks as they learn about themselves in the outdoors. I think I had begun to question the meaning of my work in experiential education because I hadn't done the risk taking and introspection that I was asking my students to do. Training with the AWE team and skiing to the South Pole provided me with the challenges I needed to learn about myself in relation to the land, and in relation to a small group of women.

I love wilderness and cold climates. Skiing in the wilderness is my passion. I knew I had the skills and the ability to enjoy the rigors of travel in extremely cold conditions with a small group of women. I believe that life is to be lived fully. When an opportunity arises to live in a way that you are ready to live, it makes sense to go for it.

Only now am I beginning to realize the real intensity of working so hard and relying on a group of four women. We each had our hard times and received the caring support of the other three. And we were each called upon to give everything we had in patience, strength and humor. We did have disagreements, but no major fights. I find that I have a deep respect and appreciation for the qualities of each of these courageous women. We are all so different, and we used our different qualities to work together as a team, drawing on each woman's strengths. Sue put her energy into efficient camping and travel, taking care to keep the equipment in good shape and getting enough sleep. Sunniva was indomitably positive and cheerful in spite of her painful illness and injury. Ann's unflagging determination and desire inspired us to continue when we were weary. I gave hugs, sang songs and tried to encourage the others. We found that although we got annoyed by some idiosyncracies, we still valued and needed each individual and the qualities she had to offer the group. Ironically, it was often the trait I admired most in a woman that would annoy me. I became irritated by Sue's efficiency, which, while necessary, seemed to be like a roommate's compulsive need for a spotless kitchen. My interest in her personal life no doubt irked her as well.

I am sure that each one of us felt held back at some time and felt that she held the others back at other times. But as Ann once said, "That's part of traveling in a group. I didn't come here to do a solo trip."

When we were tired and didn't want to go on, how did we get motivated to continue? We encouraged each other. Usually, when one of us was feeling particularly tired or was hurting, the others had the strength to cheer her on. We also remembered the support from friends and family and even strangers back home. Often, I thought of the effort put into getting us to this incredible place.

The pressure of making miles each day was always on our minds. We had to make some difficult decisions about whether to travel or rest on some days. It required an exchange of information from all of us, keen examination of our physical conditions and an estimate of the toll the daily exertion was taking on our bodies. As a result, I think I have a better understanding of what it means to set a goal and work toward it. It requires pacing, endurance, focus and concentration.

I was curious to see where my limits really were. Just when I felt I was about to break from physical, mental and emotional exhaustion, I would find another ounce of energy and go on. It must have been a deep spiritual resource fueled by the power of the land, ice, snow and wind. On December 17, day 39, I felt extremely weary of the struggle. I had skied up to sixty-nine miles with tendinitis, which produced a painful throb with each step. The ibuprofen I took masked the pain for a while, but I was not healing. I felt more and more depressed. Finally, at a break, I lay down on my sled and cried. Ann asked, "What's wrong, Anne?" Sunniva walked over to me and rubbed my back and listened to my tales of pain. Sue told me that when she had been feeling bad in the first weeks of the trip she noticed all the sparkles in the snow and it reminded her of all the people who loved and cared for her. I began to feel much better and was able to continue to ski. Later I switched medications, to Arnica Montana, a homeopathic remedy. Within four days my tendinitis had healed and I was happy once again.

Through the trip, I began to see that the way to go on in the face of adversity was to believe in myself; to trust that I would be able to continue even in pain, even in loneliness. By pushing my limits, I learned the line between discomfort and danger. For example, after each break, my hands cooled off. I had to take off my down coat and put on the sled harness and skis. My hands would often become almost numb as I began to ski. I would take off one pole and swing my arm vigorously to get the blood flowing back into the fingertips, then switch my poles to that hand and swing the other one to get it warm. I would do this as I skied. I knew the edge between very cold hands and numb hands meant the difference between pain and frostbite. I constantly checked my face as I skied, to feel if the skin exposed to the wind had become numb. A mental checklist of each part of my body kept me very aware of life sustaining blood flowing to each cell.

One discomfort we faced was the absence of a shower. It is amazing how well one can wash with a bandanna and a cup of warm water. Still I longed for a refreshing plunge in a bath. So one day I worked up a sweat, then stripped off my clothes and rolled in the snow! It was as wonderful as a sauna and a swim.

On January 13, after sixty-six days of pulling the sleds uphill, Sunniva spotted the buildings of the scientific station at the South Pole—about fourteen miles away. We skied steadily toward it all day on January 14. At 6:30 we were greeted by three construction workers who told us that they had been anxiously awaiting our arrival. As we covered the last two miles to the Scott-Amundsen base, waves of scientists and support workers came out to greet us. The warm welcome was completely unexpected. I felt very energized by the excitement these people had for our achievement. Along with a feeling of great satisfaction at reaching the Pole, we came to the realization that we had made history. We were the first all-women's expedition to ski from the edge of the continent to the South Pole. Ann Bancroft is the first woman to cross over ice to both the North and South Poles.

I was surprised to meet a friend, BK, who works at the South Pole station. BK and I had led llama pack trips together in Colorado. Seeing her at the South Pole made it feel like a familiar place. It is a small world.

A small world indeed when we could stand in one spot and be in all the time zones at once, surrounded by the flags of the original twelve nations of the Antarctic Treaty. Now forty nations have agreed to coexist in Antarctica peacefully, dedicating the continent to scientific research. Because of its significance in the climate of the globe, many people would like to see Antarctica preserved as a World Park. Organizations such as Greenpeace and others have worked to raise the awareness of public and government agencies asking them to improve practices at their base stations in Antarctica. The workers we met at the South Pole took their actions seriously. They tried to lessen their impact on the environment by reducing what came in to them, reusing items as much as possible, and recycling anything that could be processed in the U.S. As we skied across Antarctica, we took out all our trash and required the charter flight company to take out all the empty fuel drums from our flights. This is beginning to be standard practice.

Deciding to end the trek at the South Pole was the most difficult decision we made. How did we make it? We studied the records of others who had traversed Antarctica and found that it had required forty-five days of hard travel for them to make the 850 miles to McMurdo Sound. We had only thirty-two days to meet our ship. We investigated other possibilities for getting off the continent and found them both incredibly expensive ($350,000) and risky. Winter comes quickly and furiously to Antarctica. We decided not to push on. Although it was hard to give up the dream we had for four and a half years, we knew it was the right decision.

After a few days at the South Pole we flew to South America and began our trip home. As the plane banked away from the Patriot Hills, I saw mountains flash past and I knew I would remember this journey all my life. It would leave me with good memories, friendships and recollections of adventure. I feel privileged to have skied in the vast wilderness of Antarctica.

This expedition never received corporate funding, although we approached over 250 corporations. Only Marlboro, the cigarette manufacturer, expressed interest, and the expedition members decided not to sell our souls to the makers of tobacco or alcohol products. One corporate executive reportedly told Ann Bancroft, "Maybe...if you take a man along...." Other companies were fearful that if the women got hurt it would be bad for their image. Some didn't want to sponsor a women's expedition because they assumed that all the team members were lesbians. A lot of suggestive remarks were made both directly and indirectly: Two women to a tent? Gonna keep each other warm? Such homophobic assumptions weren't made about Will Steger's 1990 all-male Antarctic Expedition, or the Reinhold

Messner/Arved Fuchs ski traverse of Antarctica.

Now that I am home, people often ask me if I would do this again. I pause, reflecting that the challenges of this journey are still with me. Financing a $900,000 expedition is a major undertaking. Over half of the expedition's $900,000 budget was paid by $12 to $25 donations or by sympathetic supporters who bought the $12 AWE T-shirts. The smallest gift was $5, the largest $10,000. The AWE team members are still working hard to pay off the rest of the debt (as of this writing, we still have $210,000 to raise). We wonder what it will take to convince corporations that it is in their best interest to support women who are experienced in their field and who choose to take on new challenges and continue in the face of adversity. Through my slide show and talks I have become a public figure, which is very new to me, and not something I willingly sought out. Leaving loved ones for a long period of time to work harder than I have ever worked before, day after day, demanded that I learn to pace myself physically and sustain myself mentally, spiritually and emotionally. Still, I long to return to the ice, the cold wilderness of quiet, the pure air that carves sastrugi. I long to travel light and fast. . . .

The Cache

At 89.98° South, 74.45° West lies a cache.
Food for two to sail across an Antarctic desert.
A dream, sleeping frozen
Waiting for the right moment to awaken and begin.
I long to travel light and fast
Free from publicity, loans and fears

The cache waits patiently
On the forbidden side of the runway
Watching with puzzled curiosity
As each C-130 lands in a cloud of thunder.
Perhaps the cache will disappear,
Under the blowing snow
Neglected, unused, crushed by the weight of the dense sastrugi
A forgotten dream . . .

In the Canoe Endlessly Paddling

Alice Evans

THERE WE WERE, paddling upriver on the last day of our two-week journey through the Boundary Waters Canoe Area of northern Minnesota. We had gone out of Ely mid-May, a risky choice so early in the year, yet one that seemed serendipitous the first week as we basked in eighty-degree sun. But not the second week when the weather turned nasty. My husband and I were inexperienced canoers. We had supplied ourselves well, but the maps failed to indicate the direction of drainage. We believed that the river flowed into Lake Superior and would thus carry us downstream to our waiting car. Instead, it was bound for the drainage of Hudson Bay.

So we had struggled upstream, battling the current as well as wind, rain, hail and sleet. In addition to the already rigorous physical requirements of this journey, paddling against the current sapped our strength, pushed us almost beyond our limits, and set us a day behind schedule.

Wolves had howled that final night. Loons cut loose with messages only loons could understand—*and* those who had passed through the fabric that led into another world. Hooting as my brother had taught me, I summoned seven barred owls with whom to chat. One roosted overhead through all my dreams, calling to me softly at dawn with the trill of a lover, a song rarely heard, except by another owl.

My down bag was damp. I had slept poorly. We ate the last of our oatmeal just before we broke camp.

Then it was onto the river, the dip and pull of the paddle, the constant motion in driving rain to get out of the lake country.

I rode the bow of the Grumman, just as I had throughout the trip. I called out the rocks and submerged logs, the approach of portages, the falls.

When the portages came, I stepped from the canoe and pulled it ashore. On this last day, confused and approaching desperation, I did not attempt to keep my feet dry but stepped calf-high into the cold pools. It was lift and carry, then return for the rest of the gear. Lift and carry, then stop for a bite to eat. When we hit Basswood Lake we were down to our last cup of barley. This I attempted to cook, hands shaking with cold, almost unable to strike the match to light the stove. But I managed, knowing we needed that heat, knowing we needed that fuel for the final pull down the length of the lake.

We were stubborn in our refusal to ask for help. We passed a half-dozen motor cruisers we might have hailed in those final hours. But we held to the purity of our wilderness experience, believing as we did, that motorboats did not belong in the Boundary Waters. It would have been legitimate, a plea for help. We were cold, we were wet, the rain was driving right through us. And then there were the bow-high waves, sweeping up the lake. If either of us failed in our vigilant paddling we might swamp at any moment.

Jon steered us straight into the waves. The waves swept toward me in the bow, gray canoe on gray water under gray skies. I felt gray. Grayness seeped into my bones. My fingernails were gray. Gray, too, the color of my breath. The waves broke across the bow, swept into the boat, drenched my already drenched clothes. I paddled.

Lift and pull, lift and pull, lift and pull. The water was no longer gray, but white. White were the waves, white were their peaks, white were my hands as I dipped my paddle into the cold, deep lake. How deep was this lake, I wondered? How many pike swam beneath its white surface? Did pike eat human flesh? They certainly had the teeth for it. If Peter Piper picked a peck of pickled pike. . . .

Another white wave landed in my lap. "Paddle," I heard Jon yell from behind me. "You've got to keep paddling."

Dip and pull and lift and dip and dip and pull and lift and dip and old King Cole was a merry old soul, a merry old soul was he. Something of a dip perhaps, but his fiddlers kept pulling their bows across their fiddles, and I must pull my paddle along this bow. Lift and pull and dip and pull.

And then there was a moose, twenty yards off the bow, attempting to swim the lake in three-foot waves. "Do you see that moose, Jon? Bear, oh my big bear Jon, do you see that moose?"

"Amazing. Yes, amazing. But you muusssttt noot stooop paddling!"

One, two, three, four,
five, six, seven, eight,
nine, ten, eleven, twelve,
thirteen, fourteen, fifteen, sixteen.

Keep going, keep going, keep going all the way to a thousand, to a hundred thousand, to a million if I have to, to a googolplex, a googolplex squared, cubed and fried like the steak I wish I had. Or squid. Fried squid are so yummy.

God, my arms are numb, where do these muscles come from? How many blisters do I have on my hands? None, because I practiced. On Lake Monroe. Practiced, a dozen times, paddling. How smart we were. How smart I am. I am the one who insisted on all that practice.

But why am I here? Why come so far? Because of the loons. I'll never hear those in Indiana. Nor see bear, nor wolves, nor moose. Nor the moccasin orchid. Nor could I troll for pike there, nor taste the mmnnn, wild taste of their baked flesh.

Yes, and swimming naked in Pipestem Bay and having it all to ourselves: the wilderness, its meandering streams, those cozy little lakes and the river, the fast, mean river. I'm glad we went the wrong way on the river. Because we went the wrong way, I didn't have to worry about going over the falls. That's what almost stopped me from coming on this trip at all. The falls. It must have been that movie, *Niagara*, where, after he murders Marilyn, Joseph Cotten goes over the edge.

Going over the edge. We didn't do that, but we're close, now. Mighty close. Too close. Are we fools? Or just adventurers, willing to take risks in order to feel alive?

Alive. Yes, that's what we're after here. To feel alive. Unrestricted. After one year of graduate school, to know my own wildness again. I have felt so alive on this trip. But now I feel so close to death, so cold, so tired, so numb.

"Owlll iiii ssssss. Keee p paaad elll ingggg!"

How far, I wonder? This wind is such a beast. There's the water and the wind, and they can be your friends or they can be your enemies. You can go with them, or you can go against them. They can be behind you one day and in front of you the next.

Water you can swim in or drink, you can fish in, you can even fuck in water, and fish must do that, after a fashion. But you can also drown in water. Do fish ever drown? And if I drown, will I become a fish in my next life?

The sides of the lake are called shores. There's the near shore and the far shore. In biblical metaphor, if you travel to the far shore that means you've died and gone to heaven, or possibly gone to heaven. Paradisio or purgatorio or inferno. We're paddling alongside the near shore, but we've got to go to the far shore to reach our car. Our car is home in this instance. Going to heaven is going home. And going to our car is going home. We've got to go to the far shore to either get to home or heaven.

"Swing low, sweet chariot,
coming for to carry me hooo o mmme
swiii i ng low . . . "

"Save your strength, Owl!"

"How many miles, Bear?"

"I don't know, but we've got to keep moving. Give it all you've got. We've got to get back to the car!"

I wonder how we're going to get across the lake. These waves, if they hit the side of our boat, will tip us right over. And then it's curtains. Yes, curtains. Or maybe we could cling to the canoe and kick our way to shore. Maybe a motorboat will come along, and the captain will throw us a line. Maybe we can just forget the canoe and swim for our lives. I can swim a long way on my back. But in these waves? And this cold? People die from the cold in water like this. Wouldn't it be nice if a McDonald's just popped up right in front of us? Or a K-Y Fried?

Dip and pull and lift and pull and dip and pull and lift and pull.

Curtains. I've seen shower curtains with wave patterns like these. These waves are like ocean breakers. Only they're endless. They cover this sea. This lake, this sea, this endless sea. Two weeks of waves and water. Water above me, water below me, water all around me. My glasses are so coated with water that all I can see is water. See water. Seawater. And if I ever get off this water, I wonder if I'll ever get back on water again. I'll never get on the sea I bet.

The body is ninety-eight percent water. Is that right? Or is it ninety-seven percent? Mine's probably about ninety-nine percent water at this point. Or ninety-nine percent jelly. I feel like my arms are made out of jelly. Can jelly paddle a canoe? Yes, jelly can paddle. Jelly has proved herself capable of paddling. Perhaps I'm a jellyfish. If I were a jellyfish I would not need to paddle. Nor would I need to paddle if I were a squid. I could float. I could tentacle my way to shore. But would I go to the far shore or the near shore? I wouldn't care about reaching the far shore where the car was because home is the water and not the car on the far shore.

Does anyone ever go insane in the wilderness? Moses did not and Jesus did not. But, they battled their demons there. They wrestled with madness.

Jello Biafra is a jellyfish but it's also the name of a punk rock singer. How about Jesus Moses? Or Jello Jesus? I like Jesus even though I'm not Christian. I was raised Christian, but I don't believe in dogma. Or is that catma? If anything, I'm a Taoist. But then, Taoists always go with the flow. We chose to go against the flow, and that's a contradiction. Now we're in trouble because the weather's against us. The weather is out to kill us. Mr. Death wears a whitecapped cloak. Mr. Death would like to choke us with water. There is, though, this solace. If Death were to present itself to a Taoist, a Taoist would paddle right by Death and not get freaked out, because a Taoist knows that Death is either going to get you or not get you, and the best thing to do is to go about your business knowing all the while that Death is there, all the while. It's never not there. You simply don't give yourself up to it. It either happens or it doesn't happen. Don't let yourself get ungrounded. Ha! How to stay grounded on water? That is a question if not *the* question, certainly the question of the hour and of this day and of these past two weeks.

Paddle one, paddle two, paddle three, paddle four. What did the voyageurs do in these conditions? With their big meaty arms and their hair like fur and their fur pelts and all that split pea soup that was their gruel and thick, hot chicory coffee; well this probably would have seemed a friendly outing to them, just a little cold rain to cool them down, just a friendly little splash of cold ocean water over the bow and into the face to keep the navigator awake.

Let's see now. I was given the job of navigator by virtue of my position in the bow, whence I was put because I am the lighter of the two. I cannot see past these wet glasses, and therefore I cannot see, but what's there to know except when we get to the parking lot at the end of the lake, we're at the end of the lake and we will know that. Jon will know that and he'll tell me. My job then, is simply to paddle now. Not to navigate. Because navigation isn't necessary. Because all I must do now is keep the canoe moving through the waves. Cutting through. Cutting the water. Cutting the whitecaps in two. "Car, I'm cutting through to you ou ou ou ououou."

"When the sky is blue ue ue ue ueueue. The parking lot!"

The parking lot, yes, the parking lot. The parking lot is there because I can see the end of the lake if I take off my glasses. It's a blur but it's the end and it's there.

"The parking lot. Yes! I see it! Ha! But how do we get there?"

"Zig-zag!"

Ah, zig-zag. Zig-zag across a mile of open water, hundred-foot-deep water, water like an ocean, whitecaps pounding the sides. But what choice do we have? We can't lay over until the wind dies. It's been pounding this country for a week. The rain is now sleet, it may soon be snow, there's no food left in our packs, and I'm so cold, so wet, so jellified that if I stop paddling I will not again be able to start paddling. I must keep paddling. My teeth may rattle as I paddle, but I will keep on paddling. Zig-zag. Zig-zag.

The canoe rocks. I can feel the canoe rocking. Out of the cradle endlessly rocking. Aim it into the waves, Whitman would have. That Taoist! Into the waves. Then across the waves. Then into the waves. Endlessly rocking. Tight little zigs and zags. Where does this knowledge come from? How to zig and zag? How to keep the boat steady, bail if you must, zig-zag a mile like a crooked man and you're home. Will my back be permanently crooked? Will my back be cracked? Crouched here, as I am, bent over, head to the wind, paddling for days and days and days through wind and rain and sleet and hail like a mailman, a mail-woman, am I a male woman? Certainly my grandmother would think that you must have a penis to do what I'm doing. The wind and the rain and the jelly and now the rocking of the boat, the endless rocking that is at once both the most lulling and most frightening sensation I have experienced on this trip. This trip, what a trip, this journey in a wilderness of water, this plowing of the waves, this furrowing, this planting of seed in the water, this nurturing, this self-belief, this knowing that I can and will keep going and going and going.

THE JADED DIVER

Nancy Sefton

I SETTLE ON THE clean sand, twelve feet below the silken surface of the lagoon, as the first stingray sails in my direction, banking like a giant frisbee. It makes one pass, then returns from behind. I feel its weight as the huge animal perches briefly on my head.

Through the crystal water I notice the other rays cruising in at top speed. There are at least a dozen.

What did the dive guide tell us before we jumped in? Hold the food high, arm outstretched. Not to worry, stingrays have no teeth.

I delve into the plastic bag and pull out a limp squid. My hand receives a gentle gumming, and the slimy snack is extracted from my grip with surgical precision. As each four-foot stingray flows up and over me, slicing through the bubble stream that emanates from my scuba mouthpiece, I run my cupped hand along its wing edges, feeling the unbelievable softness, smoothness of the body, perhaps forcing intimacy where it is not wanted, or perhaps scarcely noticed. The rays, in fact, seem unmindful of my caresses. It's lunch time.

The huge creatures circle and dip among the divers,

gracefully, to unheard music. All of us, humans and fish, seem engaged in an odd ballet, a bizarre merger of souls.

Above, an audience of snorkelers floats spread-eagle on the flat surface like hovering birds, eyes wide as saucers behind the glass of their face masks. I'm a kid again, showing off. Look at me, look at me! I wonder what the snorkelers think as they watch me on the bottom, disappearing from sight frequently beneath the gregarious rays. Am I brave? Am I foolish?

I feel a little smug in the knowledge that I am really neither. I have been a scuba diver for over thirty years, and have spent the last twenty of those years in the Caribbean, going underwater almost daily. I know that I am far safer here than in the world above the surface, which is bursting with threats from my own kind.

Thousands of hours underwater have taught me a great deal. I have learned that most so-called marine monsters are undeserving of the nasty reputations forced upon them by movie moguls eager for box office hits. I openly ridicule authors like Peter Benchley who make their living by making us afraid of sea animals who cannot defend themselves. Stingrays are normally shy creatures that flee from divers.

Here in this wide lagoon, however, the stingrays have been conditioned by humans to perform and be friendly in return for a free meal. They were wolves; now they are dogs.

One part of me, the environmental purist, resents such intrusions into the lives of these wild things. The other part of me, the one that lusts for contact with creatures so unlike myself, is grateful for this marine anomaly, this human-induced mutation.

I have come to dance with rays in my continuing quest for encounters with large sea creatures. My search is nearly obsessive. In this I am little different from my fellow sport divers. Originally, we all took the plunge because the ocean was a place of mystery; once we became casually familiar with this new neighborhood, we began seeking out bigger thrills to keep the adrenaline flowing.

It began when I was a teenager with a love for the sea and the normal youthful craving for a hero. I found him; he was a gray-haired balding man with a soft but commanding voice, a voice that held me riveted to my TV screen. His name was Colonel

John Craig and he hosted a weekly series about the oceans.

This was the fifties, when a handful of fearless sport divers were taking their first tentative steps into the sea. The average scuba diver was a teenage male with tattooed biceps and a spear gun in each hand.

The rest of us were content to travel beneath the sea vicariously with the help of people like Colonel Craig and his black-and-white films. We watched divers clawing their way awkwardly through the water, wearing equipment unrecognizable today. There were glimpses of sharks, shadowy apparitions lurking just inside camera range. There were fleeting introductions to "dangerous" eels and rays, big fish and little fish, fuzzy silhouettes against a gray ocean. This was heady stuff.

Not everyone gets to meet his or her hero. I was lucky. On a visit to Puerto Vallarta, Mexico, I found myself one afternoon in a state of mild delirium on a sun-drenched beach called Playa de los Muertos. The Colonel was there, taking a break between undersea filming sessions. A circle of admirers sat around him, all of us slack-jawed, listening as he deftly spun tales of his adventures in what was then the Alien World Beneath the Sea.

That day he was filming garden eels, which thrive in profusion just beyond the breakers. The size of elongated pencils, these tiny eels have their tails anchored in the sand and tend to retract quickly into the bottom when frightened.

The Colonel asked for volunteers to snorkel above the eels in order to provide visual interest for the scenes. My hand shot up. The reflexes often react more quickly than the brain.

It didn't occur to me that I had never snorkeled before, nor that we'd be in open water that was known to be frequented by sharks. I only knew that nothing could possibly happen to me if Colonel Craig was in the same ocean.

So on that hot Mexican afternoon I waded into the awesome Pacific, paddling clumsily over a flat sandy bottom graced with a bed of garden eels that looked more like sparse grass in need of pulling. The whole session lasted thirty minutes but it turned me into a diver.

Now, when I try to reach behind me and grasp those first moments in the sea with mask and snorkel, I find that the emotional texture of it is almost completely lost to my touch, that time has had its inevitable numbing effect. There is a faint glimmer of elation, of ecstasy, based purely on the sensation of being *in* the sea, of being able to *see* what was there on the bottom. The ocean was no longer a mystery. The ocean was as benign as my living room.

For some time I remained content to be a snorkeler. It was enough, for in tropical shallows, marine life is exceedingly rich. The tiny coral animals have microscopic algal cells residing contentedly in their gut cavities, leaking nutrients that are happily absorbed by the coral host. The algae require sunlight in order to carry on photosynthesis. On shallow undersea terraces, corals and other marine creatures crowd against one another, vying for their places in the sun, forming a patchwork quilt of living tissue.

On a diving sojourn somewhere east of Bali, we were on a large ship that drifted near a tiny *cay*, or islet, bearing the tongue-tangling name of Sangisangiang. With its crewcut of short palms and girdle of platinum sand, it rose from the Flores Sea like a geological mistake; there was no other land in sight. A broad subsea shelf encircled the cay like a peacock blue skirt, the bottom gradually sloping to the edge of a drowned cliff.

I joined the divers in the inflatable skiff that would drop them at the wall's edge; one by one the cobalt blue of deep water swallowed them until only their bubbles set the calm surface to boiling, testifying to their existence.

Then the boatman steered a course for the shallows and slowed. Donning mask, snorkel and fins, I quickly rolled over the sun-heated black rubber pontoon into cool water so clear that it disappeared altogether. Just beyond my reach, the corals glowed in exquisite pastels, punctuated by iridescent blues and pinks so intense that they set my teeth on edge. I could lose my soul to the colors alone, never mind what magic creatures they belonged to.

Thick carpet anemones spread their lobes across the bottom. Bright clownfish darted back and forth to nestle briefly among the tucks and folds laced with stinging tentacles toxic and deadly to all other creatures.

The sun warmed my back as I kicked slowly alone across the shallow shelf toward the edge. It lay only eight feet below me now, falling vertically into a void. Along the crest, great headlands and ramparts stretched away, fading from sight. Shoals of tiny orange and blue fish swelled and contracted above sedentary life forms bound forever to the substrate: soft, undulating whips of coral, stony limestone sculptures shaped like tables, chandeliers, pointing fingers, floral bouquets. It was a world of diffused blue, wrapped in silence.

The silence itself was seductive. Just above the surface, my consciousness seems eternally impaled on spears of noise emanating from our machines, our shrill voices. Below the sea there is only a slow symphony of movement.

The entire reef seemed to pulse, and I felt myself become absorbed into it.

On the shelf lay a large helmet shell, the kind I've seen for sale at many a roadside stand, but had never dreamt of finding in the wild. I took a breath and dove down to examine the marine snail within. The shell was empty. It was perfect, its flat side highly polished, without a scratch or a blemish. Bits of muscle and tissue poured from the opening, remnants of the shell's architect and builder, recently expired.

I lifted my prize to the surface and flushed it hard to wash out the remaining snail residue. I was engrossed; the feeling of being watched sneaked up on me only gradually. In a flash I wedded that feeling to the active shaking of the shell, the surface splashing, the vibrations. I turned slowly in the water, sensing what I would see before I actually saw it.

The shark was suspended beyond the wall's edge. The huge head turned slowly from side to side, displaying the awkward hammer shape, which was joined to the sleek, graceful body, like an evolutionary error.

For a few seconds that seemed to last forever, we two were frozen in blue space, eyes locked, as if each were reluctant to move and end the moment.

Suddenly a silver curtain of bubbles rose between us, erasing the shark as cleanly as an image wiped from a dark blue slate. I barely saw it twist and disappear. Kicking to the spot directly over the wall's edge, I tried to see the scuba divers, but they were below my visual range.

I felt sure that the shark had gone to join them in deeper waters, and I wished that I could go too. I had felt no anxiety. Alone and vulnerable, I had watched the shark and knew with certainty that I was safe, and more important, that I had broken through a barrier. I could enter the sea freely, anytime, anyplace; never would I be a prisoner of my own fears.

My memories of that first dive on scuba equipment, after an arduous training course, are fast receding. There's only a remnant: I vaguely recall the miracle of being *weightless*, and wonder of wonders, of being able to *breathe* while submerged. Soon afterward, it was all second nature. No longer was it enough to be a fish among fishes; now, I had to collect new adventures, to add them to my memory bank. I had become jaded. Like my fellow divers, I travelled to the ends of the earth to find new thrills, to stave off underwater boredom.

On a small Caribbean island I was aided in my quest by an Englishman and fellow diver. Remote, unsophisticated little islands tend to attract people like Michael. Dreamers some call them, or escapees, but I prefer to think that they are running *to* and not from.

Michael, tall, lean, middle-aged, had been a farmer somewhere in the northern part of England, where he had a wife and the usual heavy commitments. Then they came to the Caribbean for a holiday and went diving on a particular reef where a family of large green moray eels were being fed by divers and had become somewhat tame. When Michael met the morays, something snapped inside him; some sort of sea change took place. He returned to England, placed a For Sale sign on the farm gate, said goodbye to his wife and came back alone to the tiny island to stay.

At precisely three-thirty every afternoon, he donned a scuba tank and paid a solo visit to the eels, bringing baitfish packed carefully into peanut cans. For an hour or, as long as his air lasted, he would kneel on the soft white-sand lane between two tunnel-ridden coral ridges where the eels lived, and they would slip and slide between his arms, accepting his handouts with grace and gentility. Every afternoon on the shallow reef it was tea-time for man and moray.

When Michael got to know me and was satisfied that my presence would pose no harm to his special friends, he took me with him. I felt privileged.

Each of the eels measured between six and seven feet. On my first visit, as we approached their home, two of the larger morays swam toward us rapidly in flowing snake-twists, bright green ribbons against the blue reef.

In a moment I was enveloped in softness; I had the sensation of silk yardage drawn seductively through my hands and under my arms. Both eels seemed eager to weave themselves around my body, to become new appendages. I was in awe of such intimacy. But I held very still. For I had lost my fear of eels many years before, while snorkeling seaward of the breakers with Colonel Craig. The size difference between the tiny garden eels and my new friends, the morays, seemed insignificant.

I made many return trips to the eels' lair. One day when I had finished lunching with the largest of them, I gently stroked his face just behind the gills and round button eyes. Distracted by an inquisitive grouper, I glanced away for a mere second. When I turned back to the eel, I saw with dismay that my fingers were inside his mouth and two rows of needle-sharp teeth were starting to close down.

I froze. I'd been told never, never to pull my hand away suddenly from a moray, lest I arouse his instinct to grab. Had I pushed my luck too far? In retrospect, my pale, bare fingers must have looked exactly like the baitfish. Eels have poor eyesight.

I had, of course, foolishly underrated the creature's strong instincts and even stronger sense of smell. The eel paused, its jaws opened apologetically, and it backed away.

Through seemingly endless, dream-like passages, we touch, we pirouette. We speak a silent language. Here over sun-dappled corals, entwined, we are a bizarre embrace between two worlds. What binds us? What draws you to me? The raw fish in the rusting tin can? Or is there more? (Allow me my illusions, please.) I know well, of course, what has brought me here to you: an overpowering need to touch the untouchable, embrace the unembraceable, in a place where I do not belong, where no human being really belongs.

•

For all I know, Michael still cavorts with morays between the coral ridges, but I moved on to other oceans, other thrills. Always in my mind, swaying through my sleep, was the hammerhead shark, the focal point of that long ago snorkeling trip. The great fish was now elongated by my imagination, altered, endowed with some sort of siren call. In a strange way, sharks seemed to be my destiny. I had to find them.

The crossing from Puntarenas, Costa Rica, into the wide Pacific took thirty-six hours aboard the large live-aboard dive vessel. Flying fish left skidmarks on the sea as our ship slid across an ocean that looked more like a lake. The line separating sea and sky had been erased, and we seemed to be cruising in blue space—a disorienting experience.

Large sea turtles basked on the surface, each providing a perch for a resting gull. The brown-faced booby birds hitching a free ride on the bow rail spent all day preening their feathers. From time to time, the dolphins joined us briefly, dashing under the bow, becoming quickly bored with the race, disappearing.

I had come all this way for shark encounters—not with just a solitary specimen here and there, but with sharks by the dozens, hundreds. This is the lure of remote Cocos Island.

The island loomed: bare granite thrust upward from the deep defiantly, crowned by green jungle, spilling waterfalls into the dark sea. Underwater it was a somber gray place of bold outcrops, drowned valleys and steep pinnacles, fashioned by God as a metaphor for its dominant residents, the inscrutable sharks.

The tropical light streamed into the clear ocean, only to be absorbed, extinguished by the black lava substrate. This water contrasted with the coral reefs, where sunshine dances and colors sing. The brooding marine landscape did weird things to my psyche. I suspect the darkness lay partly within me, a product of the alienation I felt underwater as the currents carried me slowly around those melancholy pinnacles, yielding no clues as to what lay around the bend.

Off a rocky point, I was surrounded by clouds of fish, big-eyed jacks in perfect formation. Looking up, I watched as they rotated dreamily like a huge silver wheel on the axis of my bubble stream.

The schools were tightly packed, a mass of fins and scales

shutting out the light. Like mercury, they flowed around me as if seeking my protection; prowling the perimeter were the sharks, four or five of them. Back and forth the schools moved, forming and reforming. On the sidelines, the reef sharks, trailed by one or two snaggle-toothed tunas, waited.

I was an integral part of a dynamic process that sustains life in all ecosystems. I found myself submerged in a stand-off between predator and prey. As the jacks crowded together, body contours dissolved into a single shining cloud. The hunters, with their relatively poor eyesight, were unable to target an individual. They were forced to be patient, to wait for one fish to stray from the pack.

As I floated through the schools, the fish parted just enough to let me pass, then eagerly closed the space where I had been. Unable to see the surface, I became disoriented and had to check my bubbles to know which way was up.

Then, at some silent signal, the shoals of fish drifted away like a metallic curtain pulled aside to reveal an empty blue sea. The predators moved with them. The current was changing.

I was on the surface returning to the boat when I looked down and saw bottom. I was confused; something wasn't right. Crossing between the submerged pinnacle and the nearby island with its granite flanks falling vertically into the sea, I was supposed to be over water hundreds of feet deep.

I peered into the depths and exhaled, sinking a little deeper, my heart beginning to race. Suddenly the broad swath of "sea bottom" resolved itself into a mass of swaying backs. I was looking down on a school of hammerheads blanketing the thermocline. There were hundreds.

I sank deeper still, and the long sedate shapes of the sharks became more cleanly defined. They were in perfect military formation, barely moving, only swaying slightly to counteract the current. I knew they could see me, knew that for them I was just another living thing in the water, something insignificant to glance at and then ignore.

Now I could make out the scars on several of the animals; these were females wounded by the males' teeth during copulation. In the sea, where most creatures are shaped more or less like torpedoes, the hammerhead seems out of tune. But seeing them now I felt their perfection, their unique design created by forces complex and beyond question.

I floated spread-eagle above the school until my air was nearly gone, trying to emboss the moment forever on my memory.

A year or two after, there was to be one more shark encounter in a more unique setting at a thousand feet below the sea.

Still afflicted by hero-worship at middle age, I was unashamedly ecstatic when I was invited to meet Dr. Eugenie Clark, diminutive professor of marine biology at the University of Maryland. She is known to every diver as the Shark Lady. Her mission: find and photograph the magnificent six-gill shark, inhabitant of Caribbean deeps. Behavior: little known. Appetite: enormous.

Would I care to accompany Dr. Clark on one of her deep submersible journeys to lure a six-gill into camera range?

I accept.

On a moonless tropical night, our three-person sub descended slowly down a nearly vertical undersea wall.

The captain called out surrounding sea temperatures: a comfortable eighty degrees all the way to 480 feet, and then, suddenly, the thermocline. We had been forewarned that the sub's interior would cool down quickly. I was glad I'd brought a sweatshirt and wool socks.

Six hundred feet. Here, the steep escarpment sloped forty-five degrees toward open sea. The great buttresses were crowned with white sediment. No one breathing from a scuba tank had ever been here. We stared out at a world visited by only a handful of people.

Behind us, a chorus of rumbles and whines assailed our ears as the sub floated farther down the precipice, slowing here and there to home in on a colony of bizarre deep dwellers.

Sprouting from each promontory, deep-water soft corals reached upward toward the dim light, bearing totally unfamiliar shapes: bouquets of thin spiraling wires or bright-orange lacy fans. The stalked feather-stars looked like white umbrellas with twenty-inch-tall handles.

At last the sub leveled off to find a settling place, a white sandy bowl atop a giant coral pinnacle. The captain maneuvered carefully so that the sub's two ski-like mounts straddled a delicate glass sponge.

We were one-fifth of a mile below the surface.

Inside, we whispered. A faint hum behind us was a grateful reminder that the life-support systems of the Perry research submersible were working as they should.

The cameras were loaded and in position. The exterior floodlights illuminated a stout steel arm projecting from the sub, extending a wire basket crammed with ten pounds of fishheads and squid dangling obscenely through chicken-wire mesh. The bait was fresh. The banquet had been laid. We awaited the Guest of Honor.

The external floodlights, which had illuminated our descent, were now extinguished. We could not talk, or make any noise that might scare away the six-gill, a creature of awesome proportions, yet in its extreme sensitivity to light and sound, as delicate as a diva.

At around seven, darkness at last enfolded us. And for the first time I asked myself what I was doing here, crouching with limbs folded in the ridiculously tiny sub like a sardine in a can, staring into a black void without features except for the faint green glow of chemical lights, waiting for some God-only-knows-how-savage creature to come and take our bait, our pathetic little offering.

Two small deep-water eels found the basket and began thrashing at it, nipping and pulling at the meat, sending out signals, we hoped, that broadcast the news of food. With luck, something else was out there, picking up those signals. Something big?

A massive shadow passed before the dome. Beside me, Dr. Clark said "Shark!" The floods went on.

Looking like a deep-water freight train, the six-gill passed before the window and then twisted away from us, toward the bait beyond. Jaws agape, it took the entire basket in its mouth and shook. The twelve-thousand pound sub rocked on its slender mounts, and we humble creatures within were jostled and thrown against each other.

It struck me suddenly how reckless we were, to come here to the deeps—how audacious to intrude and expect to be welcomed, treated with civility by creatures that know nothing of us, nor care.

It was all over quickly. The shark, finally intimidated by the glaring floods, released the bait bucket from its jaws, gave us one disdainful look and disappeared behind a white cloak of sand. The little sub sat motionless on the bottom.

I breathed again. The behemoth had come and gone. With a sudden whine, the sub began its ascent toward the surface where there was starlight filtering through a kind of darkness that I could cope with.

I have been on the ultimate dive and met eye to eye with the ultimate denizen. Where do I go from here? What is left down there to move me? Pondering the next adventure, I realize that I have lost something. I try to remember those first journeys into the shallows, the revelations, what it felt like to be weightless, to breathe, to see, to feel, to swim with fishes, any fishes. That elusive joy flares briefly like a nova, then goes dark.

I must find it again.

On the edge of a turquoise lagoon, I don mask, fins and snorkel. Then I launch myself, drifting silently on gin-clear waters, skimming the top of an elkhorn coral thicket. A two-foot-long Nassau grouper swaggers up and stares unabashedly into my facemask, its thick lips nearly touching the glass. Below, a pair of prissy-lipped angelfish slalom among the stout trunks of coral, picking daintily at the reef. They give me scarcely a glance.

A four-foot barracuda passes below, accompanied by some two dozen young bar jacks, tiny opportunists waiting to clean up after their host's sporadic meals. Suddenly these hangers-on abandon their natural bene-factor and swim over to adopt me; they huddle beneath my chest. I have been accepted without question into their world, like a piece of floating driftwood.

The 'cuda, jealous and indignant, sneers and turns tail. Confused now, the fickle jacks give me one last look and scurry after. They know where their fortunes lie.

I stand a moment, waist-deep. The shimmering sea spreads in all directions, pale satin to the horizon. There's movement below. A little stingray has sidled up to my fins to inspect them. It's a juvenile, a miniature version of my ponderous dancing partners in the broad lagoon. Slowly it circles my outsized rubber feet planted on the sand. They are merely a distraction. It turns its shovel nose and glides away.

It is an unremarkable, yet magic, moment.

Here in the shallows, beside a coral barrier, I ride a thin silver membrane between two worlds, one from which I draw my breath, the other toward which I gaze with renewed wonder, and a certain longing.

Spirit Walk

Karen A. Monk

A certain philosopher asked St. Anthony: How can you be so happy when you are deprived of the consolation of books? Anthony replied: My book, O philosopher, is the nature of created things, and any time I want to read the words of God, the book is before me.

Thomas Merton, The Wisdom of the Desert

OUTSIDE MY STUDY WINDOW a tufted titmouse enthusiastically sorts through the bin of the plexiglass feeder, splashing seed shells into the forsythia. The bird's energy is at once compelling and mesmerizing. I save the document on my computer screen and look over to see her finish her feeder dance, then take wing. I am left with the abandoned window to contemplate. The window is framed with shelves of books: Thoreau and Alice Walker, Lao Tzu and Margaret Atwood, all keeping odd company on the walnut shelves. For all their differences, these books are all witnesses to creation and its sacred source. Beyond the books, the window and the forsythia lie the sugar maples and hemlocks of the Catskill mountains. To touch the heart of the mountains—to bury my face in the mossy earth—is to touch that sacred source that breathes under the words of all the poets and philosophers.

I make my home in a small town in these mountains. Besides the tufted titmouse and myself, the town is home to a couple hundred residents. The heart of the town consists of two small general stores, a firehouse, a post office (whose accessibility ramp is longer than the building is wide), a Methodist church, and an Odd Fellows and Rebekah's lodge. To complete the cast, there are our guardians and watchers buried in the hillside meadow of Tongore Cemetery.

I share my home in Tongore with an eighty-pound German shepherd, Abbey, and an assertive calico cat, Callie. Ours is an interfaith household: Abbey is a practitioner of some primal ecstatic religion, Callie is a Buddhist, and I'm the local Methodist minister. On this day, as the titmouse has returned to play in the feeder, Abbey patiently watches me. In her eyes, in the deep darkness of her open face, I see that she is praying to *Gitchi Manitou*, the Great Spirit. She is asking for divine intervention. She is waiting for those magic words to take shape in my thoughts: "Let's go for a walk."

Abbey's petition has been heard. She is fidgety with excitement, though she obediently sits as the leash is snapped into place. Still and detached, Callie watches us from the window. Then we're off—across Route 213, through the church parking lot and over the broken gate. I set Abbey free to dance and twirl and run ahead of me down the overgrown abandoned quarry railway that will lead us into the heart of the woods.

Here, Abbey will not heel, sit or stay. I won't ask it of her. We are both cut free from our domestic lives, and give over to the instinctual. As Abbey chases invisible trails of scent through the broken leaves, something is nurtured in her—something fiercely canine, carnivore and wild. Walking behind her, I am stripped by the earth, the stones and the trees. Entering this sacred and primeval space, all the illusions and pretensions of living with trappings of human community drop away. We are simply present to the "Great I Am."

In the village beyond these woods, I am clothed with expectations: a silk blouse for a woman, a quilted cloak for a neighbor, a damask stole—the "yoke of obedience"—for a priest. They are layered across my shoulders like garments of glory and protection. But they are also heavy and scratchy and ill-fitting. And they are not a part of the original design of my creation from the dust and ash of the universe. With Abbey bounding and darting ahead of me, I drop these social roles, letting them bunch and gather at my feet, and emerge a naked soul bathed in *spiritus,* the wind, the breath of God.

The path into the woods is worn—originally from heavy carts carrying quarried stone that was built into a dam eighty years ago. A dozen villages were flooded to create a reservoir for New York City. Perhaps the exiled stone grieved upon leaving —a young friend of mine swears there is a sadness in the silent pit of the abandoned quarry. The path taken by the departing stone is used infrequently by neighbors on horseback or young men and their snowmobiles. The path begins in crushed stone, wades through blueberry bushes, then yields to a carpet of spongy green moss.

Abbey and I wander in the cool, moist passage beneath a canopy of hemlocks. We pass a tiny stream gurgling on our left and a giant fallen hardwood on our right. While the stream badgers the solemn hemlocks, I stop to touch the fallen tree. It is remarkably alive in its decomposing. I fancy I sense a pulse under my fingertips, as the tree gives its life over to new forms—moss and grub worms. The blond, damp splinters witness to surrender, to the yielding of life to life, and death to life. Receiving the gift of the tree, I bow and walk on.

As we walk, my breathing deepens, leaving my limbs tingling with the influx of oxygen. The breath opens me and shakes my dull senses until they are aroused. Every step I take echoes through my body like a drum cadence. My mind is awakening as the aroma of the evergreens floods in through my nostrils to fill the open spaces of my skull. It is as though the fragrance drives out before it all the clouds of the day's tasks.

Trotting ahead, Abbey has reached our destination, where she waits for me. She has come to the place where the hemlocks and mixed woods give way to sparse deciduous hardwoods. Among the roots of the hardwoods, patches of lichen-covered bluestone break open the earth, revealing its age. Above us the dancing leaves splash light on the rocks, the earth, and on Abbey's brown-and-black muzzle. This is a space alive with contrast and mystery.

The people who named these mountains *Onteora*—Land in Sky—brought their questions, existential and routine, to the sacred circle to seek its wisdom. In many cultures, the circle is the symbol for cycles of birth-death-rebirth. Having neither beginning nor end, the circle symbolizes eternity and unity. In counsel, the native peoples of this continent sat in a circle when decisions were made about the life of the community.

The sacred circle emerges wherever the power of the four directions converge, whether in human community or in the solitude of the forest. Particular places may focus and crystallize that power with unique clarity. The collective wisdom of native peoples tells us that each direction speaks with a particular voice, a particular viewpoint.

In these woods, Abbey and I have come to the perimeter of such a sacred circle. In this opening in the otherwise dense surroundings I have often been touched by great power. Here stands the great Teacher: this hemlock, this sheer rock face, these lichen.

Taking out my Silva compass, I walk into the clearing. In my hand, the needle bobs and twirls briefly in its casing. I know where north lies, but I need repeated confirmation. Stepping attentively, listening, I come at last to the right spot. Checking my compass, I find that, yes, there are four trees around me that mark precisely the four directions. As these four trees knit earth and sky, the circle is completed. I also note the presence of an altar of stone at the heart of this circle.

I have no special question for the circle today; I have only come to listen. Slipping the compass back into my pocket, I turn to face each direction. First the East, the place of the sunrise, of beginnings, of the spirit and of recurring epiphanies. Turning through the circle, the South speaks to the heart, to connections and boundaries within human community. Facing west, I see the sun has begun its imperceptible slide toward the horizon. The West, the place of fiery sunsets, is the place of magic and transformation. Finally, the North is the place of the mind and of cool clarity of thought. The points between the true directions nuance my experience, and the sky and earth orient this woman in the midst of the four directions.

Abbey leaves me and roams the perimeter of the clearing. Her instincts will prompt her to check on me from time to time, but she will not disturb my solitude without invitation.

Silently, I invoke the wisdom of the directions. Now comes the waiting. Taking a deep breath and exhaling slowly, I lie down on a large, flat stone nearest the western tree, my head pointing to the West. As I focus on my breathing and open my senses to the earth, wood, sky, stone, a mantra rises in my thoughts: "Not my will, but thine, Lord."

The circle speaks to me, sometimes in Christian language, sometimes Buddhist, sometimes Taoist. Often the circle speaks in a language of its own. Today the words are Christian—a prayer spoken by Jesus at a point of critical decision in his life.

My first response is to balk. After all, I am a feminist. And I am a survivor. I am a survivor of a Christian-fundamentalist journey in the Bible Belt South of my youth. I cringe at anything that reminds me of the call to obligatory, redemptive suffering as the way to the heart of God. It's not the words themselves that assault me. It is the layer of memory, the child who endured abuse because it would make her more like Christ. The child who had no will of her own because she was not allowed to set her own boundaries. The child who somehow survived and did find redemption in the face of suffering.

"Not my will, but thine, Lord." Jacob had his angel in the night from whom he wrestled a blessing. My accosting angel is this terribly orthodox whisper. I asked the circle, and she has spoken. In these sacred woods, I will wrest hope and meaning from these words, for they've come to me from the West, from the place where all is transformed. I begin repeating the prayer as a mantra, in rhythm with my breath.

As each breath moves in and out of me, the mantra takes root in my soul and the wisdom of the ancients blossoms. I realize that I cannot will myself to stop breathing. I am not in control of this life. I am not even in control of the simplest act of life, breathing. I need not try to be in control. I need only to let go and become a part of that which is pushing to flow through me. Let go into the stream. Let go.

Lying on this stone on state land, I understand. I do not control this life; I cannot control this earth. Nor can I possess it. Where I grew up, you could measure a person's worth by their assets, particularly by how much land they owned. This all seemed reasonable and natural to me. If you could fence the land

and pay taxes on it, then of course it was yours. It wasn't until I was a graduate student living in New York City that I began to see the absurdity of thinking that one owned the land. In New York, I discovered that people could lease or buy airspace above a building or lot. Airspace?

But then, if it's ridiculous to think one can own airspace, is it not equally ridiculous to own the land? Lying here I realize that I don't possess the earth; yet she is mine to enjoy. I walk her moss-covered paths, breathe her sweet oxygenated concoctions and sweat and tumble with Abbey on her dusty breast. If anything, this earth owns me, for I have borrowed the matter from which I'm made from her sticks and grasses and clouds. Someday, she will reclaim this form, as she reclaims the fallen tree in the hem-lock grove.

I know, too, all that is powerful and holy is here—breath and wind, stone and sky, trees and life. Here is God, the "Great I Am." If I flee this moment or fill it with fear and anxiety, I dis-honor it, and miss a sweet touch of eternity. I will linger in this place for some timeless time, repeating the prayer, feeling the solid earth beneath my back and breathing the gentle incense of the woods.

The time comes for Abbey and me to return to our house and our feline housemate. Abbey leads the way, and I follow. The West has worked her magic; the earth has healed her creature. The prayer lingers with me, as each footfall repeats the even cadence over moss and stone: "not-my-will-but-thine-Lord-not-my-will-but-thine-Lord-not-my-will-but-thine. . . . "

We come to the broken gate in back of the church. The little pile of social expectations is lying right where I left them, at the threshold where the wild woods give way to the asphalt church parking lot with its rusty basketball hoop. I know that when I cross this threshold, they will clothe me again, that I may not appear naked in this post-Eden world. A soft cry floats above us. Looking up, I spot a red-tailed hawk, circling high above the church steeple, then drifting down over the post office. She does not have the manic joy of the titmouse; she is steady, and singular in focus.

I stand between the worlds in which each human must live, watching the minutest movements of her pinions, the occasional flap. It comes to me, as simple and unheralded as the breeze around us: this is the will of God—to sense the breath of the sun underneath you and to move in response to it. The witnesses on the bookshelf wait to confirm this revelation.

One more breath, one more prayer, and Abbey and I step across the nexus, her leash in place, her shoulder obediently by my knee.

A GLACIER SUMMER

Barbara Wilson

I SPENT THE SUMMER I was twenty-one in the high mountains of central Norway, a landscape known as *Jotunheimen,* or "Home of the Giants." I'd taken a job at a hotel in a green valley on the road that wound from the coastal fjords through high plateaus, ice fields and the tallest mountains in Northern Europe. In earlier times Elveseter Hotel had been a large summer farm; it was still owned by the original family and retained much of its traditional character with many outbuildings around a central hall. Although there were now two long motel-like structures for the guests, there were also numerous small huts characteristic of a Norwegian farm: storerooms, saunas and bakeries, built of logs with grass roofs where goats were once tethered. A fast-moving river ran below the farm, so loudly that in the beginning it seemed to drown out all other sound. Above the farm lay other *seters,* or summer farms, alpine meadows and glacier-covered peaks.

Almost all of us who worked at the hotel were foreigners (we often speculated that the Elveseters had chosen non-Norwegians intentionally, to push us around more easily), and few of us

spoke Norwegian. I had been in Norway working as an au pair
for three months, however, and because I could get along in the
language, I was given the job of managing the souvenir shop, a
tiny glass room off the restaurant that was packed with hand-
carved wooden trolls, delicate silver jewelry and pewter bowls,
as well as postcards, film and sundries.

Aside from four Norwegian students who worked as maids
and drivers during the day and dressed up to perform folk dances
for the tourists at night, the rest of the staff was from Australia,
England and the U.S. We all had to wear costumes at work.
Mine was a striped blue and white skirt, a white blouse with
puffed sleeves and a blue bodice that laced in front. My Australian roommate Felicity, who ran the hotel bar, wore a version in
red. We looked like something out of *Song of Norway,* and tourists often remarked how authentic we looked—until we opened
our mouths. Our lack of fluent—or, in Felicity's case, even
basic—Norwegian took Norwegian travelers by surprise but, in
fact, native tourists were few and far between. They preferred to
stay someplace less authentic and were usually up in the mountains for serious hiking, not for buying hand-carved wooden
trolls and for folk dancing after dinner. What Elveseter catered to
were busloads of European and American tourists on package
tours who usually stayed only one night on the way from Stryne
to Otta.

The hotel was quite remote and from the beginning life there
had a dreamlike, disorienting quality. Although the foreign staff
had arrived with the idea of seeing Norway, the grandeur and
isolation of the landscape were intimidating. We were all from
urban centers like Sydney, Newcastle, Cincinnati and Los An-
geles, and few of us were really prepared for the light nights,
towering mountains and what seemed, at first, an overwhelming
lack of anything *to do.* The eighteen of us formed a close-knit
society—six men and twelve women, mostly students. Felicity
was the oldest of us at twenty-three, and she and I roomed together in the second story of a *stabbur,* or storehouse. Traditionally, it was the unmarried women of the household who lived
there during the summers and drew the ladder up every night
against prospective bridegrooms. Grass and wild flowers grew in
profusion on the roof, and the ladder gave us not a little trouble

that summer. Almost every time we had a party someone lost their footing and tumbled drunkenly to the bottom.

The hotel was twenty-five kilometers from the nearest town of Lom, which, other than an old white-painted church, had little besides a cafe and a few shops. The closest towns were at least a day's journey by bus or hitching, and it was difficult to arrange time off to visit them, though several of us made it to the spectacular Geiranger Fjord. The Elveseter family—wild-eyed husband, stern wife and lonely, obnoxious son—worked us exceedingly hard. We had very little free time, and to make sure we didn't run off they kept our wages for us, to be paid at the end of the summer. Meanwhile they docked us constantly for being late to work or sneaking into the walk-in fridge to steal some food. For although the guests exclaimed at the bountiful tables of sliced roast beef, shrimp and huge strawberries, we who worked at the hotel ate only bread and cheese, cream porridge and reindeer stew with potatoes. We spent many mealtimes obsessing about pizza and Chinese food.

Our small society went through various fashions and passions during the three months of the summer season. The first weeks of June were cold and rainy, and we spent a considerable amount of time indoors, drinking and getting to know each other. We often stayed up all night because it never really got dark, and plotted ways to get alcohol cheaper than Mr. Elveseter wanted to sell it to us. Lom didn't have a state-owned liquor store, so two of us were dispatched, list in hand, two hundred kilometers to Lillehammer, to order bottles in bulk. Our boxes of alcohol arrived by bus one day, much to the consternation of Mr. Elveseter. But when these bottles were gone—almost all on the big blow-out party we held around a bonfire on Midsummer Night's Eve—a more sober period set in, and we turned to cheaper and more innocent pleasures, such as learning folk dancing from the Norwegians and stitching traditional bell pulls from packages we bought in Lom. Even I, notorious non-sewer, produced one of these objects. Felicity decided our minds were rotting, and she wrote to Foyles Book Shop in London to ask for a catalog. We ordered some books, and one week four of us young women read Sylvia Plath's *The Bell Jar* and had several serious discussions about suicide. Eventually Felicity fell down the stabbur ladder while carrying a pile of newly received hard-cover novels, and somehow that was the end of reading for the summer.

Towards the end of June the sun came out, along with giant mosquitoes, and the days were hot and long. Our group began to get its bearings and to become more adventurous. None of us had ever climbed before and a few had never been in snow, but the dream began to grow on some of us that we should be trying to conquer the peaks around us. The two gay cooks from Bournemouth firmly declined to know the heights and so did two of the women, but the rest of us gamely began to hike above the farms to the upper pastures, traditionally where the sheep were taken for the richer grass. As the snow retreated, lupines and columbines, bluebells and dozens of other flowers I didn't know bloomed extravagantly in the meadows. Above the pastures there were plateaus and peaks, and the tongues of glaciers licking expectantly at our feet.

One sunny day, four of us decided to join a guided group on the ascent to Galdhøppigen, one of the mountains across the valley and the tallest peak in Norway at 2,469 meters. We were all quite unprepared. Paul from Sydney wore sneakers and a sweatshirt. David from Hull had on jeans and a windbreaker over his T-shirt, and Sue from North London had on shorts and a sweater. I was from Southern California and, in spite of having spent a snowy spring in Norway, still assumed that when the sun shone it was hot, especially in summer. I had thought to wear two pairs of socks and had the only pair of mittens in the group, but my suede boots had little tread and soon became soaked. None of us had the foresight to wear a hat.

A bus from the bottom of the valley took us up a twisting road to a hostel at the base of the mountain, and as the bus wound upward our excited joking diminished slightly. There was a lot of snow, we noticed, hard-packed and glittering, and although the sky was blue it was definitely *much* colder than down in the Bøver Valley. Paul was too macho to give up, and although Sue admitted later she had hoped the guides would refuse to let us go, none of us spoke our worry as we attached crampons to our shoes and roped up. A crystal-cold, warning breeze seemed to come off the ice, and as we skirted one bluely gleaming crevasse after the next, and as we saw the guides tap at the pock-marked surface under us with ice picks, our jokes stopped entirely. David's beard was soon frozen stiff and Paul shivered in his Fosters Lager sweatshirt. Sue's plump little knees turned blue, and I lent her one of my soggy mittens. A wet cold fog descended on us from the top of the mountain, so that even when (after hours it seemed) we reached the summit, we didn't have a view. We bought some hot chocolate from the little kiosk and cards postmarked "Galdhøppigen," and Paul, his red nose running, said this mountaineering stuff was highly overrated, give him a pint down at the pub anytime. By the time we got down from the mountain the four of us were giddy with something approaching hypothermia, but on the bus going back, Sue said to me a little shyly, "I see we have the same day off. Shall we buy some proper gear and try again?"

Then, for the next six weeks, on our days off and sometimes in the afternoons, Sue and I began to explore the high plateau of Jotunheimen above the green valley. We bought sturdy leather hiking boots, long underwear, woolen hats and gloves. We bought sweaters with reindeer designs and extra-thick socks and Freia milk chocolate bars. Our legs got strong and our faces sunburned.

The high plateau was glacier country, full of enormous granite boulders and the rubble of glacial till left by the retreating ice. Above the tree line there was no vegetation except yellow-green lichen and a stiff, scrubby heather. Here and there were streams and small lakes, milky with glacier flour that scattered the light. It was a bare but beautiful landscape, not so much desolate as simplified: in the absence of numerous things to look at, you could look better at the few things that were there.

Paths marked by cairns crossed and recrossed the plateau, and you could walk for hours sometimes without seeing anyone. Up there everything looked clearer somehow, more real and hard and definite in the thin, high air. The sky seemed close, light porcelain-blue, though sometimes storm clouds came up unexpectedly, and we had to huddle against wind and rain in our ponchos.

Often it felt as if we were on the very top of the world, and our minds cleared out and freshened, as did our lungs, as did our hearts. We used to walk miles without saying a word, and then sit and share an orange by one of the ancient-looking cairns, and ponder which way to go when every direction looked the same. Sometimes we climbed higher and came to the moraine at the base of a glacier, and the glacier itself that was like a frozen wave caught around boulders big as sofas and small houses. We walked a little ways on the glaciers, but never far, for we were full of stories of people vanishing in crevasses that suddenly opened up, and occasionally we heard the creak and break of ice and skittered back to the safety of the rocks. Sometimes if it was sunny and we were tired, we lay down on the boulders trapped in the ice, or on the tongue of ice itself. Glacier ice has no air, it is densely packed and bubble-free. From a distance glaciers look like smooth coverlets of white, but up close, especially at the edges, they are banded with dirt and honeycombed with pockets the sun has made. Yet the density of the ice makes it seem not to melt, just as the glacier itself seems not to move, but to be hard and firm like an inviting stone. We slept and when we woke the sky was still blue and the silence was endless still, echoing hugely, and there was a cool wind blowing off the glacier, telling us it was time to keep walking.

Sue and I often had dreams when we slept on the glaciers. Hers were usually of horses; she had worked at a stable before coming to Elveseter and wanted to be a vet. I often dreamed of my best friend from high school with whom I'd had a falling out just before leaving for Norway. At twenty-one I considered myself fully grown, far from the losses and abuse of my childhood and adolescence, finally free to live out adventurous fantasies of traveling and working in Europe. But Sandy had said I would never be a writer and this whole idea of living in Europe was pure escapism; it would be better if I stayed in college and got some useful degree. I was still arguing with Sandy in my dreams, still missing her. Sue reminded me of Sandy during our giggly senior year, short and stocky with freckles and a big laugh. Sue, who was nineteen and lived at home, couldn't imagine my former life and asked me sometimes to tell her about drugs, open sexuality and the Vietnam protests, which had so lately been my world. Up there in the mountains everything I'd done and lived through before I arrived at Elveseter seemed as strange to me as it did to her.

Sometimes we walked all day and didn't return to the valley below, but stayed the night in hostels and huts where we put our sleeping bags on the floor among all the other unknown travelers and slept the wonderful, deep sleep of physical depletion.

I could have gone on walking high on the top of the world for days, for weeks. But there was always the souvenir shop to return to and my blue-and white-striped skirt and bodice to put on and my trolls to sell and the tourists to talk to ("You speak English so well!" "Thank you!"). My thoughts were always outside. Sometimes, if I had only a free hour or two, I'd go sit on a rock in the middle of the swift river and I'd lose myself completely. Above me the mountains, around me the roar of the river. I'd grown up swimming in the Pacific Ocean and that had always been my private wilderness. Now I was learning another wilderness: snow, rocks, rivers and forests.

There was another young English woman at the hotel that summer, the sort with deceptively pink cheeks and mild blue eyes, who nevertheless had no sense of physical danger. Diane had taken naturally to climbing and had far surpassed the rest of us with her exploits in the highest ranges. One weekend Diane talked me into accompanying her and two Norwegian mountain guides she'd gotten to know up a mountain near the Jostedal-breen. She flattered me by telling me I must be in really great shape after all my hiking with Sue, and I forgot for a moment that what Sue and I mainly did was stroll along cairned paths and take naps on the glaciers. I hadn't been actually glacier climbing since the Galdhøppigen misadventure, but I forgot and said, "All right. I'll go."

The Jøstedalbreen is an ice field eight-hundred-feet square that sits between the Nordfjord and Sognfjord. We were planning to hike up to a mountain called Fanaråktind, along a skeletal black ridge, to a small hut on top where we would stay the night.

Because we got a late start, the two guides decided that we should skip the slow approach to the summit, which climbed up the ridge (and to my eyes looked steep enough), in favor of a faster frontal assault. This route would take us straight up the side of a mountain that looked made of white glass and black obsidian. I was embarrassed in front of Diane's eager assent—"Oh what fun"—and agreed. I put on crampons and tied the rope around my waist. With an ice pick in hand (relinquished when Diane told a cheery story about someone who'd slipped and poked out his eye with the tip), I somehow kept from falling to the certain death I imagined at every second. We crawled up past blue-walled crevasses and sheer slopes of hard-packed snow, at certain places hacking steps in the ice and hauling each other up.

I was so afraid that I have almost no memory of the experience. I couldn't be afraid of the height, because I never looked at anything except my hands and feet and the next step. I do recall several times wanting to retrieve the ice pick and to use it on Diane, especially when she called to me encouragingly, "Only a few feet more to the next flat bit!" But mostly I felt hopelessly dependent on my companions and touched by their belief in me. "You can do it! We're almost there!"

When we finally reached the summit, it was sunset. My legs gave out briefly and my calves and arms quivered like uncoiled springs. After a few minutes I managed to stumble to the other side of the ridge, where the great white ice field of Jostedalbreen spread out before us like an immense sea turning gold and rose and lavender. Further out, beyond the ice field, was the sea itself, the arm of the Nordfjord, glittering blue-violet in the late sunshine. It was the perspective you get when you fly westward above the clouds on summer evenings, and the plane keeps up with the sun, so it never seems to quite set, or only slowly, by degrees, and everything, the clouds, the sky, the sun remains the same, almost timeless. None of us said anything, you couldn't, and then we had hot chocolate, and I found that my fingers couldn't hold the cup.

Once during the night I woke up and went outside to pee. It was August and getting dark for a few hours now, but still not very dark. A half moon swung in the east and there were stars, blue and white, and the glaciers were pillowy comforters of dreamy ivory that lay softly on the legs and arms of the giants all around. I knew that tomorrow would be filled again with fear—we had to get back down!—but that night it seemed as if you should be able to just float gently off the peak into the snow below, and falling, never feel a thing.

After my ascent of Fanaråktind, I was content to rest on my laurels, and I went back to hiking at lower altitudes. Every day I could hardly wait to get out of my skirt and bodice and into my jeans and boots. Felicity and I went often to the hillsides to pick blueberries, and Sue and I continued to sleep on the glaciers. But there were more cool evenings now and more cloudy days. Summer was ending, the wildflowers were long gone and the leaves on the birches were turning golden yellow. Darkness came earlier, more and more quickly, at ten, at nine, at eight. At meals we discussed fall plans: Felicity was planning to return to Australia after a short trip around Europe, I was traveling to Spain to attend university, others were going back to school or planned to look for work.

Everything we had complained about at Elveseter became beloved. The glucy-sweet cream porridge, the stabbur ladder, the sound of the river, the strange Elveseter family, the silence and isolation. We worried what it would be like to be in a city again, how noisy and dirty it would seem. We all promised to write and keep in touch, perhaps to come back the following summer or to work somewhere else as a group. But except for Felicity, who visited me in Spain a month later, and one of the Norwegian men, with whom I stayed for a few days in Trondheim the following summer, I never saw any of those friends again.

One afternoon, a week before the hotel was to close for the season, I took a bike and made a circuit through the mountains behind Elveseter. I could feel as I rode uphill how strong my legs were and how much stamina I had. In the high pastures the leaves had not only turned but were falling thickly, and the snow was creeping low again. I felt as if I'd come to belong there in Jotunheimen, to belong in the mountains as I'd once belonged in the ocean when I was growing up. I remember resolving that I'd never let this feeling go, this lovely, intense *outside* feeling.

But in the last twenty years that feeling has come more fleetingly—on week-long backpacking or kayak trips, on week-end camping or brief bicycling excursions. I've lived an urban life, and most of my vacations have been spent in cities, it seems. I've hiked some magnificent landscapes, the Pyrénées, the Yorkshire Dales, the Canadian Rockies; I've even been back to Norway, though not to Jotunheimen. But my life is full and busy and these trips have all been short—days not weeks, and certainly not months. My glacier summer was a sustained gift, one I haven't figured out how to give myself again.

That day at the very end of August, it rained. I took refuge with my bike in a barn, with an old man whose dialect was so strong I hardly understood him. It didn't matter; he gave me some cheese and I gave him some chocolate and when the sun came out, we both smiled to see there was a rainbow. When I got to the highest peak, I took a deep breath and started to fly downhill. It was a five-kilometer stretch of joy, where green and gold rushed around me like a tunnel I could sense but not touch; the mountains were all around me, and the sound of the river was loud as always, but so familiar I no longer heard it.

LOOKING FOR DANIEL

Elizabeth Folwell

THERE ARE THOSE DAYS when everything stands out in isolated, sharp focus: when the pine smells different (more astringent, resinous) from the balsam (sweet, haylike); when the warblers' cacophony of buzzes, tweets and nonsense syllables breaks down to discrete, pure melodic notes; when each tree, bush and shrub is brilliantly evident in an individual shade of green. Those days, any opening in the woods becomes the sacred gateway to another place. I want to walk through, parting the branches, and have all the green fill in seamlessly behind me, disappearing without a trace, passing gracefully into some trackless elsewhere.

Alone in the backcountry is the way I prefer to travel: keeping my own pace, with my own thoughts for company, but I don't often allow myself that luxury. I haven't gotten truly lost—not yet—but I've had the scare of passing the same boulders twice, three times, of getting into the thick and having to stop, think, backtrack to a known place, all the while tingling with that flushed, edgy feeling. But that's been the rare event. So of course I could understand—even envy—Daniel's desire to hike a long trail all by himself, free of distractions and hoping to learn something, about the world, the woods, or himself. He did all of the above, I guess.

He was a recently divorced guy, not quite forty, who worked in a suburban upstate New York post office. His friends said that in preparation for the hike he lost thirty or forty pounds by fasting, running and working out with single-minded zeal. He wanted to go light—really light—so he took along only minimal food and equipment: a gluey peanut-butter-and-trail-chow concoction, tent, sleeping bag. No fancy freeze-dried food, no water filter, no stove, no rain gear. He carried an old guidebook for the region; I'm not sure he had a compass. He planned to do the 132-mile Northville-Lake Placid Trail that slices through the Adirondack Park like a shoulder sash, following valleys and ridges through some of the most remote wilderness in the Northeast, at a pace of about twelve or fourteen miles a day. He left in early June at the height of blackfly season, and although his friends and family swore Daniel was an experienced woodsman, his timing showed otherwise. On this hike past pond, lake and stream, he'd forgo human companionship, trading it for the boundless company of biting insects.

A nephew left Daniel at the southern trailhead, after they had cached some supplies near Blue Mountain Lake, a small town located just shy of the halfway point of the trail. There wasn't much to look forward to in the stash—more peanut-butter porridge, clean socks, a pair of shorts. The plan they had agreed upon was that Daniel would send back an occasional postcard, mailed by whatever town-bound day hikers he might meet, and that he'd catch the bus back home once he arrived in Lake Placid.

He never got there. When Daniel was a week overdue at home, his sister called the state conservation department to report that he was missing somewhere along the well-marked trail. A massive search ensued, with forest rangers and game protectors running in two-person "hasty teams," combing the trail from both ends and checking any connecting trails. They talked to other hikers they met. They shouted his name. They followed any trampled foliage or fresh tracks they spotted and poked around the far-flung lean-tos for evidence of recent visitors. They found that he had signed trail registers located at various trail junctions up to a point about thirty-five miles from where he had started. That narrowed things down—or did it? Had he just stopped signing his name, confident of his progress? Or was he down in the brush a mere half mile from his last signature, with a broken leg or sick from bad water? Planes flew overhead, but the new flush of spring leaves made ground details difficult to see. A bonfire on a lakeshore might have been visible, but a daytime smolder in a damp forest, no.

The state police ran background checks to be sure that this wasn't a stupid prank; the inevitable rumors circulated through nearby towns that he had blithely walked out to start a new life in California or Mexico, someplace warm and dry. The most reliable information placed Daniel somewhere deep in the wilderness, about fifteen miles from the nearest settlement. The crews kept on hunting for him in the woods, enlisting experienced search-and-rescue teams from across New York. The best-trained dogs and their handlers arrived, but the scents had become jumbled and faint, complicated by all the other people on the scene. Psychics from across the country phoned in with tips; one woman said she had seen Daniel in a dream and that he was alive and well in suburban Syracuse. A small gathering of local dowsers came to help, armed with maps, cords and assorted charms. Along with a lieutenant ranger, they all sat at a rickety card table at search headquarters watching their plumb bobs slowly rotate over a topo sheet of the West Canada Lakes Wilderness Area. One old water witch, a friend of mine who's got a respected skill for finding bodies dead and alive—a suicide dangling high in a spruce tree miles off the highway and a drowning victim at the bottom of Lake George, for example—got a signal of something human near a footbridge over a creek. Rangers hiked in and found a recently-emptied Jif jar, but there was no telling who it had belonged to.

From the first day, a group of eager reporters hung around at the edge of the woods, braving the insects, rain and boredom in order to give search details to an audience that was expectant of tragedy, triumph or scandal, and believing in some kind of definitive outcome. As the weeks passed, all their enthusiasm diminished exponentially, especially since there was nothing new to say.

This case was all the more baffling because the Northville-

Placid trail is well marked, well mapped and relatively well traveled. It didn't make sense that an average, healthy adult could
lose his or her way, and if a person were disabled in the woods
near the trail, he or she would have been located by now.

The call went out for volunteers. The pros needed eyes and
ears, lots of them, as the situation became critical. If Daniel
wasn't injured or sick, he was still in danger: there was the distinct possibility he had run out of food. Even with a solid working knowledge of wild edibles, living off the land is pretty iffy
since a typical deep-woods Adirondack spring offers assorted
shoots and roots, but no abundance of easily picked berries and
fruits. If Daniel could catch some fish, his chances for survival
would be better, but the searchers found no sign of him near any
of the ponds and lakes.

Search headquarters was only fifteen miles from my home; I
joined up to help on a Sunday, the last official day of the full
search. Equipped with topographical map, compass, bug dope,
whistle and matches in my pack, I didn't know what to expect,
maybe something along the lines of orienteering with a group of
strangers, but I had hiked that country and wasn't afraid of some
serious walking. I had been reading about the case in local papers
and couldn't avoid the daily radio updates. Posters showing
Daniel's face were everywhere.

Everyone in town was swept up in the mystery, and peculiar,
unsubstantiated stories circulated about details of Daniel's private
life. His friends claimed he actively fantasized about epic, life-
threatening journeys and wrote weird sword-and-sorcery tales
for fun, all of which were practice runs for the current turn of
events. Some cynics claimed he had planned the whole vanishing
act in hopes of snagging a lucrative movie contract when he
emerged sinewy and triumphant. Folks said that he had begun
the trip because he was deeply depressed by his divorce or, con-
versely, that he was so happy about his wife's remarriage that the
hike was some kind of joyous cleansing ritual. Yet another ru-
mor was that he was desperately in love with a friend's wife and
wanted to impress her with his skills. Through all this gossip, it
was clear that people were trying to create a personality that offered an explanation for his disappearance. We wanted to breathe
life into all the conjecture and to put a real man's face to what few

worked-over facts we had. This community chorus offered a motivation to search, since there's no point in trying to find a truly anonymous person. I got swept up in it too, compelled to learn what I could about this stranger and all the people who cared so passionately about him. He had become some kind of two-legged Holy Grail, our North Country version of Amelia Earhart.

The search headquarters was in a huge clearing on the northern edge of the Moose River Plains, a fifty-thousand-acre tract of logged-over land with sandy hills, pocket swamps, low mountains, small rivers and dozens of ponds. Not many people spend much time there except during hunting season and on the occasional fishing trip. Snowmobilers pass through on old logging roads and the Northville-Placid trail crosses into the plains just north of Cedar Lakes, as beautiful and remote a spot as any on the continent. It's a place where moose are seen now and again, and I would believe someone if he or she told me they spotted a mountain lion. As empty wildness on the edge of a narrow dirt road, many miles from the nearest settlement, the plains hasn't had much in the way of human presence in the last fifty years.

Two army-issue canvas tents—with that dusty, musty smell that brings back thoughts of nights in kids' camp—were the search office and kitchen. One tent held nothing but coffin-size coolers full of sandwiches, sodas and fruit, and chests brimming with candy bars, all courtesy of local merchants who never wavered in their support of the search crews as the weeks progressed. Before our orientation, all the volunteers helped themselves to the bounty, stuffing pockets and packs.

What a mongrel bunch we were. The rangers, with blackfly bites peppering their ears and necks, seemed tired and frustrated and ragged around the edges after too many dawn-to-dark days away from home. But their uniforms lent them competence, confidence, leadership. The unpaid help, though, came in all shapes and sizes. There were lanky, loping college kids, with gleaming long hair and all the proper new paraphernalia in the latest fashion colors, alongside fish-and-game types—lumpy, patched older men, stinking of Ol' Woodsman, a pine-tar-based insect repellent. The search-and-rescue clubs from outside the Adirondacks all sported matching baseball caps plus bright-colored vests with woven lanyards attached to every conceivable gizmo leading into innumerable pockets; they looked as if they might be engineers or computer programmers in real life. I was the only woman and the only local on that particular day. When it came time for the team leaders to select crews, I ended up with two rangers and an assistant ranger in my team, perhaps because they thought the risk of losing *me* was substantial.

Our training session was brief and to the point. Each team of four to six people would be doing "type three" searches in areas that had been marked earlier with grids of string. We would walk slowly abreast in a line, within sight of the person on either side, and scan the ground for any leads: scraps of clothing, a shred of plastic, a partial boot track, charcoal from an old campfire, any bit a human might leave behind. We were told to pay attention to smells and sounds; the message was that our person might be gravely ill or seriously hurt and unable to respond. The possibility that we were looking for a dead body was never discussed. This, I learned later, was so that the volunteers wouldn't be demoralized. Searchers try much harder when they think the victim is still alive.

Daniel's family, camped near headquarters in a beat-up tin can of a travel trailer, was absolutely certain he was alive. I saw his sister, a heavy-set lady, pacing back and forth that morning. A little cloud of blackflies followed her. She had been there for weeks, waiting and hoping on the outskirts of rangerland. Just looking at her made me depressed. For a moment I felt like I wanted to talk to her, but then I figured she had been badgered enough by well-meaning folks.

Our team rode for an hour in the back of a state-issue Jeep truck, bouncing over old logging roads on the shoulder of Manbury Mountain, passing through nondescript forest and three-thousand-foot rounded hillsides, about five miles from the last trail register Daniel had signed. Someone made a sick joke about our location, smirking that there wouldn't be much to bury if the critters had gotten to him. At our appointed spot—a tagged line of twine—the team hopped out.

Our section was a shady north-facing slope covered with medium-sized second-growth hardwoods, head-high witch hobble and ferns. At first, the walking was easy and it wasn't so bad trying to watch the ground to the left and at the same time keep an eye on adjacent team members so that we advanced more or less together. Initially, the rest of the crew was overly solicitous of me—they had already festooned my hat and pack with orange flagging so I appeared to be some dwarf talking Maypole—and took pains to ask me if the line wasn't going too fast, if I wanted more bug dope. Usually it was somebody who was already out of breath checking up on my well-being, but after a while we silently settled into the work at hand.

Among last year's leaves I found a rusty bottlecap, circa 1981. One of the rangers picked up a Xeroxed topo map dropped by a previous search team. Somebody else found a dime that had fallen out of a pocket who knows when. Encouraged, we joked about our powers of observation. Then the forest got thicker and darker, and our progress slowed to a crawl as we went over boulders and stumps, calling out "Hold the line!" frequently until we could count off and hear and see each other again. We weren't all walking at the same pace, as some had more scrambling, stumbling and dodging than others. On that sticky, hazy day, the bugs were fierce and there was no relief as we went deeper into the forest. Then we hit a dense, lightless spruce swamp, where we kept moving forward, through ankle-deep, then knee-deep funky-smelling water.

After another half mile of slogging, we hit—"bumped" in search parlance—another section of the string at a right angle to our side lines. This line marked the end of our grid, so we rested a moment and counted off down the line. Then we turned around to walk back over the same territory, this time scanning to our right, tromping through the mud, up over the boulders, around the stumps and back to the road. We hiked a couple of miles to hit another section of territory and repeat the process. Along the road, we did find charcoal from an old campfire. Some debate ensued about just how old it might have been, but the consensus was that the fire was probably from the previous fall. The hiking was definitely unglamorous, through places I'd choose not to visit again. This was work, tedious, unsatisfying work, and we weren't getting our job done.

As we walked, the talk inevitably meandered to other missing persons. One of the rangers, a fifty-year-old veteran who

was from the Champlain Valley, had been in on a massive hunt
for a small boy who disappeared from his family's estate near the
High Peaks about twenty-five years ago. That case was never
solved; it was as if the child had simply vaporized. Thousands
helped on that search, including Army troops, Green Berets,
planes and helicopters, but they found absolutely no clues. From
time to time rumors surfaced about a possible kidnapping, or
opinions that the child wasn't right in the head, but the old
ranger felt those were way off the mark. Maybe the boy just
wandered into the raspberries, curled up for a nap, and never
found his way back to the trail. The other rangers agreed,
though, that most of their searches are successful in a matter of
hours, with typical scenarios like locating some deaf old Joe a
couple hundred yards from hunting camp or tracking down a
teenager who went off in a pout.

And, as we chatted idly, waving away the deerflies, we noted
that the vast majority of lost people in this territory have been
men, and fit, younger men at that. In fact, in recalling the epic
searches in the High Peaks and dangerous winter rescues of
stranded climbers and backcountry skiers, the victims were always remembered as "an athletic older guy," "three fraternity
brothers," a "couple of ex-Eagle Scouts" from wherever. "Women don't get lost," said the senior ranger, "at least, not like
that, not big time." Sure, they may wander off a trail, but not
far, and certainly not forever.

That gave me something to chew on as we headed back to
headquarters. I couldn't make the gross generalization that outdoors women are more competent and better prepared in the first
place, and I can't argue that we simply don't take the same kinds
of risks, since I know plenty of rock-climbing and white-water
women who do hair-raising, white-knuckle stuff with dead-on
self-assurance. Is it an ingrained sense of responsibility, I
mused—the drive to get home in time for dinner—combined
with the desire not to be a bother to others? Or is it just mathe-
matics, that so many fewer women undertake these long, chancy
treks?

Then, the inevitable leap—what if Daniel were instead
Danielle? Would I have joined the search earlier, tried to solve the
puzzle intellectually and intuitively, thinking through what I

would do if I were the missing one? (I'd write my name every-where in the dirt, start a huge bonfire and keep it going day and night, leave Hansel-and-Gretel-like scraps of clothing in my wake, follow the water, and a host of other rational actions.) I could well imagine the coarse talk of an all-male search squad as they stumbled through the forest looking for a *girl*, and I think anger and indignation would be smack out in the open as the days wore on. I imagine that the all-purpose bugaboo "foul play" would be taken very seriously regardless of the overt evidence, since people would be far more comfortable with the thought that external forces were the real agents in the disappearance, rather than the notion that a female wanted to prove herself in the wilds. And what of public sympathy? I couldn't see this hypothetical lost woman cast in admiring, heroic terms. There is no distaff counterpart to Hawkeye anywhere to be found in American literature and Jack London's ladies were either whores or simps. No, Danielle would most likely be seen as someone to be pitied, scorned or ridiculed.

But these thoughts were a depressing diversion from the situation at hand and I had no reason to get pissed off at the rest of the crew who had proved to be dedicated and kind. This case was beating the odds. Daniel must have headed off the trail someplace and kept going, out of stubbornness or confusion, into a moist and leafy oblivion. After four solid weeks and thousands of hours of labor, the search efforts drew to a close. The cost had been in the hundreds of thousands of dollars and it seemed likely that he was dead.

During the first weekend of deer season, a hunter climbed one ridge over from the Sucker Brook Trail, which connects the Northville-Placid Trail with a state highway and a large public campground. On that October day, most of the trees had already shed their leaves so it wasn't hard for him to spot a small nylon tent and signs that someone had been there for a long time. He yelled out, fired shots into the air and got no response. Reluctant to explore much further, he headed back to camp for help and to call the Department of Environmental Conservation. Early the next day, forest rangers found Daniel's body in a streambed.

Clearly he had been dead for a while, but it wasn't until they discovered a small paperback diary in one of his pockets that they
learned he had survived for at least a month after the search had
officially ended, scrounging what he could from the surrounding
forest. I learned about the diary from a ranger friend who helped
carry out the body. Daniel had panicked, then gone crazy, he
felt. Although the hiker wasn't hurt, and only a quarter mile or
so off a marked trail, in his journal he kept reminding himself to
stay put, reassuring himself that help would come, like some
kind of desperate mantra. He heard planes overhead and assumed
that they were looking for him, so he cut a pole to make his red
sweatshirt into a signal flag and waved it frantically under the
forest canopy. Toward the end, he wrote of eating insects off the
walls of his tent. Near the body, the recovery team found
Daniel's windbreaker spread out on the ground, the word
"HELP" written in dirt and charcoal across the back.

When I learned about the diary I called Daniel's sister, suggesting that if others had a chance to read it, perhaps they'd learn
something important from his experience. She seemed to think
that was an interesting proposal. She remarked that heavy rain
might have forced her brother to abandon his plans to follow the
trail all the way to the north, and that perhaps he had wanted to
strike out on a side trail for Lewey Lake, where they had camped
as kids, and hitchhike home. After we spoke I thought, though,
that she might see other commercial possibilities—like *Readers'
Digest*, say—beyond the regional magazine that I work for, so I
didn't press her. The winter after her brother died, she and another sister connected with a high-powered attorney in order to
sue the state of New York. "Enormous pecuniary damage" they
claimed was a result of their brother's demise and they wanted to
recoup their losses.

Their suit implied that the search effort had been haphazard
and inept, that blame for the needless death somehow rested
squarely on the shoulders of the very people who had looked so
hard for him. The rangers I know were furious. I was angered
too: if the sheer combined force of will could have done anything, Daniel would have been found. The suit raised a thousand
new questions, but foremost in my mind was one about personal
responsibility.

·

Henry David Thoreau published a modest pamphlet called *Walking* in the 1850s. The essay, which he often delivered as a public lecture, begins with the familiar "I wish to speak a word for Nature, for absolute freedom and wildness...." More bits and pieces have been plucked from it—"in Wildness is the preservation of the world," "all good things are wild and free," and other recognizable phrases—to become the rallying cries of the environmental movement.

Recently, in rereading this classic of American nature writing, I came across a passage that struck me as eerily appropriate to Daniel's death. Thoreau wrote: "If you are ready to leave father and mother, and brother and sister, and wife and child and friends, and never see them again—if you have paid your debts, and made your will and settled your affairs, and are a free man, then you are ready for a walk."

Thoreau was writing of a person in charge of his own life, ready to account for his own acts. He also meant a good, long walk, and perhaps he would have applauded Daniel's choice of the Northville-Placid Trail. Wrapped up though, in Thoreau's statement are thoughts about risks, expectations and responsibilities. Thoreau saw angels and light in the wilderness, but he wrote of the demons, too, and he called nature "this vast, savage, howling mother of ours."

Only a select few in Thoreau's day chose to enjoy the wilds; today millions of us seek the solitude, beauty and challenge that only wild country can offer. In the comfort of our homes, we flip through books and magazines that describe adventures and out-of-the-way places. Catalogs and advertisements entice the reader into the outdoors—with seductive promises that a new pair of boots can make us surefooted or that a state-of-the-art compass can turn a couch potato into an explorer. The physical act of walking hasn't changed since bipedalism evolved, yet nowadays we can overload ourselves with gear and geegaws, and wrap our bodies in space-age fibers that wick away sweat, repel water, insulate and breathe. But not one of these things is an antidote for bad judgment or a talisman against bad luck.

A great number of the long trails in the Adirondacks, the

Northeast and the West, confront hikers from the get go with warnings about weather, daunting distances and lack of shelter along the route. But to many of us these are merely words emanating from some nervous, desk-bound bureaucrat. We're cloaked in competence, we think as we set out. Modern technology helps us to head into the woods with an attitude of supreme confidence, even hubris. Besides, we're convinced that we're truly prepared: we've studied the guides, heard a weather report, looked at a map. Our comfortable daily lives give us ample protection from unpredictability. Picturing ourselves invulnerable, we begin our treks without allowing for the inherent risk and spectacular irrationality of the wilds.

Most of the time we manage just fine. If sunny skies turn to a cloudburst, we get wet. If we make a wrong turn, we retrace our steps. These kinds of experiences make for great stories around the kitchen table, since we make it back to tell them, but in that way we feed the myth about the "conquerability" of nature.

Things don't always work out the way we plan, though.

Daniel's death is tragic; it moved me to true compassion. Yet I can't help concocting "what if" scenarios that would have produced different outcomes: What if he had been hiking with a companion? What if he had made arrangements to phone home on a certain day, or when he reached a specified town? What if he had taken a week's worth of backpacker meals and a stove? Just how much did he actually know about being in the woods? And the kicker—was this trip some kind of ultimate test that from the beginning he suspected he might fail?

I can't help but wonder at what point a series of small errors reached critical mass to create a desperate situation. I can replay all the hearsay and theories about what actually happened (confusion, exhaustion, hunger, illness, hypothermia), and temper them with my own woodsmanship—but I still can't come up with a good answer.

But a good answer to the proposed lawsuit was another matter. The underlying notion of a suit has to do with an innocent party being injured by the bad intentions, ignorance or negligence of another. Within that framework is the assumption that the injured party is not at fault for the turn of events, that something measurable or controllable was defective. The suit claimed that the trail itself was "unsafe, unreasonably dangerous and defective." I just don't buy it. I think that Daniel got more than he bargained for and nature does not negotiate.

A year after Daniel began his last walk, I went looking for him again, this time on a shady ridge just south of Sucker Brook. Trillium and fiddleheads bordered the trail, which climbed thirty feet above a sparkling, bouldery stream. Warblers darted through the hemlocks and yellow birches, and far off I could hear the motorboatish thrumming of a partridge. After an hour or so of walking, I found the red surveyor's tape that marked the way into his campsite; there were lots of ribbons near a modest, mossy trickle where I think Daniel spent his last days. Shady, buggy, almost claustrophobic with cherry and beech saplings, it wasn't the kind of place I'd like to call home.

I had expected that going there would give me some kind of dazzling epiphany, that a complete stranger's soul would suddenly be made clear and knowable. I had hoped that this place could be instantly understood as a dangerous trap, or as so achingly beautiful a person would never wish to leave, but of course it was neither, just an ordinary chunk of Adirondack woods. I can't answer why someone would hunker down deep in the forest as days stretched into weeks, instead of following the stream to a creek to a pond to a lake to a highway. Was this where Daniel had planned to arrive all along, to stay on forever to become one with nature in the most literal, basic sense of the phrase? I wonder.

HOMEWATERS OF THE MIND

Holly Morris

IT IS FIVE O'CLOCK on a dark and damp Northwest morning. What I thought was a brilliant idea only six hours ago now seems lunatic. As I will the coffee maker to brew more quickly, I remind myself that the invigoration of a predawn angling adventure outweighs the unpleasant exhaustion of the moment. Last night when I was going through my dusty, stiff gear, choosing a collection of nymphs, caddis and stone flies, and reframing my mind, I realized that being an armchair angler had become far too comfortable. This morning it felt just comfortable enough as I huddled under my blankets. But my father is coming to town next week, and I need to prepare.

Fishing has long been an escape for me, and of course, escape is complicated. Escape is good when it means freeing oneself from the weight of an obscure and explosive father or the constant grating of a mind embattled by memory. Escape is bad when it means ignoring the kinds of memories powerful enough to turn a life into a fortress, a man into stone. Few images of lessons fondly passed from father to daughter linger in my memory. I never fly fished with my father. We spun no stories together. No line connected us in silence. No metronome. He never knew the meter of his own life, or mine. But he inhabits my fishing life. His image rises like a rainbow to disappear elusively or be hooked and tangled with.

The day after my eighth birthday marked the first of many flights. I was in the back room playing with my new Zebco fishing rod and reel that my grandparents had given me. From the living room came a thunderous "Gaaahd Dammit!" Not the usual I've-added-this-column-sixteen-times or where's-my-other-shoe-goddammit, but the clinched jaw profanity that was just a prelude to the real rage to come. I stiffened. I knew the glint in his eyes. Although my father governed through intimidation, the threat of violence was always lurking, ready to ignite. I began to tick through the things I'd done wrong, but before I got very far he was in the doorway and starting toward me. My mother appeared, shaking, and tried to put herself between us and hold him back. Her interference signaled that a line had been crossed. She sensed violence. I grabbed her cue, my pole, and ran like hell.

After a quarter-mile barefoot sprint, I walked on the hot, cracked pavement steadying my emotions, testing the pain on my feet and concentrating on the fish that I would catch. The pond was about a mile from our house, and I doubted he knew it even existed. I made my way down a winding trail and nestled in among the swaying grasses at the water's edge. In many ways the place was unremarkable: a midwestern pond filled with bluegill and bass, surrounded by tall grasses and few trees. On other days, I would discover the pond rough and alive, gun-metal gray like a pre-tornado sky. But on that day the water was blue and still and heavy as the humid summer air. I threaded a freshly dug worm on my hook, cast my line and rested my mind on the tip of the pole, waiting for a nibble from the darkness to tell me what to do next. The thick air wrapped around me like a security blanket and at that moment, fishing became my refuge. It was my world, one that I was determined my father would know nothing about.

Twenty years later, I am driving the hour to North Bend, the launching point for a simple day of fishing the Snoqualmie River. Six-thirty in the morning and the reason for this day comes back to me. I feel lighter, happy with anticipation. Caffeine helps. A wet fog blankets the evergreens that spread up hillsides from the shoulder of the four-lane highway. The spaces between the mountains invite my eyes: rich valleys multiply and offer something beautiful and new with each one I look into, and beyond.

A dirt road leads from the highway down to where I leave my car next to the river. I know this stretch of water, but it can still surprise me. I slide into my brown neoprenes and the place that fly fishing takes me. The comfort of ritual and the draw of another world: cold and shadow, wonder and fear, currents that offer both danger and movement. Fishing offers me new ways to look at a sunrise, a small feather or a fork in the river. The rhythm of the casts and the power of place untangle the knots of my emotions. Problems get loose and wet, slide apart, become just a part of the landscape of my life, no longer the line that binds it.

I check my tippet and leader and fumble a clinch knot twice before successfully tying on a #12 nymph. Then I choose my line, that is, the line I'll travel when I enter the river. The holes and currents will frame my movement. I feel exhilarated by the strength of the river and by the cold that I think will never reach me.

My first casts are about as gracious as the Tin Man's movements upon Dorothy's arrival. Cast number five wraps around me. (Must be the breeze that has picked up.) I hook a tree branch. (Where did that come from?) Sometime around cast number twenty-two things start to go right. I begin to relax, forget about mechanics, and start to think about placement, and place.

Gray moss-covered boulders scatter the water's edge. Brown and green bushes mask the trunks of the tall evergreens that secure the banks. The fog lifts from the Cascades revealing crisp, snow-covered peaks and soppy-looking brown and green foot-hills. The beauty makes me realize I've noticed little beyond the confines of my mind for a very long time, and I feel arrogant and small. Rivers and mountain trails have always led me to places where truth means less and there exists a simple clarity. I come here to know my own life and transform it. To revive my senses, to smell, to see, to hear. To turn everyday-politics and responsibility into distant phantoms and to put the dissonance of pain into its proper place. The pull of the land, the texture of its body, the slow rhythms of growth and death—these things teach me grace.

In Montana, strip farming dehydrates the soil and intensifies its saline content. Toxic concentrations of salt enter the ground water only to resurface elsewhere in the form of salt deposits. Saline seep. When I fish, decades-old secrets and feelings bubble to the surface, and my foundation of carefully constructed logic washes away in a current of uncertainty. Emotional seep. Much of the time I choose to avoid these feelings, but, in truth they carry the ability to erode pain and leave me resensitized, feeling, able to see possibility beyond this bend, that boulder.

The last time I saw my father he seemed slight, not the towering man from my youth, not the powerful figure that occupies my memory. Was it his age or my own growth that reduced him to mortal? For the first time there emerged a vulnerable person whose navigation of life left a trail of both blunder and accomplishment, and portions of love that were by turns cloaked and confused. I saw myself as a little girl trailing behind him pausing at these strewn obstacles; hoisting them on my back to be carried along or deeming them too heavy and foreign, leaving them behind. His parting grip was gentle and his eyes seemed soaked with decades of unspoken emotion. The scar tissue that embalmed his own wounds of youth parted and he whispered "I love you." When we said goodbye that day, I packed away that new, incongruous image of my father. But that image comes to me now.

My father's world is silent and dark and has been as much a wonder to me as the primeval world of forests and fish. The latter anchors my soul and offers mysteries with depths to be plumbed; but I've let the former become a counterweight that, in some ways, still guides my movement, or prevents it.

Rousing myself from the haze of emotional seep, I move to catch a fish. I change to a Royal Wulff #10 and cast in earnest. My pulse picks up as I anticipate the unique elation that comes with the take. In spite of the preparation and forethought fishing requires, in a strange way, I never expect to catch a fish and am always surprised, and slightly panicked, when it happens. The

moment of the take is a mix of chaos and elation and a connection that never ceases to catch me off-guard. Like Spalding
Gray's sought-after "perfect moment." You never see them
coming and they are best had alone. They give closure and tell
you when it's time to go home. A sixteen-inch rainbow bearing
down on a #14 Zug Bug. That's a perfect moment.

Eight-thirty and still no action. I crouch and cast and feel that
the morning's slight breeze has calmed. A good sign. Behind a
boulder a roiling hole beckons. Was that a rise? For at least the
fifth time, I wish I'd remembered to bring my polarized sunglasses. Two false casts and the first lay falls short. My second
cast is close, but the fly immediately hooks a passing twig. On
the third try, it lands right on the sweet spot. At the same instant
of my tiny celebration about the perfect lay, the water explodes; I
see the flash right before I feel the strike. *The line sings.* I play the
fish and try to imagine her size in between the cracks of my panic
that I'll lose her. Twice she takes line and heads into deep, mid-
river current. Twice I bring her back in slowly, cautiously. After
ten minutes she's next to me, twelve inches long, exhausted and
beautiful. A rainbow of color courses down each side melting
into her sleek belly. I hold on to the moment, the meeting of our
worlds for as long as possible, but know it must be fleeting. I
gently remove the hook from her lip and revive her. She fins for
a few seconds, then darts back to another side.

After the rainbow is gone, I glide through the water easily,
my casts are satisfying, no longer stilted by tension. My
brother's words come back to me. "He's changed. He's really
trying. Come on, always making him the bad guy is the easy
way out." My brother's opinions, which have lingered in the re-
cesses of my mind for the past year, seem almost plausible. I
dare, tentatively, to imagine what it would be like to have a dad.

As I take off up-river to fish and think for a few more hours, I
wonder . . . perhaps I'll ask my father if he'd like me to teach him
to fly fish.

WILDERNESS WAY

Meryem Ersoz

"Tucker really trusts you." Sue says this to me on our third night out, as we watch our fire fade. In the Canadian wilderness, in the summer of 1986, real fires are still acceptable camping etiquette. You can also drink the water without worrying about giardia or some other violent microbacterial infection. I secretly packed my camp stove and the little brown bottle of halazone tablets, although I haven't used either of these items; they're my concession to the creeping infestation of civilization upon what's left of the world's true wilderness areas.

"How so?" I ask.

Sue sweeps her hand in the direction of the tents behind us. "Hasn't it occurred to you? You and me. Them. Tucker never sends out a girls' trip without a man to help lead it. This is the first time that I can remember."

She's right. The thought hadn't occurred to me. We listen briefly to the muffled giggling of young adolescent girls. "They never stop, do they?" Sue laughs.

Her comment means a lot to me. Tucker taught me how to read a river, how to eat fireweed and the right mushrooms and tubers, how to find my bearings when I've lost my compass, how to ferry a canoe, and how to catch the deep-water fish. He taught me how little I really need to be happy. On my first trip, he told me, "All you need to know about the woods is how to get lost with your axe and a map and still come out alive."

Tucker is the best woodsman I know. He owns a wilderness camp. It's a place where rich white kids go to develop character. Back when I was a rich white kid, my parents sent me there: I had returned, as an adult counselor (and as a poor, white English teacher this time) to re-acquaint myself with the wilderness and share these experiences with my young charges.

Tucker sends kids of all ages—from seven to seventeen—on canoe trips of four days to three weeks, depending on their ages and abilities. These trips are the real thing, complete with five-mile uphill portages, blistering sun and freezing rain, ten-hour days of paddling, and rapids that can wrap an aluminum canoe around a rock like tinfoil around a baked potato.

As a kid, of course, I took these experiences for granted, and I certainly didn't realize the danger. Rapids were just nature's roller coaster rides. And if we swamped, it was no big deal, just a quick ride down the river feet first (hold on to your paddle). As an adult, I grabbed my pleasure in between the cracks, watching the fire die beneath the simmering northern lights, getting up early before the girls to dip my line and serve up the morning's catch before breakfast, tying the canoes together and stringing up a makeshift sail if the breeze cooperated.

Talking with Sue after the girls are piled in their tents to giggle is an unexpected pleasure. When I was twelve, Sue was my junior counselor. Now, we have returned to this place at the same time, as adults. As a child, I liked Sue; I admired her and wanted to be like her. Maybe I was a little crushed out on her. As an adult, I like her still, for different reasons. We share an absurd sense of humor; we compete for the best one-liners. We love to breathe the still night air. Maybe I am still crushed out on her.

The trip that Sue and I lead together is called the Upper Mississagi, named for one of the rivers we will travel on. It's a six-day trip—mostly rivers, only three long portages and some decent rapids. The first three days have been long and demanding, but nothing unusual has happened. We have run the rapids without swamping. Our girls have complained that we didn't bring enough food for our third day. Bree speaks for them; she is their leader. She is pretty and shares her CARE packages. "We're still hungry. Can't we make some more to eat?" I look guiltily into what's left of my bowl of pasta and freeze-dried meat sauce. I am still hungry too. "If we make tomorrow's food today, we won't have enough to eat tomorrow," Sue explains reasonably. Bree doesn't look happy.

"Tell you what," Sue says, rummaging through her pack, "I think we have extra pancake mix. You girls can mix up some pancakes if you want." She shoots Bree a warning glare. "You be sure that everyone gets an even amount, OK?" She tosses a plastic bag full of beige powder to Bree. "Bring what you don't use back to me. And clean up after yourselves."

The fourth day is our bad day. Sally and Sandy swamp on the Upper Mississagi River. Sandy drags herself up on the riverbank, coughing up half the river, but she is OK. Sally is wearing the wrong boots. They are too heavy, and they get caught in the V between two rocks. Sally is face down in the water when this happens, and the water is fast. She can't fight the rapids to come up for air, and she can't release her boot. Sue is in the lead canoe and has eddied out at the bottom of the rapids. The girls scream to Sue. The riverbank is rocky, and it's difficult for her to run.

I jump into the river and manage to scull my way (feet first) over to where Sally is trapped. She has long hair. I grab it and pull her head back. She is choking and sputtering. I am terrified. The rapids are strong. I can't release her boot or hold her head up much longer before the water sweeps me away, and Sally is face down again.

Sue has managed to jump in after me. When I pull myself out of the river, I can see that Sue has pulled Sally's head out of the water again. Sue has grabbed the back of Sally's orange life vest. Her grip is better than mine. She lasts a few seconds longer before the water pounds her off the rock that she is braced against.

I scream for someone to get a rope as I do my best to run back up the bank. Someone hands me the end of a rope, and I jump back into the river, this time thrashing my way over to where Sally is drowning. I reach Sally, but the rope is not taut. No one remembered to hang on to the other end of it.

I release the rope and do my best to keep her head above water again for as long as I can. Sue is right behind me this time, and I am swept off the rock just as she arrives. Sue ties a rope around Sally.

The girls have held onto it this time, and seven of them pull back, allowing Sue to release Sally's boot just before she is swept downstream for the last time. The girls drag Sally to shore and pull her out of the river. Sally lies on her stomach, coughing and making sucking, gasping sounds. I eddy out and crawl back up the riverbank.

Sally is still vomiting when I arrive on the scene. "Get a sleeping bag," I scream. "Now, goddammit."

The girls' eyes are huge, terrified. They stare at Sally, paralyzed. I grab a backpack from the nearest canoe and tear at the bungee cords that attach the sleeping bag to the pack. I wrap the sleeping bag around Sally and ease her into a sitting position. I wrap my legs around her and pull her close to my chest, muttering what I hope are comforting phrases like, "It's OK now, you're safe. You'll be fine."

Sue arrives and starts giving orders. We still have two canoes that need to get through these rapids. We will camp at the bottom of the rapids tonight. No one volunteers to run these canoes. Sue turns to Bree. "Can't you and Liz take these two canoes through?" Bree refuses. Bree's fear makes Sue angry. "Fine. Then you can just carry them to the bottom."

I look up from where I am holding Sally. "You and I can run them, Sue. There's no path along this river, and the rocks are slippery." I am covered in snot and tears and watery puke. "The girls will help Sally walk down to where we'll camp. We can take care of the boats."

It takes a long time to get organized that night. Everyone is silent. Sandy and Sally's canoe ran over a waterfall with their packs in it. The boat is damaged beyond my ability to repair it. Their packs are lost. We zip sleeping bags together. Three young girls fit snugly in two bags that are zipped together. Sue and I plan for the food shortage. The food that Sally packed was eaten on our first night, but Sandy was carrying breakfast and lunch for tomorrow. We still have extra pancake mix. Sue sends some of the girls to gather blueberries. Three of us go fishing in the waterfall the next morning. We catch six walleye, but it isn't any fun. Sue cooks it in extra oil to give us fat in our breakfast. That night and the next day we eat fish and pancakes. We are too sick and tired to do much more.

That night, after the girls are in their tents, Sue and I talk about how we can continue the trip after what happened. "The girls are scared of rapids now." Sue looks glum. "I'm not sure what to do about it. Since their boat isn't going anywhere, Sally will have to duff with you and Bree. Sandy can duff with me and Melissa in the lead canoe."

"I'm not sure it's such a good idea to make them duff. That's admitting defeat. They should be paddling—like getting back on a horse after it throws you," I tell her.

Sue considers this and nods. "Maybe. But I'm not going to force either of them to do anything that they're not ready for." Sue gropes for the topo. "Tomorrow looks like an easy day. It looks as if there's probably lots of fast water but only one set of big rapids, and we won't hit them until late in the day when the girls have had time to settle."

"Which is exactly why they both should paddle first thing in the morning, while the water's still calm." I am feeling stubborn.

"Look, we barely survived a tragedy today. We should all take it easy tomorrow, especially Sandy and Sally."

"But Sue, we can't let them just quit and give up, not out here. The potential for tragedy is why we're here in the first place. Otherwise we would just sit in our safe little homes being fat and happy and eating pizza and watching TV."

"If that's why you're out here, then you probably shouldn't be." Sue climbs into her sleeping bag and zips it shut. "Fine. Sandy and Sally will paddle together, but I want Bree to duff for them so that they can switch around. Which means you'll have to paddle with Katie and Patrice."

"Are you crazy? There's no way those two blabbermouths can paddle together. Especially if I have to put up with them."

"Look, it was your idea to have Sandy and Sally paddle to-gether. They need Bree's support, and Katie and Patrice need a strong partner. That leaves you." Sue flops over in her sleeping bag, ending our discussion.

The next day passes slowly. Katie is a lousy paddler, and

Patrice complains constantly when she's not discussing boys with Katie or talking about Pepsi or m&ms and all the junk food she plans to imbibe when we return to our base camp.

The sun is beaming high and hot when Sue pulls up and announces, "We're going to do a little experiment. We're going to separate and stagger our canoes in ten-minute intervals. I don't want you to do any paddling, except to steer. I want you to drift. Try not to talk or make noise. Just listen to the wilderness. The point is to get a feel for what it's like to be completely alone out here." She looks at Sally. "Of course, you won't actually be alone. We'll be within shouting distance of each other. If we happen to hit any surprise rapids, I'll pull out at the top and wait for everyone to catch up. We'll float for about an hour and a half this way and then stop for lunch."

Katie and Patrice and I are in the rear canoe, so we have to wait fifty minutes before we can leave. The canoes ahead of us pull out every ten minutes. Finally, it's our turn. Katie and Patrice are still talking about clothes and food. I ask them to be quiet. Patrice splashes Katie, and Katie dumps a paddleful of water on Patrice. I tell them to be quiet. Patrice starts singing a camp song about a beaver dam, and she and Katie decide to make up a dirty lyrics version. They try to harmonize to their new version of the song.

I have had it. I scream at them. "Shut up. Just shut up. I've been listening to you two yammer all morning. Five minutes. I want complete silence for five minutes, that's all. Just five minutes. Then you can talk all you want for the rest of the day. I don't think that's too much to ask. Is that a deal?"

They agree, but it's hard for them. They snuffle and snort and suppress giggles as if one of them has just farted in church. Katie mugs at Patrice as if having to be quiet is causing her great pain. Three minutes becomes four. Their noise subsides. Four minutes becomes five. They have clammed up completely. I check my watch and give them an extra minute, enjoying the silence. Mosquitos hum. Leaves rustle. I dip my paddle once in a while. I am content.

"Fine," I tell them, "you can talk now." They burst into giggles. Patrice tries to talk about boys again, but her conversation fades. Katie says something about Madonna, but she lapses into silence.

An amazing thing has happened. When you stop and listen, the wilderness is a vacuum of sound. It's almost like a negative sound, a silence that is so profound that it is almost as imposing as loud noise. It's so absent that it's present. And we find ourselves not listening to it, I suppose, but somehow being drawn into it. I can't explain except to describe its effects on these two chatterboxes. They try to jump-start their conversation three or four times, but the words fade into the silence. We spend the next hour in silence, yet we are alert, on edge, listening. Katie's head is cocked to one side expectantly. Patrice looks relaxed and almost thoughtful. We float quietly downstream.

The spell is broken as we approach the cluster of canoes that has pulled up ahead of us. We hear laughter and the rapid-fire speech of girls. Katie and Patrice wave to their friends and resume talking as soon as we are within sight of the others. I catch Sue's eye, and she smiles at me before giving the girls instructions for making lunch.

We hit rapids in the afternoon. On the first big set, Sally walks the river bank and meets us at the bottom. The second set she runs with Sue and Bree.

Katie and Patrice and I portage our canoe over the two miles to Lake Lauzon without any arguing or complaining. We teach everybody their dirty lyrics version of the beaver dam song and manage a quavering four-part harmony. I am happy to be paddling on a lake again. I don't care if we have to face the infamous Lauzon headwinds in the morning.

The dead air between me and Sue evaporates. That night, I tell her about my experience with Katie and Patrice. She looks smug as I finish telling my tale, so I whack her with my sleeping bag roll as I say, "You expected something like that to happen. How did you know?"

Sue shrugs. "I didn't, really. We were both worked up after what happened to Sally. I wanted to remind you that we're out here to learn how to live, not just how to survive. So we had an easy day today. It happens sometimes, even out here in the big bad Canadian wilderness." Sue flops over in her sleeping bag and sighs. "This time tomorrow we'll be sucking down those big brown bottles of warm Molson and telling stories about our trip to anyone who will listen. I can't wait."

"Me neither," I mumble, executing a magnificent elephant roll of my own. "And while we're at it, maybe we could order pizza and watch a little TV."

ONE STEP AT A TIME

Lydia B. Goetze

I BACKED OUR ANCIENT VW Beetle against the snow drift near the old Glen House and left it facing downhill, ready for a push start when we came back. We quickly shouldered our forty-pound packs full of winter camping gear and trudged off into the Great Gulf Wilderness. Soon we changed to snowshoes to break trail in a foot of fresh snow. I had come to these mountains every other weekend all winter with Chris—my climbing partner, best friend and husband. Lured by the visual beauty of sparkling frost feathers and of snow plumes that veiled peaks in windy mystery, we also sought the steep slopes and wind-scoured ridges of New Hampshire's White Mountains as a training ground for bigger mountains.

We camped in gale-force winds above tree line to test Chris's new tent designs for expeditions to Alaska and the Himalayas. We learned the tricks of staying warm and comfortable for days at temperatures most climbers met only high on McKinley or Everest. We used our homemade aluminum snowshoes—it was 1967 and there were no commercially available ones then—to penetrate isolated valleys and kick steps up steep slopes to tree line where we could grapple with the wind, the cold and the ice. We loved testing ourselves against nature in the extreme. And each month we looked forward to the Mount Washington Observatory weather summary that let us calibrate ourselves against the coldest days and the strongest winds these mountains could dish out.

Chris looked a lot younger and softer than he was. Sturdily built, of average height, he had an unassuming manner that caught people unaware. He'd often been told by others who considered themselves older and wiser, that what he wanted to do in the mountains was impossible. His response was a pleasant smile that told his listener he was taking the advice to heart. But his friends knew that smile said, "You won't be able to dismiss me like that when I've done it, though, will you?"

Time after time, he did. As a college student, he'd set long distance records in the White Mountains and made several first ascents in the West. The first summer I knew him, he and six other Harvard students put a new route up Mount McKinley's Wickersham Wall. His postcard to me after the climb simply said, "Hope you didn't read the papers. We're back alive and it was a terrific climb. We all made the summit." (*The Boston Globe* had them all dead for several days before they were spotted alive and well, much higher on the mountain than expected. Fortunately, I hadn't seen the paper.)

Chris decided I'd make a climber one winter morning when I pulled on my woolen pants, soaked from hiking in thirty-three degree rain the day before. I growled, "I wish they were frozen. They'd be more comfortable." After that I'd gotten hooked on mountains from a summer of climbing in Alaska with Chris and two other men. For me, that expedition, which included several first ascents, was the Great Adventure of my life so far. (My parents saw it as the craziest, most dangerous honeymoon they'd ever heard of.)

Chris' way of bringing me up to speed as a climber was simply to take me climbing. He assumed I was bright, practical, observant and interested in my own safety. His laconic approach, common among climbers in those years, would be completely unacceptable by today's standards. After showing me how to belay and set up a climb, he led off, trusting both of us not to make any big mistakes. On my first steep slope of hard snow, where we had crampons and ice axes but no rope, he stopped halfway up and pointed. "See those rocks down there? If you fall, it's curtains. Arrange not to."

After several winters of backpacking and climbing together, we knew what to expect of the mountains and each other. On this trip, our progress was slow, perhaps one mile an hour, in the new snow. With our snowshoes and heavy packs, we waddled like toddlers in wet diapers. The first day of a winter trip was always harder work and less interesting.

At twenty degrees, the day was warm for mid-February. A few chickadees were feeding and chirping in the spruces. I startled a spruce grouse which startled me in turn as it whirred to the safety of deeper woods. Looking for things to break the tedium as I slogged along, I savored the tart taste of a spruce needle accidentally chewed in a mouthful of snow.

Gradually the miles peeled away beneath our persistence. We crossed and recrossed a frozen brook, sidehilled along its banks and progressed over the series of small moraines that ancient glaciers had left in the valley. The day unravelled in a series of companionable silences and conversations. By dark we had reached our campsite, the wooded glen at the base of the steep ice pitch that would take us above tree line in the morning.

The next day the thermometer read twenty-six below zero when we crawled out of our tent. It dropped another degree while we broke camp and continued to drop as we worked our way up the steep, icy headwall. We splayed our cramponed feet and lumbered in our bulky, warm clothes like fat grizzlies in a mountain berry patch. This half mile of trail had the reputation of being the most difficult trail in the White Mountains in summer because of its steep rocks. Now it was a blue-green wall of ice streaked with bleeding dirty-yellow stains. Every few steps one of us would have to pause to chop a foothold, wielding the ice axe surely and efficiently. Each pitch of ice was short, and we didn't bother with the protection of a belay in case we fell. I tried to ignore what would happen if I *did* fall.

As we crested the top of the headwall, a freight train of arctic air came barrelling down on us out of the northwest. There were no trees to break its fury. We consulted quickly and agreed we could make it across the half mile above tree line to descend the Osgood Ridge. This was our favorite high route out of the Presidential Range with views of the White Mountains in all directions. Chris started off.

I followed, inching along the icy ridge, bracing myself against the boisterous wind. Snow swirled high in the air, obscuring the trail beyond the next cairn. Most people stagger when the wind blows thirty miles per hour, but an experienced climber is comfortable with winds in the fifties or sixties. I was unnerved as I picked my way among the rocks, placing each cramponed foot carefully and using my ice axe as a third leg. When a particularly heavy gust came through, I crouched low. In the several winters I'd been climbing and camping above tree line in the White Mountains, I had never before seen a wind like this. Suddenly I was hurled horizontally and thrown backward against a huge rock so that I faced the frigid gale. Panic surged to my lips, but I choked it back, telling myself to calm down and move more carefully across the exposed ridge. As I started out again, I was distracted when my hat slid down over my eyebrows inside my down hood. I shoved it up hurriedly, feeling hot, claustrophobic waves of nervous sweat break out on my skin. And then I was picked up by the wind and was rolling, whirling in a jumble of body and snow across the rock-strewn terrace. Fifty yards later, I hit a big glacial boulder and stopped. *I* stopped, but the world was still doing cartwheels. When it came to a halt, I rolled over cautiously and tried to stand, but a wave of pain shot through my leg and it buckled. Then I noticed that my right hand was bare. My mitten shell was waving in the breeze, tied sturdily to a string so it couldn't blow away, but the wool mitten was gone. I hunched my back to the wind and jammed the already numb hand inside my down parka and into my armpit for warmth. What had happened? What next? Dumbly I looked around for answers. Chris was nowhere to be seen in the blowing snow. I had no time or energy for anger. I felt stupid, but I knew I had to do something fast, or I'd get frostbite or become hypothermic. It was the coldest day of the winter, and I was hurt, alone and getting cold. I took off my pack and fumbled numbly for a spare mitten. Suddenly Chris materialized.

"Let's go," he said. "It's just a short push across to the shelter of the trees."

"Hurt my knee. Can't do it."

"Come on. It's not far."

"I can't stand up. It really hurts. I have to get below the trees. That way." I pointed straight down the steep snow slope beside the ice pitch we had climbed. "First I need a mitten."

He handed me his and put his hand in his pocket. "I figured you might be in trouble when I found this." He waved the head of my shattered ice axe, which I hadn't even missed. He watched skeptically while I sidled awkwardly, like a wounded crab, on two hands and one foot, inching my way over to the tree-studded hard snow. As soon as the slope was steep enough, I slid, grabbing any handy treelet within my grasp. He followed.

When we reached the tiny glen where we'd camped the night before, we assessed the situation. I concentrated on my knee, trying to figure out whether it would be OK in a few minutes or whether it was really hurt. I tried standing on it again and gasped with pain, but thought an ace bandage might make walking possible. I pictured loose fragments of slippery cartilage sliding in all the wrong places inside my joint. I dreaded what would happen if they got stuck. Watching me suck in my breath as I dropped my heavy wool pants to strap on the ace bandage, Chris grimaced.

"Do you really think you can walk? We can set up the tent here, and I can put you in the sleeping bag and go for help. We can get back in by tomorrow morning, I'm sure." It was mid-morning now; that would mean twenty-four hours alone in the winter woods. The day before, we'd broken trail all day on snowshoes in new snow, five long miles up into the Great Gulf Wilderness where no one else went in winter. We came here sometimes just to avoid the climbers who were beginning to test themselves against the more obvious peaks, and we had never yet found the trail broken ahead of us. Nobody would come along by chance. If we needed help, he'd better get moving so he'd be out by dark. He could organize a rescue and come back at first light. Another needle of pain shot up my leg as I tried to stand on it again, and I hesitated.

We'd done a lot of winter climbing together, just the two of us, and we knew and accepted the risks it entailed. We knew that people were being urged to register for their climbs and to go in groups of at least four. We continued to climb alone in a solitary protest against the increased regulation that was coming to this last scrap of wilderness in the East. We hadn't counted on coming up with the short end of the stick, though.

Thinking about the night ahead of me, I remembered a tale from the first ascent of K-2, the second highest mountain in the world. Freaked out by the extreme conditions, Charlie Houston tried to cut his way out of the tent with a jackknife one night high on the mountain. I was afraid I too would go bonkers with the pain and do something stupid enough to get me frozen to death if I spent the night alone. I couldn't bear it. The pain of walking was better than being left alone. "No," I said gritting my teeth. "I'll be OK. Let's try it. I think I can make it if you take some stuff out of my pack and break trail."

My toes were numb now, and Chris fidgeted to stay warm. I knew we had to get moving. I strapped a snowshoe on my good leg, put my much-lightened pack on my back and tried to stride out, using my partner's ice axe and my other snowshoe like canes. It was hopelessly clumsy, but at least I didn't fall through the knee-deep snow. If I didn't try to bend my hurt knee much, it was feasible to make some progress. I'd heard that when men got badly injured in battle, some natural anesthesia came into play and made them less aware of the pain until they could treat it. Sometimes they accomplished amazing feats in spite of their injuries. I hoped the same thing would work for me.

I stomped along mechanically, putting one foot in front of the other, carefully watching the placement of my feet. My mind wandered to other times, other places. Sometimes the roaring of the wind reminded me of storms at sea or the wind in the pines outside Heidi's alpine hut. Sometimes I pretended it was summer, and I could skip from rock to rock. Or I made the bulky snowshoe and the stiff injured leg slide on phantom skis, effortlessly gliding along the trail.

I tried to let go of my concern about how far, how fast and simply walk on. I'd learned on long hikes out of the woods that it helped to let my mind go into "Hindu" time. I imagined time as a circle, cycling and recycling, instead of flying straight on like an arrow. Chris could keep track of how far we went and how fast we were going. My job was just to keep going if I were not to spend the sub-zero night alone in the woods. No matter how far I walked, this possibility would haunt me until I was out.

Once we stopped at the top of the terminal moraine and gazed back at the mountains. Plumes of blowing snow trailed off peaks capped with those weird lenticular clouds that speak of high winds. Safely down among the trees, it was hard to believe it had been blowing nearly eighty miles per hour up there. Although we knew it was very cold, too cold even for the snow to squeak, we had to take the temperature again to confirm that it really was thirty below. It didn't seem so bad when we kept moving, except that it was too cold for my nose to run. The mucus glopped up and glued my nostrils shut. I worried that my toes might freeze, but I could still wiggle them inside my boots. I kept checking. I didn't want to lose any of them. I knew mountaineers who had lost toes. Think how ugly bare toeless feet would look!

Chris made me stop every hour or so. While we rested, he offered me snacks of gorp and drinks of water, and made cheery conversation. He looked me over carefully, and asked whether I could still feel my toes. I wiggled them dutifully. I knew in some abstract way that he was watching out for me, and that this solicitude was almost unheard of for him, but I didn't have the energy to examine my feelings.

Our progress along the rough trail was excruciatingly slow, and it had taken the whole previous day to pack in. After three hours of walking, we had covered just over half the distance to the road. I had to marshal all my physical and emotional strength to keep moving fast enough to make it out of the woods before nightfall. I clung to that desperate hope, dreading the thought of the long, dark, cold night alone, with creepy noises and pain and no one to reassure me. But no matter how far or how long I walked, I still might not make it.

What I had to do was to pick up one foot, and the next, and the next and the next. I had to make a trail of hobbling footprints, mile after snowy mile, to the road and the car and the warm ride home. Never before had I needed to take my life so literally one step at a time.

The sun set. It set early during northern February days, but we were on the flat now, not more than a half mile from the car. We had come almost six hours through the snow and the cold, and we would make it! I finally knew I wouldn't have to spend the night alone. I wanted to rest, to sleep, to have someone else make decisions and take care of me. I hoped the car would start. It did, this time without a push. And the heater worked. I fell luxuriously, soundly asleep, letting my guard down at last, oblivious to the dull throbbing that continued as I slept.

The next day, I got my leg x-rayed, expecting a torn carti-lage. Wielding what looked like a giant turkey baster with a big hypodermic needle on the business end, the doctor sucked vol-umes of blood-tainted fluid out of my bulging knee. Then he told me the big, weight-bearing femur was broken. When the swelling went down in a few days, they'd put me in a cast for a month. If I was lucky that would be it. But probably there would be a knee operation, too, to remove fragments of loose cartilage. I'd be a real swinger on those crutches before I was through. But my toes were fine. As it turned out, I couldn't feel anything in them for two months, but they weren't frostbitten. Just a little skin peeled off the hand that had lost its mitten. I was lucky.

The experience took the edge off my hubris, but it was not until a few years later that I was really tested on what I had learned. Just as our younger daughter started school, Chris was diagnosed with the last stages of a brain tumor. This time I was handed both roles. First I became the encouraging companion to walk step by step with him as he faced his pain, although he still had to walk alone into the cold, dark night. Most days we went for long rambles in the woods or by the sea, trying to do a life-time of talking while we could. I remembered and tried to return the patience he had shown with me. After he died, I had to re-learn how to walk step by step back into my own life, in spite of my grief and pain. And I had to take our two young daughters by the hand to walk with me. Knowing I had done it once made me able to accomplish it again.

*E*YE OF THE MEADOW

Carolyn Kremers

These races are difficult and hazardous under the best of conditions. You will be entirely on your own in some of the most remote regions in North America. No help will be available; no rescue can be anticipated. The appropriate knowledge regarding glaciers, avalanches, crossing and paddling major rivers, bear and other animal hazards, illness, injury, gear failure or loss, self-rescue, bad weather, hypothermia, frostbite, extremely difficult terrain, and the like must have been acquired before entering. If you choose to risk your life in the wilderness of Alaska by participating in this race, that is up to you. Your injuries or death are not our responsibility.

AFTER READING THE RELEASE several times, I hesitate, sign it, then tuck it into an envelope with my hundred-dollar entry fee. I lick a stamp and press it into place.

Months later, I stand on the high bank of Jack Creek and watch Dan feel his way through roiling cold water. He wades about twenty yards into the middle, to mid-thigh, then stumbles and goes down; his eyes widen as the fifty-five-pound pack on his back threatens to pin his head underwater. Now I wish I could turn back.

I keep my eyes riveted on Dan's blond hair and yellow pack as the current sweeps him downstream. I watch to see if he will right himself, my voice muttering below the creek's roar, "Dan, stand up, please stand up." I can see his strong arms pulling, struggling to keep his head above water, straining for the opposite bank. Just as I am about to drop my pack and run downstream to try to help, he lunges to his feet like a dripping mammoth and clambers out of the rocky stream onto the other side. Now it is my turn.

If this were not the first stream crossing of the race, I wouldn't feel so chicken. We have trained hard for three months, running 10Ks and a half marathon on hilly roads, bicycling fifty-five miles in Denali National Park, testing our raft on the Nenana River, backpacking over a treacherous talus mountain pass, hiking and camping in rain and mosquitoes. I know that the stream and river crossings are going to be one of the scariest parts of this race. I've done some canoeing and basic sailing, and I'm a capable swimmer, but I flunked junior life-saving, and I don't usually go out in a boat without a life jacket—on.

One of my most panicky childhood memories is of stinging chlorinated water splashing into my mouth and down my nose when I was eight, as my mother—a certified swimming instructor and lifeguard—held my head between her iron hands in the pool at Colorado Woman's College, "teaching" me to float on my back. I was skinny and sank everytime she let go, my arms flailing in the water.

"You'll never learn if you don't try," she kept growling, grasping my head and flipping me onto my back again.

I have complete confidence in Dan's expertise in the outdoors. I would not have considered entering this race otherwise. He homesteaded in Alaska in the early seventies, hauling ninety-pound loads of food staples and building materials on his back across thirteen miles of marshy tundra to the lake he had picked out. In winter, he traps in a remote area in the Mentasta Mountains, often camping at forty degrees below zero. Of Swedish descent, he is six feet tall, hardy and weatherproof.

One blizzardy March day, my second year in Tununak, I received a letter from Dan. "I'm planning to do a long wilderness race this summer in the Wrangell Mountains. It's called the Alaska Mountain Wilderness Classic. I want you to do it with me. I think you can handle it, or I wouldn't invite you. You'll have to start getting in shape for it now, though. I'll send you more info and a list of the gear you'll need."

I was surprised. Dan had worked in Tununak the previous summer and fall as the construction foreman on the addition to the school. We had become good friends, running and snowmachining on weekends, taking walks, visiting people in the village, stalking musk ox with our cameras. When Dan left at Christmas, though, I had assumed we would never see each other again. Now he was suggesting an activity that would throw our lives together in an environment even more challenging and unpredictable than the village. And more binding. Did I want that?

The information Dan sent with his next letter was daunting:

> *The seventh annual Alaska Mountain Wilderness Classic will cover 160 miles, from the end of the Nabesna road south of Tok, over the Wrangell Mountains in Wrangell-St. Elias National Park and Preserve, to the historic mining town of McCarthy. There will be some old pack trails to follow, like the precipitous Goat Trail, which winds its way up Chitistone Pass between massive glaciers and 16,000 foot peaks and then down to Chitistone Gorge. But most of the course will be cross-country. There will be eight major stream and river crossings and four mountain passes to climb. At the race midpoint, the nearest road lies 75 miles away. The only point to drop out is 55 miles into the race at the settlement of Chisana, where a mail plane lands twice a week. Two tiny landing strips exist deep in the wilderness at Upper Skolai Lake and at Glacier Creek, but what condition they will be in and whether a small plane might happen along and be signalled from the ground in the event of an emergency is unpredictable.*

"We won't be aiming for speed, of course," Dan wrote. "Just to finish. I drove down to Dot Lake and talked at length with last year's winner. He says there are always some rookies who enter these races, besides the hard-core regulars. Every year more people enter and that's what they want: to widen the field." I thought about it. I had already made arrangements to begin graduate school in Fairbanks in the fall, and I was ready for some serious wilderness hiking. Arctic tundra and the Bering Sea had seeped into my blood in Tununak, but even so, I craved mountains. In the village, the nearest tree was a hundred twenty-five miles away, the nearest tall mountain twice that far.

Sometimes a person just has to dive in. "OK," I wrote back, "I'm game. But you'll have to help me psych myself for the water crossings. I don't feel real good about that part."

•

Now I don't feel good at all. Jack Creek is only our first stream crossing, and already Dan is soaking wet and I'm having second thoughts about the whole race. But here he is, coming back across to get my pack, more sure-footed now without his own.

"Guess I don't have to worry anymore about getting wet," he says with half a grin. Before I know it, he's back a third time, firmly grasping my arm above the elbow ("Ready?"), walking across—solid as a rock—with me on the upstream side.

There's no more time or room for dread. My legs push tentatively through the powerful current, worming into footholds on the invisible bottom. I can feel shifting gravel and big slippery rocks underneath the Vibram soles of my Cordura and leather hiking boots. Some rocks give way at the touch of my toes, making a hollow drumming sound as they tumble toward Dan. My mind is on automatic pilot, though, because I know it's better to keep up my momentum than to stop and think too much. I plant one foot and then the next, alternating with Dan. He seems to be going fast—as fast as the water—and I'm afraid he'll get ahead of me, and then I'll lose my balance.

"Not too fast, OK?" I try to say loudly but not too loudly, as the water rushes over my knees and then halfway up my thighs, plotting to knock me over. Dan seems to oblige.

"Geez, this is cold!" I yell, suddenly remembering my old karate teacher and how much it helped to yell the first time I broke a board. We get past the middle and wade out as suddenly as we waded in. I scramble up the bank and look back. If he can cross this thing five times, I can do it once.

We slog for two hours through calf-deep marsh, finally reaching the Nabesna River. Far on the other side, we can see the dots of two racers hauling out their yellow rafts. Everyone else seems to have disappeared, having floated the Nabesna on down to Cooper Creek or else crossed ahead of us.

Since I have little rafting experience, we are sharing one raft and have planned that Dan will ferry back and forth. From his pack, he unties a stuffsack smaller than his sleeping bag's and spreads its contents on the sandy grass. Our four-pound Sherpa pack raft is three and a half feet by six feet and can carry up to 385 pounds. It cost Dan two hundred and fifty dollars. With it, we can cross fast and deep rivers like this one, braid by braid. Without it, we're marooned. We each unplug a red air valve, thrust it between our lips and start blowing.

When the magical raft is inflated, Dan sets it on the river, and we lift his pack inside. He climbs in with the seven-foot kayak paddle, winks and says, "See you later." I push him off, giving him up to the grip of the brown current.

He maneuvers the raft with powerful strokes, downstream and across the first braid, then rams into a sandy bar, dumps his pack, walks upstream, puts in again and floats back down to me. I stow my camera safely inside my pack in a waterproof bag and settle into the bow with my pack between my legs. Dan gives us a push, easing himself aboard—half on top of my pack, the paddle poised—and we're off.

I try not to fix my attention on the roar of the water or the speed with which we streak down the river, shoreline receding in a blur. Rushing along backward while looking squarely at Dan's powerful hands around the bright blue paddle and the intense concentration in his eyes, I try only to relax my tense stomach muscles, breathe deeply, and enjoy the ride. It should, after all, be romantic to be ferried safely across a wild Alaskan river by a man like Dan. I have spent at least twenty-five hours practicing in this raft with him, even paddling sometimes, and I know that this is a surprisingly sturdy craft. It floats even when full of water, and the bottom is made of tough Air Force P-16 nylon which has withstood even the sharpest rocks—so far. I should be able to enjoy this.

I try it. I laugh out loud at the thrill of riding a live, hungry river. But inside, an old voice intones, "Be careful. Rivers are dangerous. You could drown. Be careful, be careful, be careful."

After we cross the third braid, I watch Dan maneuver the fourth, then walk in shallow water far up along the opposite gravel bar. He hauls the raft on its nylon rope behind him, getting ready to float back down to me.

At last, my mind is no longer inside my body. It is outside, somewhere above all this, watching and—wisely—not talking. Dan looks like he is only an inch tall. Suddenly he sinks halfway down into the water, then scrambles up again.

"I didn't stumble," he says, when I ask him about it later. "That was a quicksand hole."

Dan ferries the river braids twelve times, and finally we reach the far side and the end of our first major river crossing. We shout and laugh at each other and the raft, wring out our wet boots, socks, shorts and polypro long underwear, sit on the overturned raft and spread out lunch of crackers and cheese, gorp and yogurt-covered almonds. The three-mile-wide riverbed is bounded on both sides by rocky mountain ranges, with higher snowy mountains in the distance, and the sky is as blue as an Eskimo dress. My watch says crossing the river took us two hours. We munch and take long drinks of water, then nap a few minutes in the bright sun.

Seven hours later, after difficult hiking through bumpy tundra, tangled alder thickets and curtains of buzzing mosquitoes, I am very tired. Occasionally, I have glimpsed carpets of moss, mushrooms, ferns and wildflowers hidden beneath dense alders. We have not taken time to sink into them, though. Now, with dusk coming on, we hear rustling in a tree. Dan spots something up in the branches. Quietly he slips off his pack and pulls out a pistol. I hear two dry shots, see him reach down into the brush. Then he curls my hand around the warm, feathery neck of a spruce grouse.

I have never held a dead wild bird before, not even in the village, though I have seen many. This is a beautiful creature, layered with soft white, black, and silver feathers, a scarlet comb above its eye. I am amazed at its life and sudden death, Dan's sure aim, my lack of experience, my detachment. I know that we will probably eat this bird. I am too tired to think about it. All I can think is how the Eskimos say that an animal offers itself up to a hunter and that the hunter should be thankful, happy and full of respect. I feel respect. I also feel so exhausted I know I will fall into a dead sleep if I sit on the pillowy tundra for even an instant. I'm ready to quit for the day, but I won't let myself say so. My watch says seven-thirty. Two hours later, Dan finally stops and says, "Let's camp here."

We pitch our tent on a dry bit of rocky streambed. The Whisperlite stove and I cook chicken ramen soup as fast as we can, while Dan goes downstream to clean the grouse and wrap it in foil for baking in coals in the morning. We eat silently, huddled together on two rocks before a sturdy fire, then crawl into our sleeping bags. I pull one of our nine topographical maps out of a Ziploc bag and we trace an approximation of the race route with our fingers. Which creek is Cooper Creek? How soon can we reach it tomorrow? Wouldn't it have been easier to look for the pack trail down along the river instead of heading cross-country like this? Is this shortcut going to bring us out in the right place? Where are all the other racers? How could twenty-two people just disappear?

I don't ask Dan any of these questions, because I know that he does not have the answers. Anyway, what's done is done, as the Eskimos say. We figure we've covered about seventeen miles. We need to make twenty-six a day if we want to finish in six days. Other than that, we've already agreed that speed is not a priority. Like most of the twenty-four people in the race, our goal is simply to finish. We have at least six more days' worth of food, in addition to Dan's pistol.

We fold up the map and snuggle down into our bags, holding each other tightly. I'm proud of the water crossings I've conquered and the way I've ridden out my fear and exhaustion. And I am happy. This race is pushing me to my limits, physically and psychologically. Drifting into sleep, my mind registers one more thought. I have never trusted anyone like this before.

Midmorning the next day, we reach Cooper Creek. The map shows some sort of trail along the top but we can't find it, so we descend and follow the creekbed. Wet boots blistered my feet yesterday, and now the straps on my forty-five-pound pack pinch my shoulders into knots. I don't say anything, but my pace slows and I fall farther and farther behind as we pick our way over the rocks. Finally, Dan stops to wait for me. When I catch up to him and pull my concentration from my feet to his face, he says, "How's it going? You look tired. Why don't you let me carry part of your load?"

I protest at first, feeling guilty. When he insists, though, I give him the red food bag, lightening my pack to thirty-five pounds and increasing his to sixty-five. Now I understand why the experienced racers were throwing things out of their packs in the rain, an hour before the start, trying to get them down to thirty pounds, thirty-five max. I know that some race veterans are not carrying a tent or a stove, and their food consists mainly of store-bought protein bars. Several are travelling with a minimum of survival gear and almost nothing for emergencies. Almost everyone has a Sherpa pack raft like ours, while one team of three—including the only other female racer besides myself—shares the parts of an Ally-Pac collapsible canoe.

One ruddy fellow with blond dreadlocks and a black arrow painted across his white sun-blocked nose pops into my consciousness. Everybody called him Crazy Chuck. He carried touring skis and a parasail, three pounds of cheese and three pounds of chocolate, half a foam pad and a candle. When the gun went off at the start, he headed up Jack Creek instead of down, intending to hike and ski up the Nabesna Glacier, then sail out over the Stairway Icefall on the other side and walk into McCarthy. He hoped to cut eighty-five miles off the race route by parasailing and to finish hours, maybe even days, ahead of anyone else. I wonder if he has jumped off yet—and if he has, what happened.

Cooper Creek pounds at the bottom of a rocky canyon. As we climb higher, the creekbed narrows, increasing the velocity of the noisy water. Finally, we come to a dead end where the water scrapes the canyon wall, and we are forced to wade to the other side. The creek is numbing and fast, and we can't see the rocks on the bottom because the water is filled with glacial silt. Sometimes the water comes only up to our thighs and we're able to grope our way against the current along the canyon wall, feeling for handholds and footholds, hugging the rock, carefully working our way to the other side of the rushing water. Other times, we grab arms above the elbows as we did in Jack Creek and feel our way across together, me on the upstream side so that Dan can stagger his steps and try to block me if I fall. I teeter with my pack like a tightrope walker, while Dan seems to stand rooted among the slippery stones.

Each time we step together into the ferocious water, I try not to hold my breath. I know it's important to breathe naturally and avoid tensing up. It's like playing the flute. I have to allow my body to do what it knows how to do—give it air and space—and pay no attention to the voices inside my brain, conspiring to paralyze me like the freezing water.

Once, in mid-stream when the water is almost waist-deep and the current particularly powerful, I feel several rocks give way under my boots and hear them clatter toward Dan. We lose our balance at the same time, and everything switches into slow motion. I can feel both our bodies totter under the heavy packs, throwing our careful choreography out of kilter.

The current seizes its chance and begins to push all four of our feet out from under us, as if plucking legs off a spider. I sense a strong will taking over from somewhere inside me, though. *Don't give in. Stay standing.*

I refuse to let Dan's arm slip out of my grasp. My right foot stops sliding on the uneven bottom and wedges itself into a hole. Just as I regain my balance, so does Dan.

"Steady now," he says.

Soon we are safe on the other side. Adrenalin is shooting through my bloodstream. I gasp while Dan smiles.

"Good work, partner," he says.

Just after sunset we reach the top of the pass and look back at where we have come from. Far below us, the creek widens into forest and empties into the Nabesna River. I stop to take a picture and notice by the way Dan stands waiting, with stiff arms, that he is chilled. I have rarely seen him cold, but we have forded Cooper Creek at least twenty times today, and have gained two thousand feet in elevation. He is using more energy than I, carrying sixty-five pounds, and we haven't stopped to eat anything since midafternoon.

"I need to raise my core temperature," he says, turning to go on.

We drop down over the pass into an alpine meadow that glows pink in the nine o'clock sunset. Nine-thousand-foot Mount Allen rears its sudden snowy face. We pull on warm fleece clothes, light the stove and pitch our tent with its back to the wind. Then, wrapped in sleeping bags, we sit just inside the unzipped door and savor our soup. The air is too cold for mosquitoes now.

A raptor glides silently over, silhouetted high up against a cliff.

"It's a peregrine falcon," Dan answers when I ask. We watch without talking as it disappears in shadows, swallowed by the rocky face.

The next morning we're awake at five, cooking oatmeal and raisins in the cold. Mountains eclipse the sun, keeping our campsite in frosty shade. Just as we set out with our packs on our backs, a small herd of caribou comes trotting over a sunny ridge. The instant they see us, twenty antlered heads veer backward, and soon we spot the herd running in a thin brown line below us, over to the next hillside, out of sight.

We spring easily down the spongy slope, dropping a thousand feet. Over our heads, the sun pulls itself up above the mountain ridges, and soon it burns white as a molten nickel in the cloudless sky. Glare and heat reflect off the gravel and surrounding rock faces and snowfields, turning my bare arms red. My lips, fingers and knuckles crack with dryness. We sweat and drink liters of clear stream water, sweat and drink again.

In spite of fresh socks and patches of moleskin stuck carefully all over my toes and heels, my feet are screaming. I plant them carefully among the uneven rocks and am forced to slow down, falling far behind Dan. I actually savor the numbing cold of the shallow crossings. At last, Dan waits for me on a high bank near the confluence of Notch and Cross Creeks, dangling his bare feet in a pool. I see he has blisters, too. But he is more accustomed to pain than I. I have seen him with cracked ribs, a frostbitten nose, one finger split open by a forklift, another mauled by a wolf trap, his right ear grazed by a tree, a fragment of metal in his eye. Once he sewed up a gash in his own hand. I have never had anything worse than appendicitis and a sprained thumb. I muster a smile and remove my boots gingerly.

Yesterday and today we have seen many bright white dots of Dall sheep against green slopes and rocky hillsides, a set of black bear tracks in clay sediment and wolf tracks in the sand—along with waffle tracks from running shoes, the cooky-cuttered patterns of Vibram-soled hiking boots, one man's footprints with the pawprints of his dog and another man's prints with the punctures of a ski-pole. Now, dangling our feet in the healing cold water, we talk about our progress. We've averaged only about eighteen miles a day. We've eaten almost three days' worth of food, but our packs are still heavy, and the weight seriously threatens our balance in swift currents and deep water. With only one raft, it will take many extra hours to make the river crossings yet to come.

We consider dropping some gear in Chisana tonight and trying to pick up our pace. But the heavy items—the tent, extra food, emergency clothing and rain gear—are all things we feel we need in case something goes wrong. Anyway, the weight has already damaged our feet. They are a mass of blisters and tenderness, the outer layers of wrinkled soft skin sloughing off like cheese. And dropping gear won't solve the problem of having only one raft.

"I guess we should fly out at Chisana," Dan says. "What do you think?"

I know that Dan could have completed this race if he hadn't invited me. There were plenty of solo racers to team up with at the start. He could have walked faster and he wouldn't have had to do all that ferrying, plus he wouldn't have felt obliged to bring so much emergency gear. I know. Racing without me wasn't the point. Still, I'm disappointed, for both of us. He wanted to finish this race, and so did I. But—haven't we done the best we could?

I dive into Dan's arms so he can't see my wet eyes, and he squeezes me until my bones crack, the way he does when he wants to make me laugh.

"At least now we can relax and enjoy the view," he says into my hair. We wring out our socks, shake the gravel out of our boots and pull them on again.

We decide to celebrate and make camp early at Old Chisana, the site of an abandoned Athabascan Indian village and trading post. Soon after five o'clock we pitch our blue tent in the center of a meadow just beyond the deserted cabins. The sun still burns in its torture chamber. We stick the two ends of our collapsible kayak paddle in the soft earth, string a nylon cord between them and hang out all our wet long underwear, socks, shorts and shirts. Then we look for water.

We search the meadow, village and surrounding forest for over an hour, hunting for a spring or small stream, but find only

dry grizzly bear droppings and teethmarks on a tree. I'm thirsty
and my feet hurt, so I finally return to our camp to shake out our
sleeping bags and arrange the food, while Dan continues to look.
When he doesn't return, I sit cross-legged on the grass and write
in my journal.

A loud noise in the willows at the far end of the meadow star-
tles me, and I stand up to see two bare horses freeze behind the
branches. Their faces and backs shine in the slanting sunlight—
one black with a white spot on its forehead, the other pale tan.
They peer at me with startled eyes, then snort, paw the ground,
whirl and are gone.

I sit back down in the grass but can't concentrate on my writing. My eyes wander from the page. The meadow is ringed by
spruce trees and snow-tipped mountains. The sun bows out,
casting sudden chilly shadows. I feel as though I am at the center
of a great powwow circle.

It is dusk when I hear Dan's footsteps. He carries a round brass
bell attached to a black leather neck-strap and drops it in front of
me, jingling on the grassy floor.

"No easy water," he says. "I made a big circle around the
whole place. Whatever their source was, it must've dried up. But
I found the remains of a dead horse back there. Felt it before I
saw it. Bones scattered all over the place, like a bomb went off.
Wolves probably killed it last winter when the snow was deep.
Looks like a grizzly came in and mopped up the rest this spring.
Gobs of brown hair snagged on the trees and several pawed-out
places where he must've cached parts of the kill. White hide and
hair still on the tibias. A spooky place in this light."

We settle for cooking with marsh water and return to the
black spruce forest, looking among the mosses and sedges for
places where groundwater has oozed up above the underlying ice
lens. Dan selects a tiny pool and carefully uproots the vegetation
around it, creating a hole just deep enough to submerge our liter
water bottle. He pours the yellowish liquid into our cooking pot
and tea kettle, and fills the bottle.

Back in the darkening meadow, we prepare to make dinner.
But the stove won't light. There's plenty of fuel in the canister,

so Dan disassembles the hose and valve, holding a flashlight in his teeth. The tiny fuel orifice seems to be clogged. He needs something very fine to insert and clean out the carbon. I hunt through our first-aid kit for a needle. It doesn't go in far enough, though, and the tip snaps off inside.

"Shit. Now I need a pair of pliers," Dan says.

I remember the small forceps and package of suture needles he wanted me to buy. I begged a prescription for them from a doctor and was able to fill it at the last minute at Fairbanks Medical Supply. I pull out the miniature forceps and suture package, and hand them to Dan. He looks at me, surprised, then gives me a wink. Soon we are enjoying hot chicken ramen soup and one of our emergency cans of tuna.

Dusk turns into night. With just enough water left for oatmeal and coffee in the morning, we skip washing dishes. I stash the pot, cups and spoons in some grass away from the tent, in case any animals come.

This place is inhabited by spirits. They are filling the powwow circle, as stars push out in the blackening sky.

"I can feel the spirits in this place," I say to Dan as we cover our packs with plastic bags to keep out the dew.

"So can I," he says.

We sit down and linger a long time, cross-legged in the eye of the meadow, listening. Then, as if nothing in life were a race and our bodies were still brand-new, we make love.

The next morning, half an hour out of Old Chisana, we come to a clear spring-fed brook trickling out of a pile of rocks covered by sphagnum moss. We fill our two water bottles and our hands, drinking and drinking. Then we spend a pleasant two hours mushing to the Chisana River through muddy, verdant moose country. At the river, we find a sandy bar by a transparent stream and stop to wash our hair. I hear a throaty croak, then a swoosh, and I look up into the blue sky just as a bald eagle glides directly overhead.

The Chisana River crossing is wide. Two miles of braided channels meander between gravel and quicksand bars. There are many caribou and pack-horse tracks, plus the familiar footprints

of racers. It's fun to see how we all seem to deduce the same
routes and then run up against the same dead ends. Some channels flow deeper and faster than others, and some are booby-
trapped with patches of quicksand. But we are able to wade the
entire river, holding hands just for the fun of it, and we don't
have to inflate our raft.

After three and a half days of testing my abilities, I am more
confident in water. I can read it better, and I can wade deeper and
longer before the adrenalin bursts through. My mind works less
and my instincts more. I'm more sure-footed. Even so, I know
this is our last water crossing, and I am relieved when we finally
wade up on the other side.

A bit of fluorescent orange wind-sock beckons through the
thick spruce trees, revealing the location of the Chisana airstrip.
We discover a Cessna 206 and two Piper Cubs parked near a
creosote-smelling shack, and peer inside the dim coolness to find
a young man with a long scraggly beard tinkering with a carbu-
retor. He steps outside onto the dirt airstrip, snowy mountains
pressing up in all four directions, and waves his hand toward a
dirt road and the guide service Dan has heard about.

"People come here to hunt everything: Dall sheep, caribou,
bears—blackies and grizz. Good grayling fishing, too, and Dolly
Varden. Some folks bring the whole family. There's a German
family here now and one from Minnesota. So you're dropping
out of the race, eh? I seen two guys out at the upper airstrip this
morning, waiting for the mail plane to take them out. You say
you went fifty-five miles? Well, you come further than I ever
could. On foot, anyways."

Dan has heard stories about Ray McNutt, a guide who has
his own plane. We set out to find him. Somebody directs us to
his cook cabin, and we are greeted at the screen door by a sour-
dough in a cowboy hat and faded Western shirt with snaps.

"Well, I ain't been t' McCarthy for twenty-five years, but I
reckon I can find it," Ray says slowly. "Yeah, I'll charter you
over there. How 'bout sometime tomorrow?"

His wife offers lemonade, and he invites us to camp by the
spring on his property. Conversation eddies around the contro-
versial National Park Service, long-standing private sawmills on
what has become federal property, gold dredging regulations,

town gossip, some of the racers seen passing through. Bumper stickers plastered on the cabin door assert "Sierra Go Home!" "There's No Monument Like No Monument," "Support Your Right to Own and Bear Arms," as if this man—who doesn't talk much—is yelling. I am startled. Then I feel like laughing out loud at the free spirits inside this cabin.

Ray finishes his lemonade and ambles outdoors to do some welding. We shoulder our packs, set up the tent by the spring while batting at mosquitoes, then wander up Bonanza Creek, trying to cushion the shock of so much sudden civilization.

There isn't anything to say. It's a relief to be away from all that talk. We stand on the creek bank in the cooling shadows for several minutes, releasing our thoughts like trout into the singing water. I catch myself gauging the distance to the other side and note that rocks stick up for several feet before the creek gets deep. I wonder what Dan is thinking, but I know he would tell me if he felt like it. It doesn't seem fair to ask. We walk back.

Around noon the next day, Ray's little Cessna 185 teeters into the air with the three of us strapped into black vinyl seats, our two heavy packs stowed directly behind us above the tail. As soon as we level out, Ray asks to see our topo maps. He gets his bearings and looks for the drainages he wants to follow. The plane drones a hundred miles along the race route: up Geohenda Creek to the White River, then over Skolai Pass, the Goat Trail, the Chitistone River and Nikolai Pass toward McCarthy.

We peer down, looking for tiny stick figures or the flash of a yellow raft. But everything around us is too big. Jagged mountains as high as 16,000 feet tower on both sides of the plane, our wing-tips dangling between, so close I think we could reach out and touch the summits. Glaciers flow like rivers, and waterfalls pour out of nowhere. Dan and I give up looking for racers and strain to take in the views in all directions, shooting pictures right and left.

Ray guides the plane without talking, one hand on the controls, the other on the ham sandwich his wife packed. He has flown in the Alaskan bush for forty years, landing on all kinds of terrain in all kinds of weather.

"Looks like we're here," he says.

•

At the race banquet two days later, spirits run high. Of the original twenty-four racers, sixteen have finished. Five flew out at Chisana and one flagged down the plane of a patrolling park ranger at Glacier Creek. Two remain unaccounted for, but are expected within a few days.

Roman Dial, the race director from Fairbanks, has won with a time of two days, sixteen hours, twenty-eight minutes. He knew the best routes well, having been over the course three times before, and managed to cover over fifty miles a day carrying a thirty-pound pack. Finishing twelve hours after him is Dave Manzer, a veteran wilderness racer from Anchorage. Tied for third place are Tom Possert, a world-class race-walker from Indiana, and Adrian Crane, a long-distance runner from California who holds the world record for high-altitude mountain biking, having carried his bike up a 20,000-foot peak in Ecuador and ridden it down. The trio with the collapsible canoe has come in fourth.

Finishing last—"but with the most style," as one racer says— is Crazy Chuck with the dreadlocks. He has made three flights after bivouacking four nights in different places, without a sleeping bag. Each night he sat on his scrap of foam pad, huddled under two thin space blankets and the parasail, waiting for wet snow to stop falling and the wind to die down.

"I knew I had to fly," Chuck says. But the winds kept threatening to turn him upside-down and dump him inside his sail. "You fall into it, and it will wrap you up like a funeral shroud."

All of us sit around the wooden tables in McCarthy Lodge, finishers and non-finishers, swapping scary stories and enjoying steak and salmon, cake and ice cream, wine and hot coffee. We each receive a long-sleeved black T-shirt with a red-and-white mountain scene and ice blue lettering, and a bottle of champagne. In my own way, even I feel like a winner. And already, we are talking about next year.

Sometimes Dan says he and I are spiritual doubles. He says that's one of the reasons he's in love with me. I'd like to think that my spirit is as finely tuned and resilient as his. But now that I'm out of the wilderness and back in town and school, I'm not sure.

That's the toughest part of this race, I think: what happens afterwards.

All that wilderness I touched, inside and outside myself—it slips beyond reach so easily. My life is back to being abstract again: sedentary, indoor, cautious, hurried, not whole, out of tune. I catch myself shying away from physical risk, doubting my abilities, wincing at pain, real and imagined. At night I am mentally exhausted, but I've done almost nothing physical all day. The Northern Lights spangle the winter sky at midnight, while I'm too brain-tired to bundle up, walk outside and look.

All the things I learned in the race are still inside me, though. They may be temporarily out of reach, but they are there. I am still in the center of a great powwow circle. And the lessons are like spirits in the red coals of a ritual fire. All I need to do is stir them up with a stick and pile on wood. Then dance a Water Dance, listening and not listening, incandescent in the eye of the meadow.

Superior Spirit

Ann Linnea

Editor's note: In the summer of 1992 Ann Linnea became the first woman to circumnavigate Lake Superior by sea kayak. This is a condensation of the first three chapters of her book Superior Spirit *(Little, Brown, Spring 1995) that chronicles her self-designed, midlife rite of passage.*

*T*he flag above me *is flying straight out. Starched. How can a cloth flag do that? Fly with no ripples?*

The wind tears at my hood. Tries to rip open my shell of protection. Tries to starch everything in its path. I cannot gaze into the gale without shielding my eyes. Tiny bullets, pellets of ice bombard me. Moments earlier they were spray from raging surf, now they are piercing shrapnel.

I turn my head to protect my face from the wind, from the vision of the big lake. Gaze down the expanse of sand beach littered with ice from the long winter. The lake's twelve-foot surf pulverizes the ice. It is eager to destroy the last vestiges of winter bondage.

A gust of wind blows me backward several feet. I remember the summer. Gusts of wind that tried to knock the paddle from my hands, tried to blow my kayak over. Remember the many times Lake Superior engaged her fury and I was not standing safely on shore.

I drop to both knees, bow my head into my body for protection. In the cocoon of my thoughts, I can hear ice bullets hitting my jacket. Tiny little drums. Advance melody for the deep, steady pounding of the surf.

Pik, pik, pik, pik, pik, **Boom.**
Pik, pik, pik, pik, pik, **Boom.**

This is the symphony of She Who Is the Biggest. The symphony of She Who Changed My Life. I bow before her. Humble. Respectful. Grateful. Ready to wear the cloak of She Who Was the First.

When I stand on the shore of Lake Superior, I feel her power.

In summer the invitation is gentle. Meld with the lake. When the azure-blue sky reflects itself in a mirror this massive, the effect is infinite calmness. The calmness embraces me, cleanses out the storms of my life, fills my soul with peace. I am in awe of the clarity. I can see into my own life as clearly as into the plunging greenness before me. Ten feet, twenty feet, sometimes fifty feet down into the depths of mysterious canyons and ridges. I lower my toes into the water and am shocked back into the reality of my separateness. The lake is cold. Not cool, but cold. Temperatures are seldom in the swimming pool range except in shallow bays during stretches of warm, calm weather. And so, I feel the peace, the serenity, but I remain perched safely on shore.

During fall and spring storms, the invitation is to wildness. Ten-foot, twelve-foot, sometimes twenty-foot waves pound mercilessly against the shore, cavort with thousand-foot freighters as if they were bathtub toys. I am drawn to stand next to the lake. Drawn there like many would be to the scene of a fire or an accident. Drawn to witness something spectacular. But unlike the fire or accident, I become more than a spectator. I am soaked by the wind-driven spray. My body becomes imbued with the ecstasy, the terror of that much power. I feel safe standing on the shore, but I am not safe from the energy. I become realigned inside. Empowered in a way I do not understand. I have been touched by the wand of belief in my own vastness.

In winter the invitation is to venture out of the cave of hibernation and into the unknown. Ice is not as safe as the shore. It is always changing, especially on Lake Superior who has refused the bondage of being frozen solid every winter except one in the last one hundred years. But to know her in winter you must venture out, beyond the safety of the shore. I walk toward the open water, but not too far off shore because I'm scared. I lie down, put my ear onto the breast of this gigantic being and hear her breathe, pushing against the cloak she does not want. I hear the deep sounds she sends up from the molten core of the earth. I am connected, grounded to something much larger than the fragility of my own life.

On a quiet snow-melting spring day, the invitation is to change with the lake. The shore I stand on is encased in ice. But I can see water. The lake does not submit to the demands of winter as do her sister northern lakes. They remain frozen. She Who Is the Biggest is white only around the edges. On a sunny April day, I can see huge sections of this perimeter ice floating before me. Hundred-foot strands. Two-hundred-foot strands. Broken loose by a lady eager to regain the total freedom of movement, of summer, of warmth. I feel that same eagerness to shed the constrictions and restraints around the perimeter of my life. I want to let go of the ways winter has held me in bondage. I watch a piece of the old hole-riddled ice break free of the shore and float out into the aliveness and movement, the fluidity of the wholeness. Something inside of me releases, dissolves, transforms. The hopefulness of spring vibrates within, and I can do nothing to stop it.

Big. Big beyond seeing across. Big beyond knowing what's on the other side. Lake Superior is about the size of the entire state of Maine. To paddle around it is the equivalent of hiking the full length of the Appalachian Trail. Because it is over a thousand feet deep in some of its trenches, it contains more water than the other four Great Lakes combined. Lake Baikal in Russia contains more fresh water because it's deeper, but in terms of sheer size Lake Superior is well named.

It was not until the first white explorers arrived in the 1600s and reported that the Ojibway people called the lake "Gitchee Gumee," or "Great Lake," that a name was recorded. Explorer Etienne Brule added his own name: "The Northern Sweetwater Sea." Shortly thereafter the French called it "Lac Superieur."

At age forty-three, I set out in my seventeen-foot sea kayak to paddle around this inland sea. I left behind my husband, my two children and all the trappings of my middle-class life in search of answers to some of the tough questions that had accumulated in the cargo hold of my life. For twelve years I had lived by Lake Superior. Allowed her to play with my children, to hold the ashes of a loved one, to comfort and inspire me. But in the summer of 1992, I changed the contract. Let go of control. I asked She Who Is the Biggest to set the rules, boundaries and challenges of our friendship. I gave her permission to become my teacher. I gave myself nine weeks to be her student. I had no idea that I would never again return to the safety of the shore of my life as I'd known it.

I remember the first time I sat in a sea kayak. It was a warm August day at a camp in Wisconsin. The instructor cautioned me about the boat's balance, but my slim, canoe-wise body slid easily into the narrow hold. It was like pulling on my favorite pair of pants. Comfortable. Snug. Close to the water. My hands moved back and forth along the shaft of the double-bladed paddle. Smooth, long and lean, it curved to fit the cup between my curled fingers and palm. I found my arms and shoulders rotating automatically to the dance rhythm of the paddle. Forward with one blade. Pull. Forward with the other blade. Pull. I was delighted by how quickly the boat slid across the smooth skin of water. Naked hull caressing its partner. Slipping into line and moving, moving to the rhythm of body and paddle.

For me, who had grown up in Minnesota, swam and boated since I was tiny, this was the boat of my dreams. I had always paddled canoes. A kayak is quite different from a canoe. In a canoe you get into your boat. In a kayak you put on your boat. In a kayak you are one step above swimming. You become a creature with license to explore beyond the realms of ordinary earthbound existence. A creature that is capable of moving into small places with very little water or over immense waves on endless water.

Sea kayaking came into my life when I needed it. In the first eight years of my marriage to Dave we lived in the West. To Dave, a biologist in search of a Ph.D., the lecture hall and field trips were a source of truth and meaning. To me, a school teacher and Forest Service naturalist, time outside held truth and meaning. The more time outside, the wilder the place, the deeper the truth. The dichotomy in our approaches to life were obvious in the way we expanded on our undergraduate biology degrees. Dave kept studying things. I kept exploring them. He used his knowledge to develop his intellectual understanding of the world. I used my knowledge to become part of the world. And that brought me to sea kayaking.

We moved to Duluth, Minnesota, in 1979 for Dave's job as a university professor and adopted a Korean son and daughter within the first few years of being there. Young children gave me a whole new avenue for connecting to the magic and wonder of the natural world. They taught me, the marathon runner and mountain climber, how to saunter. But young children also put a cramp on my passion for physically challenging wilderness exploration. Sea kayaking was a perfect solution. I didn't need a partner, didn't have to coordinate with anyone else's schedule. And I was living on the shore of the largest, most dangerous lake on the planet. One early morning paddle in raging surf while children were still sleeping in the comfort of their beds could salve my desire for wildness for weeks. And so, with the introduction of kayaking into my life, I began to reclaim some of the fierceness and independence of my pre-children life.

It took me five years to get my 5'9", 125-pound frame strong and skilled enough to tackle a trip of the magnitude of circumnavigating Lake Superior. It was five years of taking short trips, of paddling in all seasons, of studying the weather. During that time, I lost my best friend to cancer, turned forty, watched my children enter adolescence and embarked upon a new career. By the time my friend and colleague Paul and I set our boats into the seven-foot surf of Lake Superior on the morning of June 17, 1992, I was ready to become the lake's student. What I didn't realize is that I was but a kindergartner in this school where I was going to discover my next life.

On June 14, 1992, the day of my forty-third birthday, I rose with the dawn and walked a block to a wooded hillside that I call listening point, a place I visit weekly. From it I can survey the lake, much of the city and the complexities of my life. Sitting on that hillside, I reflected on the last couple of weeks of trip preparation. Paul and I had packed and repacked food, gear and clothing. We were ready. We had been paddling together for five years in preparation for this trip. Five years of paddling in snow and ice, in big seas, in flat seas, in dense fog, in driving rain. And for twice that length of time we had been friends. Friends that home-schooled our children together, that taught family work-shops together, that wrote a book together. In the decade of our friendship, we had learned to navigate challenges as a team. The enormous respect I had for him would multiply many times by the trip's end.

As I sat on the billion-year-old bedrock of my listening point, I thought about my family and other friends in my life. I had sent letters to my three closest women friends admitting my fear and caution about the trip, letting them know that I'd instructed Dave to bequeath some of my outdoor gear to them if anything happened to me.

Some of the strength I drew from those last weeks before the trip came from my dream world. As I sat on the hillside sur-rounded by chest-high lupines, feeling the wind blow through the very short haircut I'd gotten in preparation for the trip, I re-read the journal entry of a dream I'd had a week ago, on June 7:

> Last night I dreamed about Betty. In the dream I was at a picnic with Dave's folks, my folks, Dave, Brian and Sally. We were all seated at one long picnic table. I was busy making a sandwich for Brian and Sally when I overheard Dave's mother say, 'Why, Betty, you look as I remember you!' I did not dare look up, kept making the sandwiches. Then a similar comment was made by my mother. This time I looked up and saw Betty's face staring at me. Nobody at the table seemed the least bit upset or surprised by Betty's presence. She looked in hairdo and age as I remembered her from be-fore her cancer, but her skin was opalescent. Angelic in quality. A tremendous calm came over me. She asked if I would go for a walk. We strode away from the table, arm in arm. She turned and said to me, 'I want you to know that being your guardian angel is my full-time job.' I was completely stunned by the information and, in that instant, she disappeared.

Betty died in 1990. She had been the closest friend I ever made. She was a dynamo: an internationally known biochemist, a fearless mountaineer, the namesake of our daughter Sally Elizabeth. She and I had taken numerous wilderness trips together during the twelve years of our friendship.

On June 15th, I rose at five in the morning. Fierce lake winds were blowing against my bedroom window. I was sure we would choose to delay the start of our trip. Still, it was important to me to begin every day between now and the end of the trip with a ceremony. I was eager to call Paul, to see what he'd say, but first I lit a candle, burned some sage and prayed for the courage to claim my dream and be safe.

Paul said the weatherband radio predicted northeast winds of twenty to thirty knots, waves of four to seven feet, and advised no travel on the lake for small craft. We agreed it was not a day to start out, called friends to let them know we weren't leaving, then drove down to look at the lake.

We stood on the beach, studying the surf. One white mountain after another rolling in and smashing itself against the sand. An image repeated again and again. Rows and rows of white mountains as far as our eyes could see. Relentless. Persistent. Loud.

"You know," said Paul, shouting over the roar of the wind. "I think we could make it out. We've done surf like this before."

"Yeah, but why give our families the message that we're going to take chances? Let's wait a day and see what happens. We've been telling everyone that we are going to be cautious."

Side by side. Two adventurers grounded.

A sea kayaker looks at raging water differently than anyone else. Paul and I did not stand there simply mesmerized by rolling surf. We were studying the water. Calculating how many sets of big waves separated the small waves. Looking to see how far out the breaking waves or the surf line actually extended. Measuring our skills against the incoming army of challenge. Thinking. Always thinking.

By Tuesday afternoon the marine forecast was calling for a wind shift. I drove down to Paul's.

"I think we should go," said Paul. "We need a shakedown paddle on big seas." I was silent for awhile.

"You're right, it's time. We weren't ready Monday. We were too nervous." Paul reached over to shake my hand. I slapped my hand into his, and we both laughed.

This time we had shaken on the contract. Two years ago we spoke about our desire to paddle around the lake. Last summer, after our fourth annual sea kayaking trip, we sat down and figured an itinerary for our circumnavigation of the lake and drafted a letter to friends and family, inviting them to join us on parts of the trip. First, a spoken contract. Then, a written contract. Now, a contract with a handshake. Each sanction of the contract had pushed us further along the river of preparation leading to the lake. Around rocks, over ledges. Over small waterfalls. Now we were prepared to drop over the last waterfall into the lake. Irreversible. One never goes back on a handshake, never goes back up a large waterfall.

Wednesday, ten in the morning, June 17, 1992. Park Point Beach in Duluth. Low clouds and fog. Strong winds. Four- to seven-foot surf breaking on the sandy beach. I knelt by my boat making last minute adjustments to her load. I moved the food bag forward to make sure the load was balanced. These little rituals were designed to convince me of my own readiness. Finally, I abandoned them in favor of hugs, kisses and goodbyes to the couple dozen friends and family members that joined us on the beach. Last minute whispers from the safety of land. From the life I was leaving behind.

"Are you ready, Mom?" asked twelve-year-old Brian. I had asked if he would help launch me. He was pleased to be asked, eager to help. I finished securing the spray skirt to my cockpit, picked up my paddle and nodded. He and Paul's son, Galen, grabbed the back of my boat and slowly slid me forward on the sand into the shallow water.

"Hold my bow steady," I said. "It's really important that I take off with my bow straight into the waves." Knee deep, then thigh deep, the boys waded into the thirty six degree water and pushed the bow within reach of the surf. Three large waves crashed in, one behind the other. The boys struggled to hold the boat straight. Three small waves. Three large waves. The boys still held me steady. The next wave was small, that was it, time to go.

"OK, let go!" I yelled above the roar of the surf.

"Be careful," I heard Brian's voice in my ear. My son. Letting go of me. Trusting me to return. With one strong stroke of the paddle, I was in the lake's power. Beyond the help of anyone on land.

The first wave crashed innocuously on my bow. I wasn't yet out to the big ones. This was the window of calm I needed and the boat was hardly moving. Stroke, Ann. Pull. Got to get out of here before that next big set of waves comes in. My boat felt like a barge. Of course, it was fully loaded! I leaned into each stroke of the paddle. Pulled the sixty-five pound boat and its eighty pounds of gear with every muscle in my body.

The next wave broke over my spray skirt. The next hit me in the face. Cold, shocking slap. No time to recover. Just keep paddling forward. Moving to get beyond the breaking surf. Can't look back to see how far out I am. Just keep stroking. Yes, I'm getting there. One more big one to get through.

WHAM—a wall of cold water hit me, engulfed me in stunned blackness. Terror. But as quickly as it hit, it was gone and there was light...and another wave coming. Paddle. Quickly up the slope of the wave. Don't let it break over your head. Yes, yes, I'm going to make it. WHAM—my boat slammed down the back side of the wave with a noise so loud I was afraid it would split. But that was all! No more breaking surf. I was free! I had made it beyond the surf, out into the rolling clutches of the open lake. "YAHOO!"

Carefully I turned my boat to face the beach so I could watch Paul come out through the surf.

Shore was so far away. When I rode a wave down into the trough, I could not see land. Up on the crest of a wave I could see dark little stick figures on the beach and Paul's boat resting on the edge of the surf. Brian's pink sweatshirt stood out next to the back of Paul's boat. It seemed forever before he got out to me. During that forever, I kept paddling and maneuvering my boat out of the reach of errant side waves that kept taunting me, trying to tip me over. But I wasn't going to tip. There was only one thing on my mind. I was waiting for my friend, my companion. I did not want to be alone out there.

Paul got to within earshot and let out a war whoop. I yelled back, and we turned our boats in tandem toward the north shore of the lake. We were partners out here, and we were going to be fine.

We held our boats in a position called "quartering." It's a bit like trying to walk along a precipitous mountain ridge when the wind is blowing forty miles per hour from the side, constantly threatening to blow you off balance. But I felt calm, skilled, and was warm inside my wetsuit cocoon, though I dared not divert my attention from the waves and look toward shore.

Gone. We were gone. Into our new lives. The sun emerged and lit up the city of Duluth to our west or left side. A benediction. One last look.

Most of the time I could see Paul because we were paddling about fifteen yards apart, but once in a while a big wave would come between us and he would disappear from view.

Paul yelled something, but I wasn't sure what. Then he motioned off to the east with his head. A thousand-foot ship loomed above the waves like some giant monster born of this storm. My God! We had passed through the ship canal barely in time. Twenty minutes later and that ship would have been barreling down on top of us. We were no more than two floating toothpicks to that ship. Invisible. It would never have seen us, never picked us up on radar, never even known it had ground us to bits.

Three hours later the clouds descended, and a cold, driving rain began to fall. At first I liked it. I felt smug about the rainhat I had bought, about how it acted like an umbrella and sent the rivulets over my waterproof jacket instead of down my neck. I liked feeling as impervious to the weather as the loons we occasionally passed.

Then, five hours into the day, I started to feel tired. This was longer than any of my recent training excursions and the longest paddle since last summer's lake trip. And it seemed to be getting colder. My hands inside their neoprene mitts were barely warm. My ears hurt from the cold. These warning signs were just distant messages. Tallies on a neon scoreboard on someone else's playing field: Lake-10, Ann-2.

Each point ahead looked prominent enough to be Stoney Point. I tried to read my deck map, to pay attention to my watch and guess how far we had paddled. But the truth was I had no idea where we were. I simply had to trust I'd recognize Stoney Point because I'd been there so often. I hoped the fog ceiling wouldn't lower any further and that no lightning would come from the ever-blackening skies. So many lessons in the first day.

As we got closer, we realized we were approaching Stoney Point, seventeen miles from our start. Place of ending the first day.

"Wait for a minute," said Paul. I didn't want to stop. I wanted to get on shore, get my tent up and get out of these wet clothes. My mind had shifted from its locked position named "paddle" to a position called "quit paddling." And it couldn't deal with anything else.

"Why?" I asked crossly. He didn't answer, just pulled back his spray skirt and lifted a large plastic bag out of his boat.

"We need to make an offering to the lake," he said pulling a rope of tobacco out of the bag. "We have a lot to be grateful for today."

I was stunned. Humbled. Ashamed. He broke off a piece, handed it to me and said simply, "For the privilege of this day." A timid ceremony. A short pause. A precedent. An important reminder.

Paul's mother was waiting on shore with a thermos of hot chocolate for us. "I have rented a cabin for the night. You will join me, won't you?"

I reached for the cup of hot chocolate without taking my neoprene mittens off. Drops of cold rain fell into the cup. I peered into it. Let the steam warm my face, said, "Bless you, Nancy. Bless you."

As I lay in the dark in my sleeping bag on the floor of the one-room cabin Paul's mother rented, all I could think about was the pain in my arms, shoulders and lower back. It hurt to roll over on my side to change position. It hurt to straighten out my arm and pull the sleeping bag up over my shoulders, warding off the chill that always creeps along the floorboards of cabins. I knew what it was like to be in physical pain. I'd run and skied numerous marathons. I expected the first week to be about pushing through pain, about adjusting our bodies to the rigors of exercising eight to ten hours a day. And so, I dismissed the pain, closed my eyes and succumbed to the relief of sleep.

Two days later on June 19th my journal read, "My body feels awful." The handwriting was more telling than the words themselves. The scrawling looked like that of a third grader who had not yet learned to properly hold a pen for cursive writing. I was in my tent writing with wool gloves on, holding a flashlight in my teeth. The temperature at the time was thirty-six degrees, just four degrees lower than the day's high.

Other events catalogued on that day reflected my discouragement:

No matter how hard we paddled, we were always on the edge of being chilled. When we pulled our boats up on the cobble beach of Split Rock Lighthouse for lunch, we went into the picnic shelter. Folks from the Duluth Gospel Tabernacle were having an indoor picnic. There was a fire in the wood stove, hot coffee brewing. I didn't want to leave. Felt only fear as we paddled beneath the light-house. Fear at the coldness in my hands. Fear at tipping in the confused water ricocheting off the cliffs. The cliffs in Tettegouche State Park were dark and foreboding. Haunting. Guarded by evil spirits. I wanted to get around them as fast as I could and find our camp for the night.

The weather was kinder the fourth day. The sun actually shone. Temperatures climbed into the low fifties. There was just a two- to three-foot chop on the water. I went from being the exhausted kayaker who could only focus on how many miles it was between breaks to the curious kayaker who wanted to explore little coves and inlets.

Early in the day we were paddling in tandem, quiet, respecting one another's need for solitude. When we came around one set of cliffs, we simultaneously gasped. There was a waterfall, a twenty-foot long wall of brown water pouring hundreds of thousands of gallons over a ledge thirty feet into the lake. The roar was audible even over the light surf hitting the cliffs next to us. And the cliffs! Their pink-grey walls were decorated with elegant orange, green and yellow lichens. Precariously clinging to their ledges was a host of cedar trees—sentinels that guarded this place.

And on this first day of summer we sat side by side below these sentinels in awe of the spectacle before us.

We stopped at Lamb's Campground in Schroeder that night for a two-day layover to rendezvous with friends. We woke the next morning to frost on the ground. As we sipped hot coffee around the campfire, we joked about picking the wrong summer to do this trip.

Our time at Lamb's was filled with important conversations that helped me refocus on the trip's intent and recover from the trip's actuality. A friend, who is an artist, asked me to talk about the physical rigors of the trip. Listening to me, she said, "We keep doing things over until we learn them."

"What do you mean?" I asked.

"Well, wilderness trips and hard physical challenges have always been important to you. Something tells me this trip is going to enable you to break through that old model of always pushing through the pain. You are going to find other ways to grasp deeper knowing."

I was sitting on a body-sized boulder of the same bedrock as my listening point. I looked out over the lake I could not see across. I knew I had lost sight of my goals these last days. Survival. That's what I had focused on. Survival.

Fear had been charting my course. Even my little ceremonies of burning sage and writing in the journal each night in the tent had been timid gestures. Exercises I felt I must do. Awkward, self-conscious procedures under the watchful, disapproving eye of Fear. I thanked my friend for her comment and said, "I hope you are right."

After the rest at Lamb's Campground, Paul and I parted company for a few days. He had to return to the university for a work obligation and agreed to meet me five days later near the Canadian border.

Solo wilderness trips have been important to me most of my adult life. Two years ago I had taken my first sea kayaking trip alone on Lake Superior. It was in late April when spring in northern Minnesota and Wisconsin was still mostly wishful thinking. My own life then felt as frozen as the inland lakes. Betty had been dead two months. I'd gone for long walks in the woods. Sat for hours by the lake. Wildness was the only embrace that comforted me in my grief. It was the only embrace that was large enough. I was searching for reassurance that my friend was somehow all right. That I was all right. That the path in my own life went somewhere beyond "Dead End."

On April 30, 1990, the day Betty would have turned forty-nine, I put my kayak into the waters of the Apostle Island National Lakeshore in search of a way to honor her birthday.

After a couple of hours, I stopped paddling, removed my spray skirt and pulled the blue denim bag with the rest of Betty's ashes out of the cockpit of my boat. There weren't many ashes left in the bag, maybe a half cup. I was glad they hadn't all fallen out when Paul and I scattered her ashes a month earlier and I took it as a sign that something was yet unfinished. I reached into the bag and dropped a pinch of the dust into the lake. Down, down into the green, infinite depths trailed this fine line of white powder.

"Where are you, my friend? Where are you, my friend?" I choked out the question . . . watched the pieces of dust stretch out before me like her hand or leg. Was that bone chip once her leg?

Out of the corner of my eye, I caught sight of a magnificent white swan floating not seventy-five yards from me. Angel white. Perfectly still. The swan stared intently at me. Through me. Past the wall of my grief. Into the center. Tears formed at the corners of my eyes, rolled down my cheeks. My heart beat hopefully in its protected cage. Neither the swan nor I moved.

After a long time, my mouth formed the words, "You're here aren't you? I feel you in my body. You're here." The swan lowered her head, turned and began to swim away. Gently, confidently. She disappeared out of sight behind Hermit Island. I looked down into the green depths. The trail of white dust was gone. Gone but not gone. Betty was not gone. I could feel her presence in my body like the faint stirring of spring wind. Barely detectable. A whisper.

After the rest and rejuvenation of two days with friends, I was eager to be solo. Eager for the kind of reflective time I'd had on that spring trip two years earlier.

My day started quietly. One- to two-foot waves. Light fog. Temperatures in the low forties. I launched my boat at what had become our customary departure time: five in the morning. I found myself stopping to rest every couple of hours.

About one o'clock I took a cup of pea soup from my thermos. I was on a cobble beach no bigger than my family car just below Cascade Lodge. About twenty miles from my morning

point of departure. The fog had been descending all day. The
wind had built waves to the three- to four-foot level. I was tired
and aware that I had already put in a long day. I was ready to
stop, but knew I couldn't camp in this small space so close to the
water's edge. So, I pushed on, optimistic that I'd soon find a
good camp spot for my first night alone—one not too close to
U.S. Highway 61, yet one with a safe beach for landing in these
waves.

After an hour of steady paddling, I realized I still had not
warmed up. I balanced the paddle across my lap and pulled a
wool stocking cap and mittens from the waterproof stuff sack I
always kept between my legs. The wool liner under my rainhat
and neoprene paddling mittens felt good. Boosted my confidence. I picked up the double-bladed paddle and resumed stroking. In and out of the water. First, reach forward on the left side,
insert the blade, pull it down next to my side. Lift. Then into the
water with the right blade and pull. In and out of the water,
sometimes doing large sweeping strokes to the side to correct for
waves. Sitting on the water. In a boat, but right on the water.
Only one inch of plastic separating me from Lake Superior's
thirty-six-degree cold. Water. Everywhere water. Below me.
On my boat. Above me. Seeping through my paddling jacket,
through the neoprene wetsuit, through the long underwear,
through my skin and into the marrow of my bones. And all cold.
Just a few digits above freezing.

"God help me," I said aloud. Three words. Nothing more.
Enough to shock me back into the present. Push on. Push on.

My mind locked my arms into an iron bar of movement,
shunted all physical sensations into a file named "denial." The
yellow kayak named Grace paddled on through the fog, rain and
waves. Alone. I felt like the only living creature in existence.

Then I started bargaining with God. "If you'll just give me
three feet of sand to land on . . . if I only have to paddle for thirty
more minutes . . . if I could have a safe place to land before it gets
dark."

Then, a black sand beach appeared. No, it was not a mirage. I
paddled closer. The waves were rolling in three- to four-feet
high and crashing on the beach. One fool move and I would be
dumped, pushed over the razor-thin line that separated me from

hypothermia. I paddled closer to shore, counted the sets of waves and carefully stroked in on the smallest crest.

"Yes! I did it! Quick, jump out. Pull the boat up and away from the waves." I needed to speak aloud. To have direction. To hear direction. To drown out the sound of relentless crashing waves, steady dripping rain and howling wind.

"Unpack the tent, Ann. Put it up. Quick before it gets wet inside. Good, now put up the tarp so you can get out of these clothes and cook supper. Damn, my fingers are too cold to tie these ropes. No, you can do it. Just one more corner to tie down. OK, now sit down on the stump and get out of your wet clothes."

I wasn't sure if the monologue was keeping me from madness or was the first sign of madness, but I didn't care. I was moving and I was not in the lake. I was on land. I was safe.

I bent over to ease myself onto the stump. "My God!" The pain. Horrible pain pulled me to the earth. The muscle spasm began in my side, spread to my stomach and thighs with the speed of a lightning bolt. The only other time I had known cramping from fatigue was swim team practice as a kid. Once my coach had to jump in after me because my calf muscle cramped so severely. And now I was lying curled up and helpless in wet grass and I could not move. Could not breathe. It hurt worse than anything I'd ever known. Worse than waking up after kidney surgery. And there was no one who could help me. My body was helpless. Never had it done this to me before. I needed help.

I looked at the young aspen trees holding up the tarp. Their branches seemed to be reaching down, gesturing. What should I do? Please help me. What should I do?

Breathe. Slowly. Just like us.

The first breath was so painful I dared not try again. But there were the trees. And they were alive. Breathing. One small breath went in. The pain was deep, but I could breathe on the surface above it.

Breathe deeper. Slowly. Down into the layer of pain. Melt it with the warm breath.

I am not going to die. I can breathe. But I cannot move. Help me. Now what should I do?

Breathe. Just breathe. Relax and breathe.

With each breath the overtaxed muscles melted their grip on my life. Finally, I could straighten out my stomach muscles. I lay back and looked directly up at the trees. "Thank you," I whispered.

I lay in the wet grass with the rain falling on the tarp above me, afraid to sit up lest the pain return. But I was calm. I was not alone. I kept looking at the trees. Listening. Knew that I would be all right if I could just keep listening. Moving slowly.

After a time, I sat up. As big an accomplishment as the first time I sat up in bed after the kidney surgery. I struggled to unzip my life jacket. Pulled my paddling jacket over my head. I was aware that a sudden movement would send me back into spasms, that the violent shaking of my hands meant I was already hypothermic.

Getting my clothes off felt as big an accomplishment as landing safely on the beach some long, long time ago. Another lifetime, perhaps. All I knew was right now. This moment. I was standing naked in the wind and fog and shaking so violently I could scarcely pull on my dry long underwear.

"Slowly," I said aloud. "Slowly or you'll go into spasms again." Finally I was dressed and dry.

"Food. I must eat something." It comforted me to keep speaking aloud. To test the clarity of my thoughts against a larger audience than my own brain. I walked over to the kayak, which rested just beyond the grasp of the angry lake, and struggled to unclasp the back hatch cover so I could pull my stove out. My hands were shaking too violently to help.

I saw the thermos sitting on my kayak seat. I reached for it. Managed to unscrew the lid. Wonderful warmth! Soothing liquid. Ancient memory of milk. Milk from the breast of She Who Is Always There.

"Tent. I must get into the tent. Turn the boat over and get into the tent."

I crawled into the tent, zipped it closed, removed my boots and rain gear and climbed fully clothed into the womb of my sleeping bag. I lay on my back staring up at the dry roof of the tent. Betty's tent that I had inherited. I reached for the pouch that still held some of her ashes, set it on my chest. Listened to the rain and wind beating on the tent. A relentless knocking. A ruth-less stalker. A giant beast that had not gotten its prey. "What if," screamed She Who Is the Biggest, "that muscle spasm had come while you were paddling?"

I cringed. Pulled the sleeping bag over my head. Rolled my body onto its side and tucked my knees up to my chest to protect my soft belly. *Drowned.* That was my response. *I would have upset the delicate, skilled balance I use to hold the boat upright. And I would have gone over. Over in the water in a totally helpless, cramped position.*

Storms worse than my own

Clarice Dickess

I shift the bill of my red cap over my left temple, desperate for shade. Behind prescription sunglasses, sweat from my brow wicks the sting of sunscreen chemicals into my eyes. More water, my dry throat begs.

"Rest break," I turn and yell to Keri and Cheryl who are roped in behind me. Without protest, they pull off their slings of hardware and sit down on their packs. This will be our heaviest load of the trip, twenty days' worth of food, fuel and climbing gear. I don't sit because that means having to get up again. I stand and stare at this world of blue and white, the Kahiltna Glacier, a desert of pure quartz sand, the sky an inverted lake without a ripple.

Stomping my skis around in a stationary circle like a plow-ox, I start at Begguya (Mt. Hunter), about-face to Sultana (Mt. Foraker), quarter-turn to Mt. Crosson, another quarter-turn to Denali (Mt. McKinley), then a few more steps around to face Mt. Francis and Kahiltna Base Camp. Though I've pored over photos and topographical maps, this still feels like a different planet, a place so alien that the beauty can only be absorbed through a filter of caution.

Many years ago, I saw the New York City Ballet's production of the Nutcracker at the Metropolitan Opera House. At one point during the performance, a little seven-foot tree on stage began to grow, rising taller and wider straight up out of the floor. It continued to grow until my heart began to race—it looked like the monstrous thing would go crashing right through the roof of the Met. Mt. Crosson does the same thing now as we ski toward its base, where we will start our climb of the Sultana route on Mt. Foraker.

We're disappointed to see another party, three men it looks like, camped within sight of our intended spot. One of the reasons we wanted to climb Sultana rather than Denali was for its lack of climber traffic. After probing a clear path through a series of crevasses between our chosen campsite and the base of the route, we divide chores and prepare ourselves for our first night of the climb. Late evening descends on us quickly and, while the sun has not officially set, it floats around behind the bigger peaks now, throwing shadows into the steep gullies and between the static waves of snow on the glacier. My nose tingles with each breath of frosty air.

Keri digs down into the snow to make a platform for the tent, and I can hear her toneless voice, though I'm paying no attention to the content of her words. She's grown so warm from exertion that she's thrown off her shapeless orange coat, and it strikes me now as it has before how deceptively frail she appears. Though she stands a couple of inches taller than me, she weighs about ten pounds less.

I remember being surprised when she first told me how old she was. The two of us were sitting out a stormy snow day in a tent in the Ruth Amphitheater, just southeast of Denali. It was three spring breaks ago, the first time Cheryl, Keri and I had climbed together. In the free time we read, napped, gossiped and attempted to groom and clean up. The ten years of climbing experience she had on me showed itself in many ways, but one I'll never forget was when she handed me a moist towelette in a foil packet. After several days of hard physical labor in the outdoors, this gift struck a chord of gratitude in me.

She was just finishing an undergraduate degree in geophysics and already had plans to continue studying at the University of Alaska at Fairbanks for a master's. She said she'd finally decided to "do" something with her life "in a weak moment." I thought she was my age, twenty-seven at the time, and so wondered what the rush was. But then she told me she was thirty-four, and when I felt discouraged after that by how much more climbing skill she possessed, I tried to remember that we started the sport at about the same age.

Her confident movements belie the look of frailty, too, I think now as I watch her stomp on the snow in a random pattern, packing the floor. She and Cheryl talk, and Keri takes the snow saw from her to demonstrate a more efficient method of cutting blocks to build walls.

Cheryl's a little taller and thinner than me, too, but we share the same dark brown coloring in hair and eyes. She still has Jersey brass in her talk, though she moved from her East Coast home when she finished high school.

I'm glad for the bit of solitude created by the roar of the little stove and the concentration the other two need to set up the tent together. For now I'm free from the pressure to talk, to participate. If I had my way in life, we would all communicate through a series of half-hearted grunts without needing to manufacture a liveliness of facial expressions. Somewhere along the way, I learned to retreat behind a poker face and a monotone voice. My inner life bubbles and froths in a cauldron of conflicting voices and emotions, but my face clamps down on that seething activity like the lid on a pressure cooker.

And people misunderstand. I inherited enough of my grandmother's Native American features to have a thin face that appears severe when I'm not smiling. I've been called the Ice Queen. Evaluations of my teaching have included a need for more "presence" and "animation." One boyfriend complained that he could never "read" me. More often than not, I'm asked to repeat myself in conversation when I forget and lapse into mumbles. I try, but it isn't easy to change who you are. What a relief to flop down on the backpack, let my face muscles go slack and absorb the splendid scale of the scene around me.

•

Two days ago, halfway to Talkeetna, the snowstorm had abated and I could look out the windshield of Cheryl's "heavy Chevy" without feeling dizzy from the flurry of flakes. The three of us sat in the front seat of the luxury car with elbow room to spare. And the back seat held the chaos of the rest of our gear, skis and all. The vehicle has remained in Cheryl's possession as a sole survivor from another life. It was hard for Keri and me to fit the pieces together when Cheryl described her former life in the Air Force, complete with husband and house and, now this was really hard to believe, china.

Now Cheryl studies archeology and anthropology, while Keri and I are both grad students. All three of us live in one-room cabins without running water, Keri and I alone, Cheryl with Mike. We belong to a network of friends who love to ski, climb, backpack, travel, kayak, take saunas at thirty-below. We're a cliché, really, and easy to spot in town. We're the ones who ride our bikes to school in the winter and wear functional clothing like ear-flap hats. Keri drives a 1970-something Toyota pickup, and I own a 1980 Subaru.

I'd been reading Dr. Peter Hackett's small book on recognizing and treating altitude sickness aloud to Keri and Cheryl. When in doubt, Hackett's three rules are "descend, descend and descend." In spite of its obvious wisdom, this phrase gave us the giggles.

"Hey," Keri said, her round blue eyes alive, "we have to come up with a name for our expedition." The way she said this reminded me of the boys I hung out with in my childhood, when a new scheme would catch fire: "Hey, let's go to the fort." "Yeah! Boss, man!"

All climbing parties registering with the Park Service before flying out of Talkeetna need some form of identification. "What should we call ourselves?" she asked. "How about The Cast-Iron Ovary Crew?"

"Oh, God," I groaned, as Cheryl cackled wicked-witch style, "no." Though I was responsible for teaching them this phrase on the Ruth trip (along with calling dried pears, monkey vaginas) I couldn't face going down in Park Service history with that kind of label. I knew Keri was goofy enough to not care.

"I know," Keri said, "we could be The Succubi. The Sultana Succubi with Cast-Iron Ovaries!" I groaned again, while Cheryl laughed.

"No, I refuse," I said. Keri and Cheryl bantered around a few more lewd possibilities. I laughed at their ingenuity, but couldn't picture writing out those words on a Park Service form.

"How about The Sultana Sisters?" Cheryl finally asked.

"Yeah," I said, approving for the first time.

"Yeah," Keri said, "The Sultana Sisters with Cast-Iron Ovaries!"

The struggle for patience begins on the first morning of the climb when Cheryl forgets how to tie her figure-eight knot to clip into the rope.

"I can't believe this," she cries, "I practiced this knot." Her head is bent over the mess of rope in her hands and tufts of wavy brown hair escape her wool hat.

"Didn't you use figure-eights when you were climbing in Ecuador?" Keri asks.

"Yes," Cheryl says, "but Mike always tied them for me."

Another kink develops over Cheryl's crampons. She can't fit them on over her stiff new overboots. Keri helps her, then we wait for her to finish getting ready while the sun's heat intensifies. I pull off layers until only a thin polypro top remains under my bibbed climbing pants. Thick coats of Sun Protection Factor 25 cover all exposed skin, including my ear lobes. Everything in my being cries, *C'mon, let's go!*, and I catch myself heaving sighs and exchanging looks with Keri.

I study the lower reaches of our route from camp to distract myself from the rise of anxiety I feel as the sun grows warmer. Yesterday's probing tracks wind about two-hundred yards through a field of crevasses to the base of a steep pitch of snow next to a rock rib. The snowslope is mercifully short, about the height of a two-story city building, and tops out on flatter terrain just beyond our view.

Finally, we're ready. Today we will choose a site for our first camp on the route and cache the load we are carrying in our packs. We'll have to climb much of our route twice, ferrying loads. I elected to carry all but three days' of my share of the food, plus a gallon of fuel, an ice hammer, a picket, and the radio. My usual trick, heaving the pack by its shoulder straps from ground to knee in one smooth arc, fails me for the first time. My heave bounces the pack a few inches off the ground. I try again, throwing all my strength into the motion, and barely clear my knee. Almost collapsing off-balance, I finally manage to shoulder the bag. It's going to be a long day.

"Let's go slowly at first," Keri says, "until my legs get used to the idea of climbing with this load." I thank her silently, resting between each heavy step as we traverse up the slope, zig-zagging sheep-style. Once we reach the top of the bench, the landscape opens up to our left, the snowy terrain rolling away and down toward the glacier bottom, while the white diamond-head of Sultana rears up to the southwest at 17,400 feet. Between the summit and the top of Mt. Crosson at 13,000 feet, snakes a ridgeline about seven miles long. Up and down, up and down, the ridge stretches like the serrated blade of a bread knife. In the heat of this early May day, against the unclouded blue sky, our goal looks awesome, yet calm and attainable.

Our immediate goal, gaining the ridge to our right which we'll follow to the top of Crosson, seems nearly unmanageable under the weight of our packs. After following the bench to the most favorable snow gully, we again begin a steep, sweaty ascent to the ridge. A very short pitch of ice, split in two places by narrow crevasses, faces us first. I made the mistake of attaching our route and cache-marking wands, three-foot sticks of bamboo, to my pack so they reach beyond my head. I place my ice axe into the ice above me, kick in a cramponed toe, step up and accidentally poke the wands directly into the slope. Very poor form. Instead of stopping to readjust my pack arrangement, I continue to bumble my way upward, avoiding the bamboo as best I can. In a few steps, the slope angle allows easier hiking, and we make our way up the snow gully slowly and painfully.

We manage to reach 9,500 feet before running out of time and energy. Chopping a shallow grave in the icy snow with our axes, we bury the heavy burdens in our packs and quickly head back down to camp, rejoicing in the near-emptiness of our packs.

I love returning to the tent; it's like coming home after work. The three of us pile in and create chaos in the tent while changing into warm clothes and getting hot soups and dinner made. The success of our first day on the actual climb makes for a celebratory mood.

"Puppy pile!" Keri hollers, and we cross our legs over one another so that we all have room to half-sit, half-lounge while the stove hisses in a corner, melting snow in the dinner pot. We've used up the daylight and can barely make out each other's features. Over dinner, Keri and Cheryl begin to spin high school tales.

Keri's family practiced the Baptist faith, and her parents, fearing their teen-aged daughter might wander from the fold, insisted that she attend a lecture on nature versus nurture. Apparently, Keri happily followed her parent's religion until listening to the lecture swung her in the opposite direction.

Cheryl's mom disowned her legally when she was a teen. After her parents divorced, Cheryl did a lot of acting out. "My mother filed a complaint against me, then my dad had to come get me and take care of me from then on. My mom couldn't handle me anymore." Again, I have to try to fit the disparate pieces of Cheryl's past into the current picture I have of her as being a relatively well-adjusted individual.

As Cheryl and Keri giggle and laugh together, I'm grateful for Cheryl's presence on this trip, for her ability to entertain Keri. With her here, I'm more free to glow to myself without having to be highly vocal or animated.

The next morning we bury our climbing non-essentials, like extra food, fuel, a flask of rum and the sleds. Breaking camp, we pack loads much lighter than yesterday's and head up our broken trail. Again, we're bathed in hot sunlight, but the southern horizon froths with grey clouds. Travel today is so much easier that we make our ascent quickly. Perhaps too quickly, as both Cheryl and Keri ask me to slow down more than once. My concern about the weather has been growing along with the clouds that have now blocked out direct sunlight, hanging in the sky around us in great dark shapes. Worry, worry, worry. My steps quicken in cadence to thoughts about tents and wind and snow caves and exposure as snow begins to fall in slow and lazy flakes.

We reach the ridge at 9,000 feet in four hours, almost half the time of the day before. The flakes fall harder now, while milky gray swirls of storm close down the mountain world around us, leaving us with a few feet of visibility. It's time to make camp, even though our cache still lies about five hundred feet above us.

Once we're settled in to our first camp on the route, the storm kicks up a big wind, swirling the fast falling snow into drifts around the tent. In the white-out, we must limit our activity outside the tent to a small circumference for fear of blindly stepping off one of the ridge's cliffs. We won't be climbing anytime soon, it appears. I lay back in my sleeping bag with Annie Dillard's *Pilgrim at Tinker Creek*, enjoying the sound of thousands of snowflakes dive-bombing the tent.

The tent. The first time I saw it, spent a night in it, I worried about suffering through three weeks of living in it with two other people. It's a Stephenson design, shaped like a ten-foot-long caterpillar. An inverted V-shaped door, which requires a person (even a small one) to supplicate before it on hands and knees in order to wriggle in or out, occupies either end. The double-walled fabric supplants (in theory) the need for a fly. Living in this rectangular space, somewhat like a trailer home, just feels wrong after sleeping in dome-style tents for ten years. We sleep opposing heads and feet in order to maximize space.

The tent belongs to Keri, as does the new MSR XGK stove, both of which she cheerfully offered for group use for our trip, neither of which she will allow Cheryl or me to carry in our packs for fear of damage. The caterpillar comes with three poles, but Keri only brought two because the middle pole busted through the tent during a bad storm before and because she wants to save weight. So, now, in this heavy wet snowstorm, the roof of the 'pillar sags, sadly scarred by its repair tape.

Suddenly, we're scrambling, belongings flying into the sacred center of the tent.

"My sleeping bag is soaking wet!" cries Cheryl. In fact, everything in contact with the tent's walls and floor is lying in a puddle of water.

"My tent leaks! I'm sorry, you guys," Keri says as we stuff our things into waterproof bags and survey the damage. On climbing trips, moisture is the enemy. Though we're warm now, the temperature could easily dive to sub-zeroes in a matter of hours, freezing our wet gear and leaving us hypothermic.

We need to dig the tent out from under the weight of wet new snow pressing into the sides. I pull on my mountain layers, squirm through the rear door, and begin shoveling, taking care to keep the metal blade away from the tent's tender hide. A headache throbs in my brain, the same one I've had for about twelve hours.

"Uh, Clarice, wait," Keri says. "Don't get the shovel so close to the tent. You have to scoop the snow away with your hands and feet," she instructs, demonstrating. Reminding myself that it's her tent, I try to do it her way, though her lack of faith in my judgment and experience annoys me. As does the wet living quarters. As does this damned headache. I feel an ugly blackness begin to build pressure inside me, the swollen, out of proportion anger made of many small, suppressed frustrations.

Back inside, Cheryl and I are treated to a tent lecture.

"I paid four hundred and fifty dollars for this tent," Keri says, "and at the time it was the strongest, lightest tent on the market."

It's a piece of shit, I say to my headache.

"I've spent hours talking with friends about how to use this tent, and our lives depend on it. So if I say I want it dug out a certain way, I don't think anyone should resent it," she says.

Yeah, yeah, yeah, I think, *aren't you rational and reasonable*. I feel a force inside sliding out of control. I've passed the Point of No Return.

I start flinging my stuff around in ostensible readjustment against the wetness. I'm not so far gone that I would damage the tent; it's more my refusal to make eye contact, grabbing clothes and pulling them from underneath my partners without letting them move first, yanking things they hand to me with force. I'm probably wearing my most vicious scowl, the one I copied from Mom when she used to scare me with her mean look.

I thrust myself inside my sleeping bag and yank it closed with a loud zip, then fling my body onto the pads and down jacket doubling as a pillow. Keri and Cheryl fall silent and exchange looks at my rude behavior (I see this out of the corner of my eye though I've now got my face stuck in my book).

After the Point of No Return and an aggressive display of anger, I enter the stage of Silent Withdrawal. This is a powerful technique that drives anyone who cares about me crazy. When I'm here, I will show no response to anything you do or say. Secretly, behind my poker face, I'm waging war with myself. Rational Me begs and pleads with Stubborn Me to stop being an asshole. Rational knows how destructive this behavior is to relationships that I care about, but her voice remains meek for awhile. The duration of Silent Withdrawal depends largely on how much punishment my ugly side thinks the injurer deserves. In this case, I needed overnight to recover and was ready to be human to Keri next morning.

Blue sky reflects my change in mood. After checking the weather through a slit in the door, I get dressed and nudge the other two.

"We should get going now," I say. "There's no telling how long this window will last."

I squirm outside and begin organizing my gear. Yesterday, the weather forecast on our radio called for a short break between storms today, then three or four more days of snow and wind. We have to make a dash for our gear above us to retrieve more fuel and food, as we're already low on supplies after weathering this first storm for two days.

"How many days' worth of food should we bring down from the cache?" I ask from outside.

"Maybe we should just bring it all down," Keri says. She's suggesting we end the trip.

"I'm really disappointed in you, Clarice," she says. "I've never climbed with anyone with your attitude before."

I sigh and stop preparations. Keri responds to my anger last night with anger, and I'm going to be made to pay for getting pissed off. Given these dynamics, perhaps going down is a wise choice. When I return to the tent, Cheryl talks first.

"Well, I'm not ready to give up yet. I think we should talk this out and keep going. We're bound to get mad and frustrated on this trip, and I think we should be able to do that and go on."

I'm impressed with Cheryl. She seems to have her head screwed on straight. In spite of her lack of technical knowledge, her presence on this trip as a mediator may well carry it further than it might otherwise have gone.

Keri sits up in her bag and talks at me. She dredges up a comment my boyfriend once made about my climbing abilities. "I think Randy's done you a disservice to call you an intermediate climber," she proclaims. "Some of the things I've seen you do . . . Cheryl climbed that ice pitch the other day better than you did."

I'm shocked by this put-down. No one has ever talked to me this way before. Part of me understands at some vague level that her words are untrue, and that they're weapons, lashing out because I hurt her the day before. Another part of me feels wounded, and yet another part of me turns rock hard. I resolve to continue the climb, though, because of all the work and expense we put into getting this far, and we're *here*, dammit, in this incredible place. I try to think of Keri as a business partner instead of a friend, the arrogant kind that one must deal with in order to get the job done. We all decide to keep climbing.

After ferrying the cache to 10,500 feet the day before, we pack up our first high camp and head up the ridge on day seven. Finally, we have the white-on-blue of the peaks and sky again. The gang's all here in white crystalline glory: Denali over our right shoulders, Kahiltna Base Camp and Begguya behind us, Sultana over the left shoulder. There's a bit of cold in the dry air, and I stomp around impatiently, trying to keep warm until Cheryl's packed and ready to go. In spite of tentbound instruction and practice, I still have to tie a bowline knot to secure the extra coils of rope around her.

Once we're moving, life feels wonderful. Our trail stretches ahead and up, now broken and familiar. We climb steadily through the rock rib until Cheryl's crampon falls off. This time it's not critical, but the potential for danger in other places makes this a deadly faux pas. We stop and wait for her to fix the spikes, then move on. When it happens again in a few paces, Keri climbs up from behind Cheryl and teaches her how to use the straps properly. I sit down and lean against my pack, marvelling at Keri's patience. I was enthusiastic about having Cheryl on the trip, but now I realize I wasn't prepared for the responsibility that climbing with her entails. I had never climbed with Cheryl without her boyfriend Mike along. He must have taken care of her more than I realized. I wasn't prepared to be her teacher and coach as much as it's now apparent she needs.

We're still climbing without protection; that is, we're not anchoring our rope to the mountain via hardware like pickets, slings, deadmen or ice screws. So far, we'd have been able to stop a fall on the slope by dropping into the self-arrest position: ice axe, knees and toes driven into the snow, butt up. A black rock spine juts above the snow here and there, but we crunch steadily up, up, up. By midafternoon, we've reached our cache and second high camp. There's barely room for the tent on the narrower ridge, and above us the slope steepens sharply. A rock horn crowns the horizon line, like the prow of some huge ocean vessel cresting a violent wave in a storm. The rest of our climbing will require protection.

Digging in, our shovels bounce off of hard black glacier ice just two feet down. I don't like it. Last year I endured the collapse of a tent during a wind storm in the Deltas of the Alaska Range, the most frightening mountain experience of my life. I don't want so much exposure to Sultana's legendary wind storms.

"Let's dig a snow cave," I suggest, searching the slope for a likely spot.

Keri looks up briefly from her digging, and quickly scans the area. "No, the slopes are too loaded and avalanche prone," she declares. "We'll have to make snow walls with blocks."

With hours of bright daylight left to spend, we decide to build our walls, then rope up and carry a load as far as we can get it. Keri wants the lead.

"I feel so inadequate," she says a couple of hours later, confronted by the slick black face of a steep pitch of rock. Leading to the right would require hip-deep wallowing in unstable conditions, that's clear. The rock itself offers little for hand or footholds, and no way to protect the leader.

As I wait for Keri to work out her moves up the rock, the

fingers of my ice-axe hand begin to grow numb through the thin polypro glove, and I suddenly feel the drop in temperature. The skies have been layering up in shades of grey, once again swelling with the menace of snow. We've got to find a good cache spot and get the hell back down to camp before we lose all visibility. My stomach flutters with a chill, nerves and hunger as I watch Keri make her way up the rock, crampons scraping on the glazed surface like fingernails on a blackboard. If *she's* nervous here, Cheryl and I are in for a thrill.

In minutes, though, Keri crests the top of the short wall and disappears from view. The rope moves smoothly forward in front of me, as I match her pace to approach the mean black face for my turn. The rope movement pauses. She must be setting up a belay. As I grope the wall for protruding chunks of rock, or cracks to jam my hand into, or depressions to hook my ice axe onto, I can feel my breath coming fast and hard. It's not that bad, I try to reassure myself as the first couple of moves come fairly easily, but it's hanging here, not wanting to let go to search for the next seemingly non-existent place to put my feet, that's hard. My scraping around the rock beneath me with my right foot suddenly feels much like ballet exercises meant to develop turn-out, the setting strange but the tugging on the strings inside my hip and thighs familiar. There's nothing there, and my grip above is failing. Time to just *go*, don't stop moving up. Soon, I'm over the lip and there's Keri in her sitting belay, anchoring us to the mountain.

She continues to belay Cheryl, who moves up and over the rock with a smoothness that belies her beginner status. "Wow, you flashed it!" Keri says to her, and Cheryl grins.

We have to keep moving. The terrain up ahead widens to a broader slope, and it rises up in domed snow and ice terraces, like white-ribboned hard candy. Partly shrouded, Sultana towers to our left closer than ever, and now we can see the hanging walls of blue ice that break and spread thunder across the valley between the massive peak and our Crosson ridge. At a place beyond our view, the two ridges connect, bridging a sinuous walk from here to there. The very air around us seems to snap with the power of Sultana's presence; it draws and repels at the same time, a roaring clash between beauty and force.

We don't get far before hitting the crevasses. They litter this slope, large and small. Some we easily step across, spanning a blue yawn as casually as a frost-heave split in one of Fairbanks' city streets. Others take several steps to cross canyons of black and blue, steps of anticipation, of hope that the snow bridge is thicker and stronger than it looks. "Tight rope!" we keep yelling to each other at the brink of ice lips, and I try to construct a Z-pulley system in my mind, the way the three of us had practiced in town. I pat my hip, where my mechanical ascenders are holstered.

Finally, we have to settle for chopping out a tiny niche in the ice for our gear; it's getting later, windier, and snow has started to fall. And we're hungry. While I pull on nearly all of my extra clothing, I listen to Keri's plans for the descent back to camp.

"Going down is the most dangerous part of climbing, you guys," she reminds us. To me it's also the most frightening. "I'll go last," she continues, "because you want the most experienced person in the belay position." I'm glad she's going over all of this. Cheryl offers to lead, and that sounds fine to me—I just want to get down and get down as fast as we can safely. Keri turns to me.

"Clarice, would you lead down?" Surprised, I look up at her. She says to Cheryl, "Since she knows how to place pickets and slings..." then back to me, "you can just reverse the placements I made on the way up."

"OK." I nod. I'll do it, because that's really the way it should be done, but I kind of wish I didn't have to. We shorten the rope between Cheryl and me, while Keri stays further behind to belay at the steeper pitches.

We proceed slowly, taking granny steps. A fall on one of these steeper sections could be disastrous, but our cautious pace and the anchors available protect us from falls. Suddenly, the yellow roof of the tent above its snow walls appears below me, a tiny speck from here, barely visible in the dim snowy distance. Home! Though Keri's out of sight above us, with one of the steeper pitches of the climb between us and her, Cheryl and I whoop with relief, knowing the rest of the way is a walk, relatively.

After we return to camp, we just have time to zip up the tent doors behind us before heavy snow and strong winds begin to batter the tent. Our fatigue is outweighed only by our hunger, and we stay awake only long enough to eat.

But we're awakened later by the sounds of the tent fabric flapping, and the wind howling over our heads. In spite of our snow walls, gusts of wind pummel the tent, distorting it into slanted flat shapes, like steep A-frame roofs, that it was never meant to assume. I expect the fragile fabric to rip at any moment. Keri seems to have more faith in its structural integrity, but we both dress, put on goggles and face masks and scramble outside to check our shelter. We dig out the fresh load of snow lying around the tent and, bracing against the wind, try to build up a sagging snow wall. As we work, the wind calms somewhat, and I decide to stay out and cut more blocks when Keri goes back to bed. I put on my crampons and cart the snow saw and shovel out to the wind-packed slab of snow a few yards from the tent. This snowpack cuts dense, textbook-perfect blocks, and the weather improves as I work. I begin to feel a sense of peace as the walls grow taller and stronger with the new bricks. A couple of hours later, I crawl back into the sleeping bag with numb toes, a growling stomach and a calm heart.

I get a few hours' sleep before awakening again to vicious tent slapping in the early morning. The wind has changed direction, now attacking our weakest flank and gusting with stronger force. Leaving Cheryl to attempt to cook breakfast, Keri and I again don armor and head into the storm. I immediately feel better out here, even though the wind's force pushes me off-balance. A few feet away from me, Keri's coat blurs in my vision, the rest of the world an out-of-focus black-and-white photo. She's struggling back and forth behind the tent, pulling snow blocks from one wall to build up the opposite one where the wind vents its fury hardest. I follow her lead, "robbing Peter to pay Paul," as she puts it, stumbling under the sudden blasts. I feel a pure excitement, leaning in against the howling wind.

"Don't step outside the snow walls," Keri shouts to be heard, though she's standing right next to me. As forceful as the wind is within the walls, it is still a broken version of the unimpeded white madness beyond. We manage to eat a nervous breakfast inside the seasick tent. By mid-morning, we're again spared the storm's fury, and we emerge from the tent into a sucker-hole of blue sunshine, blinking and groggy. This time, I think, this time we've got to build an impenetrable fortress. Saw in hand, I set to work in our snow quarry, mining blocks. I make a game of trying to stay ahead of Cheryl as she carts the blocks from the mine to Keri at the tent. As the sun soaks into my back, I peel off layers, and it's harder to feel the need for this work when the weather's so good.

"Maybe that's enough," Keri says after about an hour of hard labor. But it's still sunny, the exercise feels good, we're safe.

"Hey," I say, "I'm into overkill." I try to communicate my paranoia from past experience, hoping to convince both of them to give this storm business the fear it deserves. It works for awhile longer, anyway. Keri has built a double-thick wall with the big blocks, and the fortress is taller now, too, about as tall as the tent. Exhausted, we crawl back to bed.

By nightfall the storm returns. A new cycle of tent flapping sets in. It's noisy, but we fall into an uneasy, broken sleep. Early in the morning, we can no longer ignore its increased force. Later, the media would dub this the worst storm in ten years, reporting winds in excess of 110 miles per hour. Keri dresses and goes out to try to reinforce the wall receiving the worst blows, leaving Cheryl and I to support the tent walls from the inside. I fear for Keri's safety, and hurriedly dress in all my clothes with one hand, holding the tent with the other. A wide-legged squat seems to be the most stable position. I lean all my weight back against the force of the wind while it pummels my head and neck the way neighborhood boys used to do when they tried to dunk me underwater. The floor of the tent rises from underneath me, and I keep feeling like we will take off like a kite and go sailing over the ridge. "It happens," a little voice inside my head keeps telling me as I recall a story of that very thing happening to a guided party on Denali last year.

"Cheryl, get dressed," I bark, my voice sounding sharp in my ears. She's still in her sleeping bag, doing her best to support the other side of the tent, and several times during the worst blasts our eyes meet, brown to brown and full of fear.

I'm relieved when Keri finally re-enters the tent. The bridge of her nose is bloodied, the result of a snow block being blown from her hands over her head. There's nothing to do now but wait. Even Keri's blue eyes show some concern, as we sit amid the rubble of our gear.

Then the worst blast yet pitches Keri and Cheryl forward suddenly. A crash and rip. Behind Keri, the snow wall has collapsed onto the tent, breaking a pole and tearing the fabric. She leaves the tent to remove the pole. She shouts something to us, but the wind is no longer gusting, instead blasting over the mountain in one steady stream of force. I feel a panic rise and claw at the door. I want out, out, out. Stepping outside into the direct force of the storm is much easier psychically. The world beyond the tent boils in a mass of gray air and water, but at least I can see the enemy.

"What did you say?" I scream into Keri's ear. She's pulling blocks down onto the tent to keep it anchored to the mountain. I do the same on my side, then we lie down back inside, pulling the loose fabric between our legs and gripping the top with our hands. The closer we can hunker to the ground, the less likely we'll go for a flight. I take false comfort in the ice screws that anchor the tent—the tent loops there could rip right out.

I think about Randy, and Rowan, his Australian climbing friend, weathering this storm on Begguya. God, I hope they're OK. *No, we're not OK*, I answer silently to the question I know Randy must be asking, too.

"Pretty desperate," Keri comments, as we lie there, three inert figures in a row, listening to the storm scream.

Though we seem to be holding firm, I worry about our reaching a state of hypothermia and frostbite. The other pole is still working at one end of the tent, but running a stove looks impossible as we watch the floor and loose items on it dance a crazy jig. And we don't really want to let go of the tent. My hands, raised above my head, are beginning to go numb. I think about the other climbing party, the three men we saw at basecamp, now camped just a few feet away.

"Maybe we should go see if they'll let us stay in their tent until this blows over," I suggest.

Keri agrees, and one by one we gather the items we need to take along. She asks for help getting the other pole out of its sleeve to prevent further damage, and Cheryl volunteers. Out of her earshot, Keri turns to me.

"Would you do it, Clarice? It's easier for me to explain things to you." I nod. I know what she means.

We only have to spend a couple of hours with our neighbors before the storm calms enough to allow us to dig a couple of caves. When we return to the site of our camp in a state akin to shell-shock, we can hear the whop, whop, whop of choppers. It looks like two of them are active around Kahiltna Base. We're afraid that others must've fared worse than we, and I wonder again about Randy.

I have to change into my boots, as I weathered the storm in my warm down booties and homemade overboots. I have to warm the inner boots first, wrapping them up with my feet in the sleeping bag and sliding in two chemical warmers. Cheryl comes and sits beside me, and now we are safe enough for our emotions to surface.

"I can't go on," she says.

"Well," I say gently, "don't make up your mind right away. We're pretty shaken up right now, and it's not a good time to be making decisions like that. Let's just get a cave dug and get some rest and not think beyond that yet."

"You're right," she says. "I don't think I'll change my mind, but I'll wait."

"You know, somehow I knew this was going to happen. I told Keri we should dig in, but she didn't listen to me." I guess I need to vent my nervous energy, too.

"I put her up on a pedestal," Cheryl admits.

"Well, she's an excellent climber with a lot of experience," I say, "and I don't argue with any of her climbing decisions. But I have plenty of snow camping experience, and I have different ideas about how things should be done, sometimes." It is such a relief to be talking about this, to be listened to.

"You guys, I want to keep going!" I say this as I cook dinner in our cave, after an afternoon of rest. Keri's face lights up immediately, and she smiles.

"Me, too!" she says.

"We should be digging caves from now on, anyway," I say.

Seeing our enthusiasm, Cheryl cheers, too, and agrees to continue. Keri hugs Cheryl and squeals with delight, and we talk about our plan of action.

"We'll just have to make sure we can run back down to the last cave if we can't find a place to dig a new one along the route," I say.

"Yeah," Keri agrees. "Maybe we can find caves between here and the summit. If not, at least we didn't just quit."

We have clear skies again the next morning, day eleven of our trip, and decide to catch up to our cache and carry it higher, scouting out the cave possibilities at the summit of Crosson. We should be able to reach the top today, as our cache is already above 11,000 feet. The helicopters chop through the air again this morning, lending a somewhat gloomy edge to an otherwise fine day. Cheryl must be feeling good because she wants to lead. It seems a bit ambitious for someone who's never placed protection on a climb before, and who's never followed someone placing protection before this climb. But Keri doesn't object, and neither do I. We've already climbed this section up and down, so she should have a good idea of where to put in the pickets and slings.

But she has trouble with the first picket placement. She's trying to drive it into hard ice, not recognizing that the softer snow just steps below her would take a picket and hold it well. Keri and I stand and watch her for a few minutes.

"Try stepping back a few feet," I yell up to her.

"Thanks for saying something," Keri says to me out of Cheryl's earshot. "I get tired of having to tell her these things all the time."

Cheryl seems reluctant to take instruction from me, though, and she hesitates, perhaps waiting for endorsement from Keri. We sigh and wait.

"She doesn't seem to be able to figure things out for herself very well," Keri comments to me. It's true, and I feel vaguely guilty as we discuss her lack of independence in decision-making, attributing it to dependence on the men in her life, first her ex-husband and now Mike. It seems sort of two-faced of Keri to have this conversation with me, given that Cheryl has seemed like something of a teacher's pet for Keri, and Keri an idol for Cheryl. And this chummying up to me belies her feelings on the day she rated my skills as being little better than Cheryl's. But, it also feels good to vent the impatience I've felt about Cheryl all along on this trip.

When we reach the crevassed area again, Cheryl turns too early and points up the hill to ask, is that the cache? No, no, I shake my head, it's still way up there. The bump she pointed to was not marked by wands, as our cache is. Our nerves are frayed when we finally arrive at the wanded mound. As if to reflect the state of our minds, we find that the grave has been violated by ravens, and cracker fragments and Sorbee candies from my lunch bag litter the snow. Sensitive to our impatience, Cheryl tries to explain why she did things the way she did. She's upset by our unspoken disapproval of her performance.

"You're a little out of your league," I finally say, while attending to the disinterment of our food, fuel and gear.

"Oh? Why is that?" she snaps back.

"Well, the first step in leading protected climbing should be to follow someone around who knows what they're doing and pay close attention."

"Oh," she says, her voice hard and brittle, "I thought that's what I had been doing." She looks to Keri as if for her support.

"But we haven't been doing that kind of climbing much at all yet," Keri says.

"If I'm out of my league, then I have a right to know why," Cheryl says.

"One thing you could try to do is see if you can answer your own question by looking around before you ask it," I say.

"Oh, so I shouldn't be asking questions!"

"Well, when you asked about the cache...." Keri reminds her. Cheryl seems to deflate then, seeing that Keri supports my perceptions. Instead of impressing us with her desire to lead, as she had hoped, she has only reminded us of how much she has yet to learn.

With Keri in the lead, we climb on to new territory, and though the rifts in our feelings for each other still sting, it's hard to feel anything but exhilarated by the views of all the peaks and the close-ups of Sultana. The number of crevasses on this slope impresses me and keeps an edge of tension tugging around my psyche. Then we reach a true-blue short pitch of fifty degree ice. For this we need our second tools, the ice hammers, and it requires the technique of front-pointing on our crampons, heels resting on nothing but a cushion of air. Keri leads up the pitch without hesitation, placing the ice screws and displaying a grace in her movements that shows her for the talented and experienced climber she really is.

Cheryl and I, too, move well up the ice. Once I climb beyond Keri's belay spot, probe for cracks and sit down, she says without turning around, "You gotta hand it to her. She really loves this stuff." She's right; Cheryl is full of potential, her agility a natural talent. Once she's studied and put in her apprentice time, she'll be hell on wheels.

A potential cave spot presents itself here, somewhere beyond 12,000 feet. We can't be far from the summit of Crosson now. After a few probing shovelfuls, I tell them, yes, let's dig here. We get a start on the cave, then scramble back down to camp, pack, and head back up to our new home where we sleep with our cache for the first time. We finish digging the cave around midnight, stay awake long enough to cook, then collapse into deep sleep.

The next morning is another sunny beauty. Slowly we begin to stir and to organize our gear. This time, a first, we're going to carry everything we need from now to the summit and back to this cave on our backs. We've spent so many of the twenty days of our trip bank on bad weather that our only chance of making Sultana's summit, across that long, up-and-down ridge, is to go for it alpine style, light and fast. We leave a gallon of fuel and other absolutely non-essentials in the cave.

Keri nudges me to lead from camp. It's an excellent place for me to do so, the slope steep enough to require protection and crevassed enough for leader thrills, yet certainly within my range of confidence and skill. Unlike Keri, I feel no aggressive need to get out there in front, though I'm aware that leading is important for developing all the vital climbing skills. As one of my expert climbing friends has said to me, we're all really soloing out here, and a feeling of dependence on the rope, the hardware and the other climbers in the group is a dangerously false sense of security. Belay systems can fail, ropes can get severed, climbing partners can die, leaving you to find your way down alone.

But it *is* fun to load up with ice screws, pickets, 'biners, ice axe, ice hammer and slings and go clanking up in the lead like some medieval warrior, making the first steps that the others will put their feet into. In the lead, no one blocks your view of the scene ahead, and you set the pace, the rope trailing behind and down. You're empowered and burdened with the route-finding decisions; it's up to you to recognize the cracks and figure out where to place the pro, and how. As I head out, Keri and Cheryl holler at me as if I'm some kind of hero.

My lead ends when I come upon a yawning chasm of a crack, twice the width of my widest stride, that creates a big step up onto the next platform of the slope. I don't mind jumping over cracks, but I can't jump up and over this one. Here's where my experience fails me and, unsure of how to proceed, I belay Keri up to switch leads. To my shame, without hesitation, she hikes up over the crevasse on a bridge of snow that I was unwilling to trust. As we climb on, the terrain challenges our route-finding skills. With Keri's reminder, I'm trying to memorize all the bumps and curves of the route for the way down. We go around this serac on this side, and if you look back it looks like this. . . .

But this year the weather is ornery, and another storm moves in on our idyllic climbing day. After climbing for only three hours, the wind forces us to dig in again. Our frustration levels rise when snow and wind barrage the ridge, trapping us in our icy den for another full day. Desperate for activity on our second morning in the cave high on Crosson, we pack up and try climbing, but poor visibility turns us back.

We spend a few hours digging the cave bigger, hoping to try climbing later in the day, putting off the inevitable. Had the weather cooperated this morning, we would've carried on, building momentum, perhaps. But hanging around our cave makes the unknown ahead, the more difficult climbing we expect on the ridge, amplify in its threat. Soon it will be too late to get anywhere today, and the prospect of another night in the cave depresses us.

When the weather forecast on the radio calls for more of the same, our motivation flags. We gather in a group on the slope, talking and suffering from a strange mood of inertia.

"Well, we're up here because we want to look at the views,"
Keri says, "but we're not going to see anything if the weather's
always bad, so we might as well go back."

I'm glad to hear that Keri feels ready to turn around, too.
That seems to make the sentiment unanimous. "I'm ready," I
say. I feel, more than anything else, relief. The discomfort, the
emotional vulnerability I've been forced to live with for fourteen
days is almost over. Under the shadow of this release from the
goal, my feeling of regret for quitting is only a pinprick. We're
right; it's time to go. When the visibility clears enough to travel,
on day fourteen, we turn our backs on Sultana to face Denali and
Begguya.

On the descent we get all the way down to our first high
camp at 9,000 feet, covering in a few hours the territory it took
us two weeks to gain. The most disheartening part is carrying
down a heavy load after all the sweat of carrying it uphill—
we've still got a few days' worth of food and fuel left over.

Keri and I take on some of Cheryl's load; we can't afford her
knee to give out. Keri nags at her impatiently when she has
trouble in the now-rotten snow at the lower elevations. We reach
camp that night exhausted and irritable. We set up the patched
tent, and Keri notices a few new nicks. "Probably from shoveling out," she says.

The next day the down-climbing worsens. The gully we
climbed has rotted, the snow losing its tensile strength. As it
turns out, the downclimbing here is fraught with hazards: falling
rocks from the climber above; massive snow moats which collapse under a climber's weight, plunging her into its sloppy
depths sometimes as deep as her shoulders. Landing wrong could
easily injure our legs. Worst of all is the snow's complete refusal
to allow us to take sure steps—each step threatens to slide out
from under. It's like trying to stay upright while walking barefoot down a steep slide coated with Crisco. A fall in this steep
gully could send us all shooting down the slope, and Keri's lack
of confidence in us makes her nervous and irritable. She picks on
Cheryl again, and they bicker, Cheryl on the defensive. I try to
remain neutral and concentrate on the climbing so that we can
just get out of this hell.

It takes us most of the day to descend what took us two hours to go down in good snow conditions. But we finally cross those two crevasses at the bottom of the gully, and then we're free. Down to the glacier, dig out the sleds, load up and ski back to Kahiltna Base Camp.

Annie, the Base Camp Manager, greets us warmly. But she also has bad news. During the sixteen days we were gone, seven people died on Denali and eight were rescued. One of the seven was the world-class American climber Mugs Stump, who died when the snowbridge of a crevasse collapsed under him. Huge blocks of ice plunged down after him, and an attempted rescue proved fruitless.

That evening, The Sultana Sisters drink hot nog and rum, sitting shoulder to shoulder on a blue foam pad outside the tent. All around us, domed tents in blue, gold, gray and yellow sit like a village of pods nestled behind snow walls, chattering voices sifting around us in the soft air. Contrary to prediction, the summit of Sultana clears as the light fades, until the white peak reverses to a black silhouette against the pale luminescence of the night sky. We're so safe and comfortable here, no wind to chill us, our bodies accustomed to the colder temperatures up high.

Gazing in comfort at the calm diamond peak makes the past two weeks feel like a dream. Soon, the three of us begin to relax and laugh together again. I can't shake the feeling that our camaraderie is somehow forced, though, as if we're putting a happy veneer over unresolved resentments. I have little experience in the resolution of conflict. Usually, once I've lost control enough to allow someone a glimpse of my black inner self, I run. This time, my life depended on staying with these two climbing partners—in close quarters with no escape.

Cheryl flies out the next morning, alone, after a round of hugs. Keri cries. "It's so sad to say goodbye," she says. I marvel at her heart-on-her-sleeve emotional response. My reaction is more one of relief; intimacy wears me out. I remain at Base for two more days, hoping to link up with Randy until I find out that he's been hired by the Park Service to assist with rescues; he will remain at the medical camp at 14,000 feet on Denali for an undetermined number of days. Keri plans to stay on and climb Begguya with a long-time climbing friend.

She doesn't cry when I fly out, but she does give me a big hug. When the plane taxis out and lifts off, I look back to see her jumping and waving until we're out of sight. I'm still not ready for that transition, somehow, even though she had said earlier: "Except for those two blow-ups you were wonderful, Clarice." Strange, even after risking our lives together out there, I still don't trust her.

The cabin looks strange when I get home. I feel numb. For the first time in years, I succumb to a depression at home, still angry at Keri, scarred by my inner flares of violence, and missing Randy. I feel an unreasonable abandonment, afloat in this sudden, unfamiliar summer. No snow, warm, easy. Maybe this is how an amnesiac feels, wandering through the cabin, touching things and saying this is my radio, this is my couch, my pillow.

The trauma fades after a few days of rest; one can hardly sustain a state of suspended identity for long. Randy returns; I start my summer teaching job. We close the summer with a successful climb of a new route on Mt. Brooks, on the north side of Denali, with two friends. The mountain grants us tame weather; we have no group upsets.

But the climb on Sultana remains a new part of my psyche, where I finally met with storms worse than my own. They tore my walls of shelter down, opening me to conflict without the option of escape. My relationship with Keri remains strained, but Cheryl and I have slowly rebuilt a friendship. She's one of a few who are helping me to learn to risk the bridge to others over my crevasse of darkness. I'll have to keep learning how to carry the discomfort of exposure.

RIVER OF FEAR, RIVER OF GRACE

Geneen Marie Haugen

*Fear slithers across my path, hissing. Sheds
light, glides away. Oh, mercurial companion.
Oh, sacred journey.*

SUMMER HIT THE HIGH Rockies hot and fast, sending deep
fields of snow sliding off mountains, gushing down gullies and
ravines, pouring into raging streams that rushed toward the
Grand Canyon of the Colorado.

In June of 1983, we were deep in the Canyon, days on the
river, when the water started rising. We could only guess why.
The Colorado River had long been tamed by the dam at Glen
Canyon; the normal flow was predictable, controlled, and there
had been no rain.

When the thunder of the helicopter drowned the roar of the
river, I shivered in spite of the heat. Helicopters do not fly in the
Canyon without reason. We knew something was wrong before
the red-flagged, baggie-wrapped message dropped out: the dam
managers had begun releasing great volumes of water to ease unexpected flooding upstream, to relieve the sudden swell of Lake
Powell. Secure boats and gear high above the river, the message
read.

That night I did not sleep. I scrambled out of my bag repeat-
edly to check the lines holding our three boats at the shore.

Of our seven-person group, I was not the only one prowling the sand in the darkness. Headlamps flickered on and off, darting about like nervous fireflies. The rafts that had looked so substantial when we loaded them in the sunshine at Lee's Ferry somehow grew smaller as the night rumbled by and the river kept coming.

Earlier that spring, I said *yes* to the float trip through Grand Canyon, though I had never floated the Colorado before and hadn't been on any river in a couple of years. I had been away from backcountry too long, pursuing a film and video career. I was eager to introduce my then-partner, Allan, an urbanite, to river life. I desired, even needed, to re-encounter my own wild edge. I said *yes* to the river and began weight training with cast-iron frying pans. I bragged, a little, that I would row my man down the Colorado.

Years before, I had been hired as a whitewater guide on Wyoming's Snake River, replacing a boatman whose anatomy had betrayed him with a hernia. He groaned in disbelief when informed of his successor. I strutted with secret pride to be the first female guide hired by my company. That I was paid less than my male counterparts did not diminish my enthusiasm, as my employer well knew. About the same time I was hired, another company engaged a woman guide. Before us, there had been only one other professional "lady boatman" on the whitewater section of Wyoming's Snake. She was such a rarity in that male terrain that we heard an outdoor adventure TV show had filmed a special segment about her.

In those days, on that river, it seemed unthinkable to acknowledge uncertainty or fear—especially for the anomalous lady boatman, who was scrutinized for any trace of weakness by dozens of territorial rivermen. I never spoke of the breathlessness I felt at the top of Kahuna or Lunchcounter rapids. As summer wore on and highwater receded, the male guides yawned with boredom. For me, the sound of the river, the waves that popped unexpectedly, the changeable flows always carried me to the edge between excitement and fear, although I feigned boredom, like the others. I learned well to hide my wariness, even from myself. But nothing is suppressed without dulling the senses to other things; that summer, I lived in a cocky daze.

One day while I ran trips on the whitewater section of the Snake, a commercial boat flipped upstream—in the calmer, flat water of Grand Teton National Park. The guide apparently panicked. People drowned. When I heard the story my stomach lurched, my heart raced and I understood the terrible secret I had been keeping from myself: people were entrusting their breath and blood to me. My employer had never asked for first aid or CPR certification; no one had practiced rescues with me. Could I actually retrieve a dozen people if the boat flipped? Could I revive a swimmer whose lungs had filled? Could I even save myself? In the deep place I had hidden it, my fear hissed and coiled. I could not allow the enormity of it, and forced it once more below the surface.

In June of 1983, in Grand Canyon, the Colorado River rose to levels not seen since the gates of Glen Canyon Dam had closed some twenty years before, but I had never seen that river before and did not know its slower life. The sixteen-foot red Achilles raft I rowed flew down the river without much push from me. All my attention concentrated on steering that hypalon donut through rapids the size of houses; through monster whirlpools that sucked the raft tubes under, threatening to flip us even in flat water. The rising water buried tamarisk, carried sand and whole beaches away. The current was so strong that often one or two of our boats could not catch the eddy that would have carried us to the safety of our night's camp. Then, we would all have to push our rafts back into that raging water until we could find another rare beach downriver. As the river rose, our maps became less useful. We did not know what to anticipate beyond the next bend. Riffles churned into surprising waves and holes, while some known rapids washed out altogether. Where would the next campsite be—or the next uncharted peril?

Of our seven-person group, only my longtime friend and river mentor, Michael, and I had ever rowed a raft before. We had three boats; Kalib, an absolute river novice, piloted one of them. Lorraine had begun kayaking in her fifties and had since kayaked extensively, but for most of our trip she strapped her kayak to one of the rafts and rode as a passenger. The rest of our crew—Janet, Mary Lou, and Allan—had never run a river at all.

Blindly, we raced what would become known as Fool's Flood downstream, into the chasm, into the ancient stone heart of Earth.

Unfolding in stratified layers, scoured by time and water, the geologic history of the planet reveals itself in Grand Canyon. Once an ocean floor, the Colorado Plateau received deposits of sediment from primeval seas, then crumpled, heated, and shifted along tectonic lines. The plateau rose, water ran, and a great river began sculpting a kaleidoscopic, textured canyon. The eroding water exposed lava flows, fossils of marine creatures, reptilian skulls and mammal bones, forests petrified in sandstone and shale. One third of Earth's 4.6-billion-year-old story appears in Grand Canyon, including some of the oldest exposed rock in the world—1.7-billion-year-old schist risen from the bottom of a Precambrian sea. Forty million years in the making, the Canyon itself is a relative newcomer to the Colorado Plateau, but now drains the largest and most arid section of North America. Even in its aridity, Grand Canyon *is* water. Every boulder, each grain of sand, every smooth wall or crack, every layer of exposed sediment has been shaped by water returning endlessly to the sea.

That June, echoes of water filled the mile-deep chasm. Had I looked up, I believe I would have seen the ghostly primordial river flowing above our heads, carving the Canyon whose depths we now descended; but I was too preoccupied with the river at my feet.

Daily I uncovered layers of myself: a carefully constructed facade of courage, now exposed by the relentless river. The canyon of Self deepened and the walls closed in: dark, steep, primal. A serpent of fear slithered up to greet me, *hissing*, like the water.

The Colorado River reared up and terrorized me, but I could

scarcely admit it. If I were not invincible, how would I survive? There was no way out but the river, no one to replace me at the oars. I could not let fear seize me or I would become immobilized. I did my best to ignore its lurking presence, anesthetizing the rest of my awareness as well. I blistered my hand with boiling water, bloodied my shins on the boat's hardware, stubbed bare toes on rocks and cactuses.

I was consumed by desires too late to actualize: I wished I were stronger; I wished I'd had more river-reading skill; I wished I had run more big water.

I wished I hadn't brought Allan, a novice outdoorsman. On the first afternoon, Allan hiked away from camp without a word, below the rapid at Badger Creek. He climbed a huge boulder and fell asleep until nightfall. Without a light, he couldn't come down. Michael and I tracked him by flashlight, over sand and sandstone, up the side canyon. When we found him, we shined our lights while he climbed off the rock. Had we not found him, he told us, he had already decided to jump.

There it was again: the appalling awareness that, unknown to even himself, someone had entrusted me with his breath and bones.

But who would save me?

The walls leaned, menacing, overhead. The Colorado River surged, a muddy artery circulating the blood of the continent. Side streams plummeted from ledges hanging high above the river. Grand Canyon dwarfed me and rattled the unexamined bravado that had brought me to the river. I descended the artificial strata of myself: eager naïveté, arrogant confidence, blind machismo.

The river roars her own story. The river's story cut through mine. At the center of myself, I discovered I was out of control, a grain of sand rocked by the tide.

Seventy-seven miles and many days into the Canyon, we floated to the lip of the first major rapid. From the ledges above Hance, we watched the river pour over boulders, careen into hydraulics and churn with waves from all directions. I could not believe *anyone* would row a raft into the biggest whitewater I had yet seen. Michael told me it would be worse downriver. I could not imagine.

I rowed into Hance with two passengers. On top of the first wave, the boat stood straight up and turned sideways. For a critical second, the raft was too high for the oars to reach water; I could not straighten out for the next wave. As we slid sideways into the break, I yelled, "Sorry, you guys." The rapid exploded over us.

Ejected by tons of water, I cartwheeled into the river. I fought for the surface, came up with my head pressed against the bottom of the raft. I pawed my way to the side, pushed my face out of the water, gasped for air. I saw Allan clamber back into the still upright boat. Swept along, in front of the raft, I registered the danger of becoming pinned between a rock and the tube. I made myself move—swimming in slow motion against the current—to the side. Allan and Janet, the other passenger, unclipped a plastic bucket from a D-ring in the bow and began to bail, unsteady with the turbulent river. Neither looked behind them. Neither knew I was not at the oars.

I shouted for Janet to row, to pull us away from a steep ledge on the bad side of the river. Allan was too dazed to drag me in; I struggled into the boat, over the rowing frame and gear. Janet yanked the oars. We bucked haphazardly through Hance.

I yelled for Michael, on the lead raft, to pull into an eddy at the bottom of the rapid. He did not seem to comprehend my shock and exhaustion and continued downriver. Later, when I confided my terror that someone might be harmed by my lack of skill or knowledge, Michael informed me that whatever happened to another was their own karma. I was not soothed by his revelation.

Below Hance Rapid, Vishnu Schist suddenly rises out of the river, lining the Inner Gorge of Grand Canyon. As the Canyon steepens, the Colorado speeds up, squeezed between the black walls. In the first recorded exploration of the Colorado River, Major John Wesley Powell wrote at the entrance to the Gorge in his expedition diary: "We are now ready to start on our way down the Great Unknown.... We have an unknown distance yet to run, an unknown river to explore. What falls there are, we know not; what rocks beset the channel, we know not; what walls rise over the river, we know not...."

In June of 1983, nearly 115 years after Powell's expedition, I felt as the Major might have felt, entering the formidable Gorge. Although I knew the names and locations of the big rapids only miles or days ahead—Horn Creek, Granite, Hermit, Crystal—I could only hope I would come out of the Canyon alive.

In 1966, a thousand-year flood had washed down Crystal Creek, delivering huge boulders to the Colorado and transforming a riffle into a cataract. Crystal Rapid became legendary. Its fierceness haunts the boater's dreams. Tales abound. All are true.

In Grand Canyon, rapids are rated on a scale of 1-10, the rating variable with water flow. At best, Crystal Rapid is rated 10, maximum difficulty. At "normal" high water flows, the rapid becomes a 10+. By the time we reached that ferocious drop in June of 1983, the river had swelled far beyond normal.

The water rampaged so wildly that we could not see the length and depth of the rapid from where we scouted above the river. We were not aware that the rapid was rearranging itself in the revived force of the river. White foam spewed off unseen obstacles. I knew nothing of the hidden rocks and holes, and had only the words of others to inform me. It made no difference. Fear was so large in my throat I could scarcely breathe.

Somewhere there is a photograph of a sunburned woman in a pink shirt and blue shorts, with glacier glasses tucked uselessly under her chin. She squints against the glare, watches the river at Crystal. What is that look on her face? The photograph records a moment of unbearable awareness: this river could claim my life with violent ease.

Worse, I could not confront Crystal Rapid alone. Each boat needed the weight of a passenger or two to help keep the bow down, and presumably, the raft from backflipping. In the highest water since Crystal had formed, someone would have to entrust their life to me, a Grand Canyon initiate whose entire prior river experience consisted of day trips down Wyoming's Snake, a week-long float on the Green River, and a few inner-tube rides down the irrigation ditch behind my adolescent home.

The river sucked my breath away even as I stood on the rocks at the shore.

That afternoon, we made camp on the ledges above Crystal with a commercial rafting party. The outfitter's head boatman, with the unforgettable name of Jimmy Hendricks, splashed and laughed in Crystal Creek with his new wife, also a guide. I could not fathom their nonchalance. Later, I cooled in the creek and spent most of that evening alone, on the boulders above the river. My heart pounded in rhythm with the rapid I could not escape. My stomach knotted. The ammo-can latrine got more than the usual offering from me. The deep-breath calming meditations I knew were of no use. I could not get Crystal out of my ears and eyes. By morning, I shook with exhaustion and terror.

We stood on boulders and plotted our route through the maelstrom. The apparent entry was a narrow slot between rocks and a boat-swallowing hole. I didn't know if I could hold the raft in that tiny margin of safety. From above the river, I couldn't tell if I would see the correct line once I was in the boat, eye-level with the water. I couldn't tell if the current would inexorably suck us toward the hole, and a certain flip.

As we scouted Crystal, we agreed that the commercial party would run first. If none of their boats flipped or lost passengers, they would eddy-up to wait for our private trip to come through.

Lorraine Bonney and Mary Lou Long—in a bold demonstration of female solidarity, I thought—fastened their life jackets and stepped into the boat with me. I never asked why they chose my raft, but I was grateful. Perhaps I visualized running Crystal right-side up. More likely, I was too stunned to think of it. We untied, shoved off. I mechanically lined up to follow the raft that rose on the swell and then disappeared over the edge before us. The current caught. We were committed to gravity, to the river, to Crystal.

We rode the first wave up and up, then fell off the backside into the trough. Nothing but seething whitewater, above our heads, all around. Mary Lou and Lorraine, crouched low over the bow, gripped the lifelines that encircled the raft. They turned to look at me from a great distance.

I looked up that steep, long wave, at least two boatlengths from trough to breaking crest. Somehow time stretched and slowed, and I saw light on the smooth tongue of that towering water. I felt how centered the raft was. I felt the oars easy in my hands. I knew we had already missed the first killer hole. My body's dullness vanished as we climbed water to the sky.

Sliding up that sparkling tongue, I was transported beyond myself, rising into grace. I *became* the boat, the oars, the river. Then, again, myself: a human woman immersed in living wild. My fear shrank to a small blur, a tiny hum, in a vast spectrum of sensation.

The river roared and went silent, an amplified stillness. Out of the resounding hush I heard a call—the river's voice, my own: Geneen. If you can do *this,* you can do anything.

We flew down the wave, up another, down, up, undulating through the rapid named Crystal. I rowed into the eddy at the tail of the waves. The new bride of Jimmy Hendricks, one of few female guides I saw that June in Grand Canyon, stood up in her boat and applauded.

Perhaps some people are born fearless. I am not one of them.

Sometimes hot fangs of fear pierce me, lancing my sides, burning deep, making me run crazy without thought or direction, desiring only to escape, escape the sharp weight and pain of the fear I carry. Sometimes I cannot discern the source of my terror, it is just there, a cruel phantom. Sometimes a sensation of falling sweeps me. And sometimes clear danger—a child drowning, a hand raised to strike, vehicles nearly colliding, thin ice.

Yet some fears, at essence, invite even as they cast alarming shadows. Where lie the watersheds of the sacred journey? The siren beckons. A paradox: to creep along the safe rim of danger or leap into its unknown abyss. To die? Perhaps to fly, to be transformed, to become . . . a new self.

•

The Colorado River showed a remnant of her untamed past that spring, surprising everyone: dam managers, boaters, Park Service employees, residents along the lower river. Rafts piloted by professional guides with years of uneventful trips in the Canyon flipped often and unexpectedly. At Crystal Rapid, three commercial "baloney boats" capsized, one person drowned, dozens were evacuated by helicopter. I heard a boatman tell of a hiker who had come down Havasu Creek to the river, kneeled to fill a water bottle and fell in. The dory that chased her downriver never saw her again. I met an older gentleman with a prosthetic leg who had run Lava Falls in a life jacket after his guided boat flipped at the top of the thirty-seven foot drop.

I was blessed by luck and the river goddess; the raft I rowed stayed upright the entire journey. Fear was my constant companion. It snaked along beside me, riding the currents of air and water. But so, I discovered, did grace. One became the other.

By the time we got off the river at Diamond Creek—at mile 225, the first possible take-out, fifty miles earlier than we'd planned—we heard the Park Service had stopped all launches. The flood eventually crested at a post-Glen Canyon Dam record: more than ninety-two thousand cubic feet of water per second flew by.

We did not know until much, much later that the Bureau of Reclamation had allowed Lake Powell to fill to near capacity before the upstream flooding had even begun. We did not know that a plywood barrier had been erected atop the spillway gates of Glen Canyon Dam to hold back the swollen water. We did not know that the force of the release had broken concrete out of the spillways. We did not know that the cliff that anchors Glen Canyon Dam had shed sandstone boulders the size of houses. We did not know that we had ridden a historic release of the Colorado River that would be called "Fool's Flood" in honor of the disastrous mismanagement by BuRec. We did not know that no one—not even the builders of the monolith—had been certain the fifty-story dam would hold.

•

The Colorado River flooded me, drowned who I was and baptized who I became that June, as I plummeted down the dark canyon, into my deep watery self. I could not say I liked it.

But there: a watershed.

I dreamed the songs of canyon wrens and longed for the feel of timeworn, sunbaked boulders under the soles of my bare feet. I lusted after the warm blue water and pale travertine of Havasu Creek and the Little Colorado. I wished to touch the ancient gneiss and dark schists. I wished to explore the stony strata of myself. In October of 1987, I returned to the Colorado, but that is another story.

Each year, my name slides up a long list and I get a little closer to a new permit to run the river that carves Grand Canyon. I have floated other rivers whose mysteries run deep.

I grow older. My hands might not hold oars against the rip of big water again. No matter.

I journey into canyons of dreams: landscapes of fear, and of desire.

The serpent inside hisses. Slips out of old skin, emerges transformed. Grace slithers across the path. Slides away, blends with shadow. Submerges, enticing the traveller to follow: surface is safe illusion. Breathe deep, dive below. Oh sacred journey. Oh mercurial companion.

CONTRIBUTORS

Deborah Abbott works as a psychotherapist in Santa Cruz, California and is a raft and sea kayak guide with Environmental Traveling Companions. Her poems and stories have appeared in many anthologies including *With the Power of Each Breath: A Disabled Women's Anthology, Touching Fire: Erotic Writings by Women* and *In Celebration of the Muse.*

Lucy Jane Bledsoe, who will do just about anything to pitch her tent in exciting places, has snow-camped all over the U.S. Her fiction has appeared in magazines including *Newsday* (as a PEN Syndicated Fiction Project winner), *Evergreen Chronicles, GirlJock* and *Conditions,* and in anthologies, including *Dykescapes, Afterglow* and *Women on Women 2.*

Anne Dal Vera is an explorer and outdoor educator. She works as a cross-country ski instructor at Vail and as a wilderness ranger for the U.S. Forest Service. She was a member of the American Women's Antarctic Expedition, the first all-women's team to ski from the edge of Antarctica to the South Pole. She was co-leader of a 1987 all-women six-hundred mile canoe expedition in Northern Canada. She has worked as a guide for Woodswomen and has taught wilderness courses for the National Outdoor Leadership School (NOLS).

Gabrielle Daniels was born in the city of New Orleans in 1954 and since age seven has lived in urban areas of California. Her work has appeared in the anthology *This Bridge Called My Back: Works by Radical Women of Color,* and in several other publications. She is an alumna of Hedgebrook Farm, a writing retreat for women, where the greater part of her essay was written. She is at work on a novel.

Clarice Dickess lives in Fairbanks, Alaska, where she is working on an M.F.A. in nonfiction at the University of Alaska. She began her outdoor experiences at an early age and as an adult has taught downhill skiing. She spends all of her spare time outside.

Meryem Ersoz was a dedicated camp-fire girl throughout most of her youth. She is currently residing in Oregon, where she is pursuing a Ph.D. in literature and exploring the Cascade Range.

Alice Evans is a mother, poet, journalist and fiction writer living in Eugene, Oregon. She holds an M.A. in journalism from Indiana University. Her writing has appeared in many journals including *Clinton Street Quarterly, Mr. Cogito, Poets & Writers*, and numerous anthologies. In the early 1970s, she co-authored a wilderness study of Hoosier National Forest, making several appearances before Congressional committees as an advocate for both that proposal and the sanctity of wild rivers.

Elizabeth Folwell is senior editor of *Adirondack Life* magazine, a job that leads her into the wilds on a regular basis. She lives in Blue Mountain Lake, New York.

Kathleen Gasperini has worked as an editor at *Powder, Snowboarder, Rocky Mountain Sports* and *Women's Sports and Fitness*. She lives in Boulder, Colorado.

Lydia B. Goetze has been climbing and backpacking in the winter in the White Mountains for the past thirty years. She made first ascents of several peaks in the Hayes Range, Alaska in 1964. She teaches biology and chemistry at Phillips Academy, Andover, and has been an instructor and former head of their outdoor program that is modeled on Outward Bound.

Jean Gould is a former college teacher and now a freelance writer and editor who lives in Natick, Massachusetts. Her published work includes *Divorcing Your Grandmother,* a novel, and a number of short stories, essays and book reviews. With her daughter, she is currently working on a book in which they explore the meaning of fatherhood. In the fall of 1993, she returned to Nepal on her way to Bhutan.

Geneen Marie Haugen has traveled by river in Alaska, Northern Saskatchewan, Arizona, California, Utah, New Mexico, Idaho and Wyoming. *Adventure* was the first multisyllable word she learned to spell. She watches birds and weather fly by from her home in northwestern Wyoming, where she is currently finishing a novel and working on a collection of personal essays.

Carolyn Kremers writes creative nonfiction and poetry and teaches at the University of Alaska in Fairbanks. Her writing has earned her a fellowship from the Alaska State Council on the Arts and a special citation from the PEN/Jerard Fund award for emerging women writers of nonfiction. "Eye of the Meadow," is from her book manuscript *Place of the Pretend People.*

Gretchen Legler is currently finishing a Ph.D. in English at the University of Minnesota, where she received a master's degree in creative writing. She teaches creative writing, literature and composition, and courses in women's studies. Her essays about the outdoors have appeared in *Indiana Review* and in the anthology *Uncommon Waters: Women Write About Fishing.* She recently won a Pushcart Prize for an essay "Border Water."

Susanna Levin grew up in Long Beach, New York, and graduated from Swarthmore College in 1985. She wouldn't have survived either without sports: softball, soccer and volleyball. She has worked as an editor at several magazines including *McCall's, Walking* and *Women's Sports and Fitness.* She now lives in San Francisco and works as a freelance writer.

Ann Linnea is the author of several hiking and skiing guides and co-author of the award-winning book on environmental education for children, *Teaching Kids to Love the Earth.* She is an ecofeminist committed to helping women love themselves and the planet as a form of healing and activism. She lives on an island in Puget Sound where she offers Women and the Planet and other seminars (under her business name, Peerspirit). She is the mother of two school-aged children.

Karen A. Monk is a United Methodist clergywoman. She lives in the Catskill Mountains of New York, where she is pastor of a rural parish and an Emergency Medical Technician. When she is not walking with Abbey, meditating with Callie, playing with friends or writing, she is studying and training as a spiritual director.

Holly Morris is the editor of the anthology *Uncommon Waters: Women Write About Fishing* and the forthcoming collection *A Different Angle: Fly Fishing Stories by Women.* She hikes and fishes the Western states and lives in Seattle.

Terri de la Peña birdwatches with her partner Gloria Bando on weekends and on vacations. She is the author of *Margins* and *Latin Satins,* both published by Seal Press.

Nancy Sefton is a nature photographer and outdoor/travel writer whose work has appeared in *Sea Frontiers, Oceans, Skin Diver* and *Northwest Travel.* Her photos have appeared in *National Geographic World, Smithsonian, Omni* and *Natural History* magazines. She has received the Arts Award from the Underwater Society of America for excellence in undersea photo-journalism. She teaches writers' workshops in the Pacific Northwest.

Sherry Simpson moved to Juneau, Alaska with her family when she was seven and has lived in the state ever since. She worked for several years as a newspaper reporter in Juneau and Fairbanks before entering the master's program at the University of Alaska in Fairbanks, where she is pursuing degrees in nonfiction creative writing and northern studies. She and her husband live in a cabin in the hills outside of Fairbanks.

Marti Stephen is the mountain bike editor for *VeloNews,* an international newspaper dedicated to competitive cycling. She is a native of Colorado and has a particular fondness for red dirt. She also has some regret that in her youth she was a teenage intellectual, because she realizes now that the best years of her racing career were buried in books—although she has some confidence that those same books and ideas have finally come to life in sport.

Barbara Wilson is the author of two novels, a collection of short stories, and five mysteries—three featuring Seattle sleuth Pam Nilsen and two featuring Cassandra Reilly, the traveling translator. Barbara Wilson is also a translator and received the Columbia Translation prize for her work on Norwegian author Cora Sandel. The cofounder of Seal Press, she now lives in the Bay Area and is at work on a new novel.

Note: The following writers' essays were published in different form in *Adirondack Life*: Gabrielle Daniels, Elizabeth Folwell, Terri de la Peña. Nancy Sefton's essay appeared in different form in *Scuba Times* and Carolyn Kremers' essay appeared in different form in *Sonora Review.*

Susan Fox Rogers is the editor of *SportsDykes: Stories from On and Off the Field* (St. Martins Press, 1994). Her writing on rock climbing has appeared in the anthologies *Leading Out: Women Climbers Reaching for the Top* (Seal Press, 1992), *Sisters and Brothers* (Harper San Francisco), and in *GirlJock, Climbing* and the *Village Voice*. She works as managing editor for an academic journal and lives in High Falls, New York, behind the Shawangunk Ridge.

WHEN WOMEN PLAYED HARDBALL by Susan E. Johnson. $14.95, 1-878067-43-5. This book is a celebration of the brief yet remarkable era of the All-American Girls Professional Baseball League and a remembrance of a sensational championship series. Filled with colorful stories and anecdotes by the ball players, as well as play-by-play action and insightful commentary exploring League culture, *When Women Played Hardball* honors a unique chapter in sports history.

THE CURVE OF TIME by M. Wylie Blanchet. $12.95, 1-878067-27-3. This is the fascinating true adventure story of a woman who packed her five children onto a twenty-five-foot boat and explored the coastal waters of the Pacific Northwest summer after summer in the late 1920s.

LEADING OUT: *Women Climbers Reaching for the Top* edited by Rachel da Silva. $16.95, 1-878067-20-6. Packed with riveting accounts of high peak ascents and fascinating narratives by some of the world's top climbers, this exciting collection is an inspiring testament to the power of discipline and desire.

UNCOMMON WATERS: *Women Write About Fishing* edited by Holly Morris. $14.95, 1-878067-10-9. A wonderful anthology that captures the bracing adventure and meditative moments of fishing in the words of thirty-four women anglers—from finessing trout and salmon in the Pacific Northwest to chasing bass and catfish in the Deep South.

WATER'S EDGE: *Women Who Push the Limits in Rowing, Kayaking and Canoeing* by Linda Lewis. $14.95, 1-878067-18-4. An inspiring book that takes us inside the world of competitive rowing, kayaking and wilderness canoeing through ten candid profiles of women who have made their mark in these sports—from pioneering rower Ernestine Bayer to Arctic distance canoer Valerie Fons.

DOWN THE WILD RIVER NORTH by Constance Helmericks. $12.95, 1-878067-28-1. In 1965, Connie Helmericks announced to her two teenage daughters: "We are going to make a canoe expedition to the Arctic Ocean." This is their remarkable story of a wilderness adventure down the Peace, Slave and Mackenzie river systems in a sturdy twenty-foot canoe.

RIVERS RUNNING FREE: *Canoeing Stories by Adventurous Women* edited by Judith Niemi and Barbara Wieser. $14.95, 1-878067-22-2. This spirited collection spans a century of women's canoeing adventures. Whether they embark on back country wilderness expeditions or leisurely canoeing trips, these women eloquently record the personal boundaries canoeing has inspired them to explore and push beyond.

SEAL PRESS, founded in 1976 to provide a forum for women writers and feminist issues, has many other books of fiction, non-fiction and poetry. You may order directly from us at 3131 Western Avenue, Suite 410, Seattle, Washington 98121 (add 15% of total book order for shipping and handling). Write to us for a free catalog.